T0369714

HOT FUDGE SUNDAE IN A WHITE PAPER CUP

Hot Fudge Sundae in a White Paper Cup

A SPIRITED BLACK WOMAN IN A WHITE WORLD

Gwendolyn Calvert Baker

The University of Michigan Press

Ann Arbor

Published in the United States of America by
The University of Michigan Press
Printed and bound by CPI Group (UK) Ltd, Croydon, CR0 4YY

2017   2016   2015   2014   4 3 2 1

A CIP catalog record for this book is available from the British Library.

ISBN 978-0-472-07237-8 (hardcover : alk. paper)

ISBN 978-0-472-05237-0 (pbk. : alk. paper)

ISBN 978-0-472-12067-3 (ebook)

OLIVE LEVI CALVERT THOMAS

My grandmother Thomas, as I knew her, was the mustard seed of my life. Her tender loving care helped me acquire the spirit necessary to live successfully in a world that is neither black nor white.

The seeds of her love and care are reflected in the lives of my three children to whom I dedicate my life's story. Their success reflects mine and theirs. THANK you Grandma Thomas. Thank you JoAnn, Claudia, and James.

CONTENTS

PREFACE

The purpose of this book is threefold. First, to tell the story of how my life was influenced by the University of Michigan. This influence was not limited to receiving degrees from this institution: it was much more than that. Second, I hope that anyone who reads my story will join me as an advocate for encouraging young women and men, especially those who come from limited financial backgrounds, to achieve an education. And finally, I want to encourage individuals to explore ways to challenge and transform their negative experiences so they can shape their lives and careers in positive ways.

There were times when I found it difficult to believe how attending a May Festival Concert on the campus of the University of Michigan when I was in fifth grade began my lifelong connection with U of M (as we call it). I never realized that the excitement of checking coats at a "J-Hop" on campus, and almost jumping for joy when one of the students tipped me a quarter, would be surpassed by actually attending one of those dances as a student.

These experiences were just the beginning of my association with the U of M. Sixty years later I can proudly claim two awards: the Ann Arbor Teacher Award in 1964, and the Alumna Award in 1991. I earned a bachelor of arts degree in 1964, a master of arts in 1968, and a PhD in 1972. I received an honorary degree of law in 1996. From 1976 to 1978 I became a tenured associate professor at the University of Michigan and served as the assistant to President Robben Fleming for affirmative action.

As I review similar memoirs, I have found many that tell the story of an individual's life, but none that attaches the experiences of a writer to one major university. Not only are my experiences strongly tied to my relationship with the University of Michigan, but my career clearly represents my education and exposure to experiences received at this institution.

One of my favorite authors is Maya Angelou. A writer and a poet, Ms. Angelou has shared many of her life experiences with readers through numerous publications, and I have the privilege of knowing Ms. Angelou. Her admirable success and her achievements tend not to be attached or attributed to her earned degrees from a major institution. In Dorothy Height's memoir, she clearly outlines the events that served to highlight her career. I also knew Ms. Height. Several of my experiences mirror hers, especially her work with the Young Women's Christian Association. Yet again, her life is not closely attached to a major institution.

Paula Giddings writes primarily on sex and race. Her writings contributed to my way of thinking on many issues; however, she provides a more general historical description of what most women have experienced. Her writings are also quite different from my story. *Beyond the Wall*, by Dolores Cross, another colleague, is an interesting memoir. There are similarities between our life stories, but hers is not connected to the influence of a single institution.

Anne Summers's book, *Ducks on the Pond*, is beautifully written. Her writings are much more historical and political than mine could ever be. Her background as an Australian provides an interesting point of view, but we write from two different frameworks. In their book *Swim with the Dolphins*, Connie Glaser and Barbara Smalley portray women in corporate America from a particular point of view, as does Patricia Reid-Merritt, whose focus is on African American women achievers. These three authors have included me in their books.

I do feel my memoir contains events and experiences quite different from these books, and from many others about women. Again, I attribute my success to growing up in Ann Arbor, and to having been heavily influenced by the environment, experiences, and education afforded me by and through the University of Michigan.

ACKNOWLEDGMENTS

It is impossible for me to acknowledge and thank all of the individuals who contributed to this manuscript. This is my memoir, an overview of my life. And I thank all . . . you know who you are.

When I considered working on this manuscript, I focused on how I would begin to tell my story. It was not until I had written my introduction and the first three chapters that I thought about needing an editor. My first thought about searching for an editor was very short, and it had a very short ending. A newly met neighbor overheard me talking about my memoir at a social gathering. Joyce Portnoy came up to me and offered to edit my writing. I was thrilled at the offer. Joyce is a professional editor, one among many of her skills. We worked together on the first three chapters and all was moving along quite well when a family tragedy forced her to resign. However, Joyce continued to be interested in my work and was able to introduce me to another talented editor, Ramonda Talkie.

My sincere appreciation and thanks to Joyce Portnoy, my neighbor, my first editor, and a dear friend.

Ramonda and I have worked together for about a year. We have worked together like the ingredients of a hot fudge sundae. She worked a great deal like Joyce. She was fast and good. However, we didn't know how fast and efficient she was until Thomas Dwyer, the Executive Director of the University of Michigan Press, called to inform me that the University was going to publish my manuscript. We had less than a month to submit my completed work. Ramonda and I learned what fast and good was.

There are times when certain situations require more than a giant thank you and this is one of those times. I simply could not have made the deadline for submitting a draft of the book without Ramonda's help. My dear friend and editor has truly earned my sincere appreciation, not only for her editing, but also for her continued support of what I was trying to achieve. With her help we did it.

After a conversation I had with Tom Dwyer, he introduced me to Steven Moore, a copyeditor who would do the final editing before publishing. I was extremely fortunate that Tom engaged Steve to do the copyediting. I thought I knew what fast and good was, but my definitions became even more refined when I worked with Steve Moore. What an amazingly quick and good editing process I experienced. Steve left no stone unturned. He did a most professional job editing *Fudge,* and I learned a great deal from him.

Thank you, Steven Moore, for putting the final touches on my book. My gratitude and appreciation to you.

I was introduced to the Faculty History/Memoir Project through Scott Ham, Acquisition Director of the University of Michigan Press. I met with a former President of the University, James L. Duderstadt, and discovered the interesting work this Project is doing to record and share the work and history of university faculty. I am grateful to President Duderstadt and to Anne Duderstadt for the leadership they are giving this Project. I also appreciate the support and interest I have received through the Memoir Project for publishing my memoir.

Finally, working with Tom Dwyer has been a pleasure. Early in our working together, Tom introduced Ramonda and myself to Christopher Dreyer. With Tom and Chris we have been able to form an excellent working relationship. I am most appreciative of their professional guidance. As I am nearing the completion of this manuscript I am grateful to Marcia LaBrenz for giving me the support I needed to finish this project. Also my thanks to Aaron McCollough for his continued support.

My respect for the University of Michigan continues to flourish. I am so proud to have been a student and to have earned three degrees from the University. My pride was extended by receiving an honorary degree.

The proceeds from the sale of this book will go to Rackham Graduate School and the School of Education. My thanks and gratitude go to the University of Michigan for having played such a prominent and important role in my life as a student and faculty member.

Introduction

School was out for the summer. It was a warm and sunny Saturday in mid-June, and I was about to take a ride on my new bike. It really wasn't a new bike, but it was new to me. My parents had given my two brothers and me each a secondhand bike for Christmas. When I saw the three bikes around the Christmas tree in our not-too-large front room—today we would call it a living room—my heart jumped with joy. But I knew a gift of this size would make my tenth birthday gift even less significant than usual. You see, my birthday is New Year's Eve. Most of the birthday gifts I received from my parents and my Grandma Thomas were included in my Christmas presents. I always thought this was unfair, but it was something I could not do much about.

I quickly put this thought aside and examined my blue-and-white bike. I was really happy—so happy, in fact, that as soon as I got the bike outside I rode across the street to my Grandma Thomas's house so she could see it. At first I thought I might have trouble riding the bike because of my height. My long legs actually were a blessing, because the bike was rather large. Grandma Thomas, my father's mother, and I had a special relationship. I think this was because I was the first grandchild in the family. Grandma Thomas married Mr. Thomas after my father's father died. That meant I was not only the oldest, but the only Calvert grandchild. My grandma was almost as happy as I was about my gift and offered to buy me a bell for it.

This was a Christmas before my mother became a Jehovah's Witness. I guess we were lucky to have received anything at all for Christmas, because when my mother converted from being a Baptist to joining the Witnesses, we no longer celebrated holidays.

On this particular Saturday in June, I was about to ride down the street to Betty's house. Betty Williams was one of my closest friends. She also had a bike, and we rode them together. I heard someone call me. In my younger years, my friends and neighbors called me Gwennie. I realized it was our neighbor, Mrs. Shoecraft. I parked my bike and ran quickly to where she stood on her front porch to see what she wanted. I took one look at her face and knew she was at it again. Mrs. Shoecraft often drank a little too much. When she drank she yelled and said nasty things to her husband.

As I neared the porch I could see she was waving a dollar bill at me. I greeted her with a "Mrs. Shoecraft, did you call me?" As she extended the dollar with one hand, I noticed she needed to hold onto the porch railing with the other. That confirmed my suspicions. But it was really no concern of mine. I was interested in the dollar. I knew she wanted me to go to the corner store for her. Whenever I did an errand for her or for most of our neighbors, they always paid me. As I got a little older I referred to my pay for errands as a tip. That sounded more grown up.

Mrs. Shoecraft wanted me to go to the store. Her words were a little slurry, but she managed to ask me to get her a loaf of Wonder bread and four slices of garlic bologna. She handed me the dollar and reminded me that she wanted the garlic bologna sliced not too thick. She really didn't need to tell me that because I had gone to the store many times for her for the same thing. As I turned to go she yelled out, "Don't bring me anything but Wonder bread!" I never knew why she liked that soft, gummy white bread. My father used to tell us it was like eating uncooked dough. Sometimes he demonstrated this when my mother served Wonder bread. He tore out the center of a slice, rolled it in his palms, and held it up, saying, "See?" Then he dropped it on his plate. My mother stopped buying Wonder bread.

I decided to walk to the store instead of riding my bike. My bike didn't have a basket, and I didn't want to take the chance of having the brown paper bag tear on me. I walked fast because my thoughts had turned to how much Mrs. Shoecraft would pay me for the errand. This was very important. I had a secret plan that I'd been thinking about for a long time. I needed eleven more cents to carry out my plan. I was pretty good at arithmetic. I could add numbers in my head. I tried to figure out how much change Mrs. Shoecraft would give me. The loaf of bread would cost fifteen cents—at least that's what it cost two weeks before when I ran an errand for Mrs. Day. That errand earned me five cents toward my plan. I could always count on Mrs. Day for at least five cents. She was such a nice lady.

Mrs. Day lived next door to Grandma Thomas. Her husband was in a wheelchair and she took really good care of him. If the garlic bologna was five or six cents a slice, the total would be about thirty-nine cents. Gee, if this worked out I would get sixty-one cents in change. I knew that Mr. Corwin, the owner of the store, would give me a fifty-cent piece, and with the rest of the change, if she gave me all of it, I could carry out my plan. As I got closer to the store I got more excited. I ran the rest of the way, carefully crossing the highway. The store was on the corner, and almost everyone in the neighborhood went to Corwin's when they needed only a few things. They shopped at the A&P when they needed more. You couldn't get four slices of anything at the A&P, you had to buy it by the pound. I was finally in the store. There was only one person before me paying for her groceries, so I wouldn't need to wait long.

Sometimes Mr. Corwin was not nice. I guess running a store all alone was difficult. But I thought he was making lots of money and that should make him happy. Some of the neighbors gossiped about him, saying he was not getting along with his wife. The Corwins were white, and they lived in the back of their store. The neighborhood was home to all kinds of people, white, Greek, and colored. Sometimes I would hear the colored neighbors complain about Mr. Corwin getting rich off colored folk.

This morning Mr. Corwin was in a good mood. Before he sliced the bologna, I reminded him that she wanted the garlic kind. He said he knew what she wanted. While he was cutting the meat, I put a loaf of bread on the counter. As Mr. Corwin wrapped the bologna in the pinkish-colored paper he ripped off from a big roll next to the meat case, he asked me if she wanted anything else. He put the meat and a brown paper bag flat on the counter. Then he wrote down two numbers and added them up. Just as I had hoped, it came to thirty-nine cents! I put the dollar on the counter. As he rang up the sale, I put my hand out for the change. When he put the fifty-cent piece in my hand, I could feel myself smile, and the smile got bigger when he added two nickels and a penny. I carefully put the change in the bag for safety's sake and thanked Mr. Corwin. Grandma Thomas told me to thank people, even when they should be thanking you but did not.

On my way back to Mrs. Shoecraft's, I decided to walk down the other side of the street for a change. I was so happy at the thought of getting the two nickels and a penny that I skipped all the way. Mrs. Shoecraft lived right next to us. I mean literally *right next* to us. Sometimes I could see her in her dining room when her curtains were open. As I got closer to her house, I heard her yelling at her husband. She must have been really mad at him. I heard her say, "You go to hell you son-of-a bitch, and if you don't like it, get your nigger ass out of here." Wow, I thought, what a thing to say.

Mrs. Shoecraft was a big fat white lady with long, stringy, gray-and-yellow hair. Her husband Cagey was colored, with something else mixed in, like Indian. A small man with reddish-brown skin and straight black hair, he never ever yelled back at her. I wasn't sure if I should go to the door and knock, or wait until she cooled down. Finally, after I heard something that sounded like a pan or pans hitting one another, I decided to knock. Mr. Shoecraft opened the door, took one look at me, called his wife, and disappeared as she came to the door and opened the screen. She held out her hand for the bag and reached in for the change. I always put the change in the bag, so she was used to this. She counted the money, and picked out the two nickels and the penny. "Here," she said, "this is for you, and thank you." Her speech was clearer this time. I guess her anger used up some of what alcohol does to some people. I thanked her and moved quickly down the steps to think more about my plan.

I rushed home, almost knocking down my bike that I had parked on the front walk. I wanted to get my coin purse, the one Grandma Thomas had given me with a nickel in it. Little did she know what her gift was going to help me do. I sat on the bed in my little room next to the kitchen, reached under the pillow, opened the little leather purse, and shook out two nickels. One was from Mrs. Day and the other was from Grandma Thomas. I wished more would roll out, but that was okay. I now had twenty-one cents. My plan would cost fifteen cents. There would be money left over. I was so excited. The plan was my secret and I would not tell anyone until after it had succeeded.

All I had to do now was decide when I would carry out my scheme. The place had already been selected. My stomach was bubbling. I didn't think I could sleep that night without doing it. I decided to carry out the plan that Saturday afternoon in June. I was not quite eleven years old, but I looked older. I was tall for my age and I walked as I was taught by Grandma Thomas, as though I were trying to hold a dime in the crease of my behind. She really meant crack, but Grandma Thomas would never say "crack" in reference to that place.

I looked through the tiny closet in my small bedroom. My father had made this closet for me with a broom handle and a couple of pieces of wood. It didn't hold much, but I didn't have a lot of clothes. I picked out one of my nicer blouses for the occasion. I sat down at my vanity, which consisted of two orange crates, an old mirror and a stool. After brushing my hair and giving my face a once-over with a washcloth, I dusted my Sunday shoes and picked up my purse. I was ready.

My mother was at the A&P and my dad was under his truck trying to fix something, so I didn't have to explain why I had put on one of my nicer blouses and brushed my hair. I walked out of my house, thinking and walking like a proper young girl. My destination was Crippen's Drug Store. I had gone to this drugstore with my father many times. Each time I had been there, I wished I could sit at the counter and order a sundae. Well today was the day I would make my wish come true. Today I was going to sit down at the counter and order a hot fudge sundae. Little did I know that my wish, my plan, would become a compass that would guide me for the rest of my life.

I ordered a hot fudge sundae that transformed me into a spirited black woman in a white world.

ONE

At First Glance

I don't remember much about my early years except that I lived with my parents in a small house on a dirt road just off Harriet Street, a long street located in Ypsilanti, Michigan. It took me some time to learn how to pronounce Ypsilanti, and an even longer time to learn how to spell it. At that time I lived with my parents and had two brothers and one sister. I wasn't born in Ypsilanti; in fact I was born in Ann Arbor, Michigan, a few miles west. My family had moved to Ypsilanti for a brief spell when my parents were having a difficult time finding suitable and affordable housing for our family.

During the time we lived in "Ypsi" (this is what we called it), I started school. I was enrolled in first grade at Harriet Street School. I remember how excited I was walking up the hill to go to school. I loved school because I loved my teacher, Miss Campbell, the nicest and prettiest teacher in the entire school. To this day, I think my respect and love for Miss Campbell is the main reason I decided early in my life to become a teacher. Miss Campbell always greeted me with a smile, gave me a little hug, and seemed to like me a lot. I always did my best work so I could get another hug and a bigger smile from my favorite teacher in the whole world. My world, at first glance, was the three or four blocks surrounding "my school," which was named after the street it was built on, Harriet Street.

Next to remembering "my school" and "my teacher," I also remember

Evelyn. Evelyn was my very best friend. She lived in a big house across the street from our smaller house, and at times it seemed that she was rich. Evelyn's mother was very nice and made sure that Evelyn wore a fresh dress to school every day. There were times when I had to wear a dress for more than one day, but I was always neat and clean. Evelyn and I walked to school together every morning and spent hours playing after school, mostly in her house or in her yard. Sometimes we would talk about Miss Campbell and wish she would marry the principal of the school, Mr. Beebe. He was a large man who did not have much hair, but he had a smile as broad as his face. Evelyn and I were disappointed when we learned that Mr. Beebe already had a wife, so that put an end to our dreams of happiness for Miss Campbell and Mr. Beebe.

The neighborhood that comprised my world in those days also included the large house next to ours. My mother's parents, my Grandfather and Grandmother Lee, lived in that house. When I was not at Evelyn's or playing in her yard, I was sitting on the porch with my grandmother. I liked to sit with my grandmother because the porch faced Harriet Street. My grandmother knew everyone who walked past the house, and she would always carry on some kind of conversation with them. She also knew some of the people who drove cars, and when they tooted their horns, my grandmother and my grandfather, when he was there, threw up their hands and gave a very hearty wave. I liked being a part of all that.

I was fond of my grandmother and loved to hear her laugh. She had a loud and heavy voice that could be heard for blocks. My Grandmother Lee liked me too. I remember one Christmas when we went to visit her; she called me into her bedroom, shut the door, and presented me with a gift. I was only somewhat surprised, because she always gave my brothers, my sister, and me each a small gift. However, this year, as she explained to me, she invested all her money in a gift for me because I was the oldest. "Money" in those days really meant the points she had earned by buying staples and dry goods from the Tea Man, who had a covered truck loaded with goodies for sale. He drove through the neighborhood, and the women bought things from him. He kept a record of how much they bought and gave them points to use like cash to purchase articles that were not for sale.

My grandmother had saved up enough of points to get me a beautiful quilted bathrobe. The robe was light blue, with large pink and red flowers on it. It was the most beautiful robe I had even seen. I was so proud of that robe. But I was overcome with guilt. How could I walk out of her bedroom with this beautiful gift in front of my siblings? What would they say and what would they think? To this day, I'm not sure what their reactions were. I think my mother handled the situation so it wouldn't be quite so obvious that I'd been singled out for special recognition.

At first glance, I liked my world and felt very comfortable in it. The people around me were warm and friendly. Not until years later did I realize that my first glance reflected a world filled with people who looked like me. We were all colored. Some were lighter and some darker. I was a colored girl. I lived in a colored neighborhood and went to a colored school. But we were all people. I hadn't really noticed any differences because I was just me—Gwendolyn Joyce Calvert, and at first glance, I loved the world I lived in.

About the time I was old enough to enter second grade, my parents moved to Ann Arbor, which was not too far from Ypsi, meaning we could visit my grandparents, my relatives, and my friend Evelyn on weekends. By this time my father had a car, which made it possible for us to take those very long ten-mile trips on a weekend.

At the time of our move, I had no idea that we would be living in our very own house. This time our house was not next to my mother's parents, but across the street from my father's mother's house. Grandma Thomas, as we all called her, had been married twice, which is why her last name was different from Calvert, my father's name. From what little I've been told, her first marriage did not last long. The man who would have been my Grandfather Calvert divorced my grandmother and moved to Canada. Most of Grandma Thomas's relatives came to Michigan from Canada. And most of their movement was involved in the Underground Railroad. Ann Arbor was close to Canada, and Michigan had been part of the Underground Railroad network. This group helped transport slaves to Canada, so many people who looked like me lived in and around Windsor, Canada, in cities like Detroit, Michigan, and the surrounding areas.

My Grandma Thomas had a fine house. She had hardwood floors, a front parlor with a piano, a front porch, and a pretty backyard with flowers and grapevines all along the fence that separated her yard from her neighbors. She also had a garage where she kept her Model T Ford.

In addition to her fine house, Grandma Thomas was a fine lady. She was my special friend, and I was special to her. Whenever I went on a school trip or did something out of the ordinary with my Sunday school class, Grandma Thomas made sure I was dressed appropriately and had the perfect lunch, with a dime tucked in my lunch box for whatever extras I might need. Why, I even wore white gloves to church. You see, my Grandma Thomas was an important lady in our church. She was the secretary and treasurer of the Second Baptist Church. I didn't learn until much later in life that all colored churches were always the "second" whatever. The "First" Baptist or Methodist was always a white church.

My grandmother took me to church with her every Sunday, and sometimes on Wednesday evenings for prayer service. We never missed an event at the church, whether it was a service, a wedding, a funeral, a dinner, or a tea. I learned so much going to these affairs with her. I could sing almost all the verses to the songs, I could recite Bible verses from memory, and I learned how to eat and drink properly at all the special functions, especially the teas. The church would usually have a tea party on Sunday afternoons in the social room.

The women made special sandwiches with all kinds of toppings and fillings. Some sandwiches were filled with ham salad, others with chicken. The open-faced sandwiches were so pretty. They were spread with cheese toppings and decorated with pimento and sliced olives. Some sandwiches were shaped like a cloverleaf, a star, or a plain old circle. The tea table was covered with a beautiful lace tablecloth. At one end there was a gorgeous silver tea set complete with tray, coffeepot, and a large teapot. At the other end there was usually a bowl of fruit punch, and along that side of the table were the delicious little cookies and slices of pound cake baked by the ladies of the church.

There was a special manner for approaching the table. I was taught to advance in line, according to my turn, toward the end of the table that held the liquid refreshments. I could then pick up a plate and ask for tea. I usually liked hot tea. After I received the cup of tea on my plate with lemon and sugar, I could move to the other side of the server, select my sandwiches and cookies, and place them on the plate. I learned very early not to take more than three or four different items at one time. And, oh yes, I had to have a napkin and a spoon with me as I approached the tea server. I was learning how to become a lady. Little did I know at the time that there would be many occasions in my future when the skills I learned at church and with my grandmother would benefit me greatly.

Grandma Thomas worked at different kinds of jobs. She often cooked for rich white people when they entertained on the weekend. She needed help in the kitchen, and even though I was only nine or ten, I was dependable enough to help her set the table and clean up the dishes. This was not a chore for me but an opportunity. I accompanied my Grandma Thomas to her weekend job. She made the dos and don'ts very clear while I was with her. The rules didn't bother me one bit, nor did the work, because I loved being in those beautiful homes or cottages on the lake.

The most important thing was having the opportunity to eat the food served at a party. I ate frog legs, wild rice, leg of lamb, mint jelly, and all kinds of foods that were a very special treat for me then. The experiences with Grandma Thomas in the kitchens and homes of these white people helped me begin to define what I liked. Not just the foods, but the kind of environment I wanted to be in. I was developing a taste for a lifestyle that was taking hold like a dream, even though I had no idea at the time that these experiences were shaping who I wanted to be.

My grandmother later worked for a department store in downtown Ann Arbor. One day when I was going downtown I saw my grandmother on the street. I ran up to her and called out, "Hi, Grandma." She answered, but acted somewhat distant. She said she was in a hurry. When I went across the street to see her later that day, she told me never to call her Grandmother when I saw her downtown. I didn't understand why, but I accepted it. Sometime later, after I had begun to realize what racism was all about, I understood that when she was downtown she was "passing." Grandma Thomas was very fair. She looked like most of the white women I saw. However, skin color didn't mean anything to me. She was my Grandma Thomas, I loved her, but I was confused. I was brown. I had never thought about my skin color until she told me not to call her Grandma when I saw her downtown. I didn't understand the burden she was under, trying to make a living in a racist world, until racism raised its ugly head not long after this confusing experience.

Our house had a large stone porch where we all loved to hang out, to play games, and be together. We had two bedrooms and an attic, what today people would call a loft. My mother and father had one bedroom, I had the small bedroom off the kitchen, and my two brothers and my sister shared the attic. Mother explained my assignment to the second bedroom was because I was the oldest. I felt special, but tried to keep these feelings covered up. I loved having my own room, even though it was only large enough to have a set of double decker beds, a handmade closet, and a small vanity. I had no time to think about where I lived, how I was living, or who I was, except for the fact that I lived with my family on Fourth Avenue in Ann Arbor, Michigan.

At first glance, my world was an enjoyable one. I had three brothers and a sister, a mother and a father. We lived in our own house, had our own car, and had all kinds of neighbors. The family next to us was what we now call an interracial couple. All I saw at first glance were Mr. and Mrs. Shoecraft.

Next to them was an African Methodist church. Having a church in the neighborhood was really cool. Whenever the church held a service or program, cars lined our street. I got excited because I could sit on our porch and watch the people get out of their cars and greet one another. I liked to see what they were wearing, especially the women, who almost always wore fancy hats. The hats they wore on Sundays were fancier than the ones they wore during the week. And the hats and outfits they wore to weddings were something else. In those days women didn't wear slacks to church. Some wore long skirts, others wore short dresses, but not as short as most women wear today. It was fun living almost next door to a church. This was all part of my world.

On the other side of our house was a much smaller house that our family owned. I took great pride in the fact that this little house belonged to us and we rented it out. There was usually a single man or a couple living there. However, the family I remember most was a family with five children. My mother was friendly with the mother, Margaret, and they spent hours on the back stoop or sometimes the front porch, talking about everything and everybody. I often wondered how seven people could live in a house with one bedroom. I never got a chance to see how they slept, but I could imagine.

This family went to a store once a week and came home with lots of groceries that didn't look like ours. They had sacks of beans, and large chunks of cheese and butter. I later learned they were on welfare. I didn't see much of the father. I thought he was working. I found out he didn't work much and often wasn't home. I often wondered where he was and what he was doing. Sometimes I heard Miss Margaret, as we were taught to call her, tell my mother that she was five cents short of buying a box of cereal at the corner store. My mother always made sure she had what she needed for the box of cereal and other things. This was part of my world and while I accepted it, I learned very early on that welfare was something I didn't want.

I asked myself many questions, such as why Margaret and her children were on welfare. Why didn't she have enough money to buy cereal to feed her children? Why didn't "Mr. Margaret" come home? Most importantly, why didn't he have a job? The answer to these questions came later in my life. However, one thought continued to stay with me: I would do whatever it took to avoid welfare.

Besides the Shoecrafts and Miss Margaret and her family, our neighborhood was very diverse and warm. Of course in my early years I didn't know what "diverse" meant. I just knew that, at first glance, I lived in a wonderful world.

The Kuehnes family lived in the large white house up the street from our house. Bobby and his older brother Harold lived with their parents and one of their grandmothers. The Kuehnes were white, but at that time in my life, what they were, other than people, was not important to me. Because Bobby and Harold were boys, they spent more time with my brothers than with me. However, the family was very friendly and often shared the lovely roses that grew in their backyard with our family.

There were lots of other interesting people in the neighborhood. Some of the families had children and some consisted of two older people who had raised their families and were settling into a quiet time of old age.

One of the most interesting families on the block was the Baker family. The Baker family lived in a very large house. When I was finally able to count all of their children, they had twelve. It was hard to count all their offspring because it seemed one or two or more had gone into the army. I really didn't get too involved with the Bakers because they had lots of boys. My brothers were often at the Bakers' home playing basketball in the driveway or doing other things with Mrs. Baker and her family. The girls in the family were older than I was so there was no reason for me to spend time with them until a few years later.

The Baker family was well respected because it seemed they could afford almost anything they wanted. While most of us had a family car, ours were old ones, while the Baker family got a new car every other year. I soon realized that Mr. Baker was a businessman. Not a businessman in today's terms, but he was part owner of the Ann Arbor Foundry. I wasn't sure what a foundry was, but I knew it must have paid him well. I was impressed when a picture on the front page of the *Ann Arbor News* showed a television set being delivered to their house. This was the first television on our street and there were not too many others in the city.

Maybe half of the people who lived on Fourth Avenue, my street, were older, like Mr. and Mrs. Day, who lived across the street in a very neat house. I used to do errands for Mrs. Day because her husband was not well and she could not leave him alone for long. I liked to go into their house because it was so lovely. They had carpeting on their floor and the neatest kitchen I'd even seen. Everything was in place. They rented out an extra bedroom to students. You see, Ann Arbor was the home of the University of Michigan, and at times some its students needed a place to stay. At that time, I didn't realize that black students could not stay in the university dormitories. However, having these students in our neighborhood added a degree of interest that was intriguing. We watched them carry stacks of books to and from the campus. I wondered how they found time to read all those books. I thought carrying the books and attending the university was very interesting. Soon I started thinking that I might go to a university one day. I never thought it might be the University of Michigan, but that comes later in my story.

Speaking of students, it was also about this time that my favorite uncle, Mallory, graduated from high school. Uncle Mallory was my Grandma Thomas's youngest child and I was the apple of his eye. He asked me to clean his room and paid me twenty-five cents to hang up his clothes and make his bed. Twenty-five cents in those days was a lot of money. But my little hustle soon came to an end. Uncle Mallory announced that he was going to college in Virginia. I'd never heard of Virginia, but I had some idea of what a college was because I'd heard it said that those of us who lived in Ann Arbor lived in a college town. In those days, we did not distinguish college from university. All I knew was that my Uncle Mallory was going to college, and that made me think even more about the possibility of my going to college.

I did wonder why Uncle Mallory was going away to college when we had one right there in our own town. Even the explanation that he was going to a Negro college didn't make any sense to me. It wasn't until some sixty years later that I learned the reason he went to Virginia State College. My Uncle Mallory liked to play basketball and he was very good at it. He wanted to attend the University of Michigan but at that time they would not allow him to play basketball because he was what they called colored. This situation played an extremely important part in determining his future. After a year or so at Virginia State, he enlisted in the US Army, where he became a commissioned officer and reached the grade of captain. He married a very nice woman and the two of them traveled all over the world.

During the years he was stationed in Japan he sent me lovely gifts. He also brought me special presents when he came home for visits. I still have a beautiful evening jacket made out of material from Japan that he gave me. By this time I was about to graduate from high school and I wore the jacket to my senior prom.

Because of the University of Michigan's decision not to let my uncle play basketball, he didn't finish his college degree until sixty-three years later. How proud I was when he marched in the graduation procession at Eastern Michigan University in December 2003, at the age of eighty-three, to receive his bachelor of arts degree. This was a very special occasion in his life, and in the entire Ypsilanti and Ann Arbor community. This ceremony was also special for me because I witnessed my youngest child and only son, James Jr., graduated from Eastern Michigan University.

As a small child learning about racism, I didn't understand what I was experiencing. Even more devastating was the impact racism was about to make on my own life. Most of my friends lived on my street, Fourth Avenue, around a five- or six-block area. This was in the 1940s. Our neighbors were white, black, and mostly Greek. We played together, went to school together, and never gave a thought to the fact that we were anything other than people who lived in the same neighborhood. It made no difference to us that all the black kids attended one of the two black churches in the neighborhood, that the Greek children attended their own church, and that the white children either went to the Catholic church or to one of the other white churches in the surrounding neighborhood. We were totally unaware of the impact these conditions would have on our lives.

One thing that didn't make any difference to us when we were younger was the location of the park where we went ice-skating as often as the weather permitted. During those days, the city would freeze lakes in the city parks for skating. In many neighborhoods they also built shanties with wood stoves and benches for warming. The park at the bottom of Fourth Avenue was one of the skating parks. As soon as supper was over, the neighborhood kids raced to the park and skated until it closed at nine o'clock. If we wanted to skate, we had to do our homework after school, before supper. For those of us who had part-time jobs during our high school days, this was a problem, but we learned to manage our time well so we could skate together. In fact, the park is where I got my first kiss and started skating with the man who was to become my husband and the father of my three children. But I'm getting ahead of my story. Back to the neighborhood and the skating environment.

A slaughterhouse where they killed pigs bordered the park on one side. During the day and in the summer we heard the pigs squealing, but at night there were no noises, just the ominous presence of the old ugly slaughterhouse. To the right of the slaughterhouse and across the street was a junkyard. While a wooden fence surrounded the junkyard, we could still see car parts and other things sticking up and beyond the fence. We noticed but we did not notice. On the opposite side of the junkyard a street ran parallel to the railroad tracks. The sounds and smells from this area became part of our daily lives and play times. We never noticed that most of us who frequented the park lived in that neighborhood, and the majority of us were colored.

I recently read an article paying tribute to the mother of one of my friends, Mrs. Richard Dennard. She lived in a house on the fourth side of the park, with the slaughterhouse in front of her, and the junkyard and railroad on each side. The article noted that when the Dennards bought their house some sixty years ago, it was in the only neighborhood in Ann Arbor where "colored people" could live. It did not take me sixty years to realize that where I lived as a child and the city in which I lived for over forty years practiced housing discrimination. However, housing discrimination was not the only form of racism that we, as blacks, experienced; as I reflect on this form of racism today, it controlled almost 100 percent of who we thought we were, what we wanted to do, and what we aspired to be.

I guess at first glance I accepted my world as it was presented to me. A young girl doesn't usually question much, but rather accepts what is. I liked my neighborhood and the people around me. Some days I liked my parents and siblings and some days I didn't think much of them. Most of my feelings about my family were controlled by what we did together and what I was allowed or not allowed to do. Of course I was happiest when I had my own way about things. This was often when we did things together, like going nut hunting.

When I was about eight or nine, there were still a lot of country roads. We could avoid the highways, which were somewhat rare, except for long-distance traveling. This gave us the opportunity to take long country drives together for fun. I especially liked our Sunday drives in the fall when the trees were changing colors. We discovered that at this time, the walnut trees were also shedding their fruit. Our family threw large gunnysacks in the trunk of the car and when we found a tree whose walnuts had fallen, we stopped to fill the gunnysacks with these nuts. We used cloth gunnysacks because they could bear the weight of the nuts without tearing, and we could store the nuts in them until the outer shell of the walnut became very dark and dry enough to peel. Once the nuts were peeled, we let them dry for several weeks before we cracked them. We did this in our basement and enjoyed eating what we could. We saved some for the fudge we made when Mother gave us the sugar we needed. Making fudge on a cold winter weekend night was a lot of fun, almost as much fun as making potato chips. We never had the money to buy potato chips from the store, so our mother taught us how to peel potatoes real thin and cook them on top of the kitchen stove. Our kitchen stove was really neat. On one side there were gas burners and on the other side was a smooth grate surface that kept food warm. When we fed the fire with lots of wood the grate became hot enough to cook the thinly cut slices of potatoes so crisp that the result was homemade potato chips.

My parents both liked to fish. They gave each of us our own fishing pole at a very early age. The pole was a long lean cane with a fishing line attached that was easy for us to handle. We were also given a bobber, usually made out of cork. We learned how to put a sinker on the line, which was a small piece of soft metal that could bend around the fishing line so the hook could sink in the water. When everything was ready—the bobber, the sinker, and the hook—we were taught how to tie a piece of old cloth around the hook to keep our fingers safe.

The entire fishing process involved two more steps. We had to have bait. For that we used worms, or even better, night crawlers. Some people bought worms by the can, but since economizing was important in our house, we found our own source of worms and night crawlers. We needed to dig for worms, which meant that we needed a spot to keep the dirt moist for several days before digging. Our father gave us a spot behind the garage for this purpose, and we were careful to keep the spot very damp. Each day we carried cans of water and watered our special spot of dirt. When it was ready, we took turns turning over the soil with the shovel and very quickly digging in the dirt to find the worms. Some were tiny and moved very fast, but we were faster. Once we finished digging up the worms, we put them in a can with some dirt and turned our attention to hunting the night crawlers.

Night crawlers were much larger than worms. One night crawler could be split and used several times, compared with a one-time use for a small worm. Hunting night crawlers was really fun because we had to stay up past dark to catch them on our front lawn. We watered the front lawn a couple of days before the hunt. When we were ready, we crawled over the grass with a flashlight. When a night crawler appeared on the surface of the lawn, we carefully pulled it up and out of the dirt. We had to be very careful not to break the night crawler because it was more valuable in one long piece.

Once we had enough night crawlers, we were almost ready for the trip to the river. We lived near the Huron River and on our Sunday rides we had spotted several places near the shore where a car could pull up close to the river and park.

Now, no fishing trip is complete without something to eat. We needed food because it often took us several hours to catch enough fish. Of course the end result of the fishing trip was to return home, clean the fish, and fry them for a delicious meal. So the final step to prepare for the fishing trip was to pack a picnic lunch. I'm sure we had lots of food, but the two things I remember most were the baloney sandwiches and the wonderful orange or strawberry Kool-Aid. (When I became an adult, I learned that what we called baloney was really bologna.)

I still remember the thrill of watching my bobber go under the water, telling me a fish was eating my bait. I pulled up my fishing line quickly, but not too quickly, just enough to hook the fish in the mouth when he started to nibble. What fun! I learned the names of some of the fish: we caught sunfish, bluegill, catfish, and small bass. The catfish were the most difficult to take off the hook. Usually our father had to do this for us. However, my siblings and I were really good fisher people, and we could bait our own hooks and take the fish we caught off the hooks. I learned to enjoy fishing, but I never could master the art of using a rod and reel. Later in life, when my husband and I were able to own a small cottage near a lake, we often went out early in the morning in a flat-bottomed boat to catch enough fish for breakfast.

During that time my world, at first glance, was okay with me. I was learning more than I could begin understand. However, it didn't take long before I took a second glance.

During my tenth year, many interesting things started happening to me. This was the year I became a woman. My mother must have prepared me well, because when I first saw a spot of blood on my underpants, I didn't go into shock. I seemed to know what was happening to me and took it in stride. I reported my condition to my mother and she took me under her wing. In today's world, when this occurs to a young girl, the mother has a supply of sanitary napkins. When I started to menstruate, I was introduced to the process of making my own sanitary napkins. At the early age of ten I was well into becoming self-sufficient, independent, and economical.

Because I was maturing well beyond my chronological age, I had the desire to branch out from my neighborhood and venture into what we referred to as uptown. Uptown was really the business section of Ann Arbor. There was the business section that surrounded the university campus, but we didn't go into that part of the city to shop, at least not in those days. My ventures often took me to into Woolworths, the five-and-dime store, where I would spend hours walking around and looking. There were many other shops in this section of the city, but I usually stayed close to Woolworths and enjoyed window-shopping. I felt comfortable in this section of Main Street because our dentist had an office above Woolworths. I often wondered how my parents could afford the dentist when it was obvious money was not plentiful. For some reason, keeping our teeth in good condition was a priority for my parents. Our shoes were half-soled more than once. I think learning to set priorities is critical and helps making the right decisions. This may be one of the reasons I invested a great deal of time and money in my teeth, and why at my age I still have most of them.

There was a section of Main Street with several restaurants. Most of them were owned by Greeks and they prepared the most delicious-smelling food. Once or twice, whenever I had a dime, I would go to the restaurant that displayed their wonderful-looking dishes in the window, and order a hot dog with mustard and chili sauce. They were generally very nice in filling my simple order. When I say I went into the restaurant, I mean I slipped quietly inside the front door and placed my order with the man behind the counter. No one ever told me not to go in and sit down, but somehow I took the hint from what I observed. There were only white-looking people in the restaurant, and this must have been reason enough for me not to venture inside to the seating area.

In the block past the cluster of restaurants, there were several small shops. One shop was a bakery, another sold only fresh cuts of meat, and there was a drugstore. I was familiar with the drugstore, named Crippen's, because this is where my father bought my mother perfume. Whenever they argued a bit, and sometimes on a holiday, my family stopped into Crippen's and purchased some Evening in Paris perfume. (It was more like toilet water or cologne.) My mother liked it, and the gift, for whatever reason, did the trick. I thought it had a terrible smell. This was also the drugstore where we went for medicine. A man in a white coat stood behind one of the counters, surrounded by bottles of medicine. I later learned that this man was a pharmacist. However, in those days, my father simply talked to him about the problem and he recommended several remedies. My father usually purchased something from the other side of the store.

Sometimes when I went into the drugstore with my father or by myself to pick up what my mother had written on a note, I found myself staring at another section of the store. There was a long counter with several black stools in front. On the other side of the counter were lovely serving glasses, cups and saucers, and tall containers filled with all kinds of colored drinks. I soon learned that this was a soda fountain. I watched the man behind this counter, who was also in a white jacket, fix a cold drink and serve it to someone seated on one of the stools. Sometimes he scooped ice cream into a fancy dish, put chocolate or a fruit topping on it, and served it to a customer sitting on a stool. I liked what I saw. I liked being in Crippen's Drug Store because all the people seemed very nice.

One day I had an idea. It came to me that I should sit on one of those stools and order me one of those dishes of ice cream with thick chocolate fudge on top. I made up my mind that I would do just that. But first I needed to save up the fifteen cents to buy the ice cream. By the time I saved the fifteen cents, I had learned that what I wanted to order was a hot fudge sundae.

So one day I decided that would be the day I'd go to the drugstore and have my sundae. I did not tell one soul what I was going to do, and I did not ask any of my friends to go with me. I'm not sure why I wanted to do this all by myself, but I think I was somewhat intimidated by the thought of what I was about to do. I wasn't sure what was going to happen, but maybe I didn't want to be embarrassed in front of my friends if this did not turn out all right.

What was I reading from this totally white environment? I was more cautious than when I went into the Greek restaurant to purchase a hot dog. But now I was not going to ask for something to take out of the store, I was going to sit on one of those stools and place my order. After all, why not? I had the money. And I had the desire to eat a delicious hot fudge sundae.

With fifteen cents in my little worn-out coin purse in one hand and my nerve in the other, I marched my ten-year-old self uptown and entered the drugstore. As I write this, I am reminded of so many other times when I had what was needed in one hand and my nerve in the other as I approached a situation, and almost always I was alone.

I sat down at the first stool I came to. I think I did this because I was nervous and I might have fallen if I tried to sit farther down the counter. The man in the white jacket approached me and asked me what I wanted. With my shoulders very square and sitting as upright as I could, I ordered a hot fudge sundae. The man told me that it would cost fifteen cents. I proudly opened my purse and counted out the correct amount. I had a couple of other coins in my purse, on purpose, so he wouldn't think that I had only enough for the sundae. I didn't dare place the money in his hand. I put it on the counter. I looked straight ahead and saw my reflection in the mirror. I was thinking and acting like a big girl. And I liked what I saw in the mirror.

It didn't take the man long to make my sundae. I watched him put two scoops of vanilla ice cream into a white paper cup that was in a black holder. He was generous with the hot fudge, and I remember smiling as he poured the thick sauce over the ice cream. Then, to my surprise, he placed a red cherry on top. He gently tapped the cherry with a spoon to secure its place in the center of all this beauty. When he placed it before me, I took a deep breath and started with the first spoonful of this delicious creation. I could have gobbled the entire sundae up in no time at all, but I wanted to look like I belonged there and knew how to eat a hot fudge sundae.

Before I took my second mouthful, I noticed that a young white girl about my age or a year or two older was sitting at the opposite end of the counter. I didn't hear what she ordered, but before I enjoyed the second spoonful of my sundae, I saw that this girl had also ordered a sundae. Hers was covered with strawberries. The strawberry sundae also looked delicious. But there was something about her sundae that looked different from mine, and it was not just the strawberries. The sundae served to this young white girl was in a very pretty glass dish.

For some reason, though I continued to eat my sundae, it did not taste the same. I kept looking at the girl, then at the strawberry sundae in the glass dish, and then back at my hot fudge sundae in a white paper cup. I finished my sundae and slowly got down from the stool. I took one last glance at the girl, noticing the obvious fact that she was white, and for another second or two I focused on the strawberry sundae in the glass sundae dish.

I walked backed to my neighborhood feeling so uncomfortable about this difference that I wasn't sure whether to discuss it with my mother. But I felt under such pressure to find an explanation that I finally approached her.

My mother, in her very careful way, began her explanation by pointing out the differences between the girl who sat at the opposite end of the counter and me. The main difference was our skin color. My mother explained that this in itself was enough. There were people who felt that because of my skin color I was not entitled to the same treatment as a white girl my age.

She tried to make me understand some of the differences between the ways blacks were treated in the South and in the North. As a young girl of ten, I did not easily understand the comparisons or explanations. All I knew was that the world I had put so much trust in had deceived me.

At that moment, nothing seemed the same. My world began to change almost immediately. I grew up in minutes, in hours. My second glance at the world I loved and felt so comfortable in had changed me forever. My life became a battlefront. I was determined to show the world that I was as good as any white girl. Whatever I had to do to achieve this would be my claim to the future.

Coda: It was not until my mother was ninety years old that I had a conversation with her about this experience. She told me that this incident was the reason the soda fountain in Crippen's Drug Store later closed. She said that several people in our community had protested, and rather than face what might have developed, the drugstore closed the soda fountain. I had no idea the soda fountain no longer existed, because I never went into that drugstore again.

At the tender age of ten, with fifteen cents in one pocket and my nerve in the other, had I made in a quiet way a contribution to the civil rights movement? It certainly was a major contribution to the life of a spirited black woman in a white world.

I SAW MY FUTURE THROUGH THE GLASS

Sitting there at the counter, savoring the sweetest
        concoction ever
  boy did I think I was smart, cute and clever?
I was on top of the world; a mocha chocolate
        Brown-eyed little girl.
  I wanted to linger, not eat too fast;
until I looked to the right and saw the glass!!

By Sherry Harvey-Tuley

TWO

Taking a Look at the Real World

Whether or not my first real experience with racism was a small step in what later became known as the civil rights movement, it was a giant step in shaping my future. My world was never the same. I had difficulty believing the reason I was served my sundae in a paper cup while the white girl was served hers in a glass dish was because of the color of my skin. What difference did skin color make in deciding how I would be served?

At that time, no one would have anticipated that a "civil rights movement" would occur some twenty-five or thirty years later and would make such a tremendous impact on how Negroes were treated in the United States.

When I was a small child in the 1930s, people who looked like me were referred to as "colored" people. By the time I entered junior and senior high school in the 1940s, we were trying to get used to being called "Negroes." When I began teaching school some fifteen to twenty years later, the term had been changed to "black." Many of us who had just become used to being called "Negro" had great difficulty with the new designation that was replacing it. It was somewhat easier for the younger generation to accept the term "black" because by the mid-sixties, after the passage of civil rights legislation, the mood in the country was different. People discussed race openly. Soon the term "African American" replaced the term "black American." The term I will use as I write this story will in many ways reflect the mood of the country and the status of civil rights in the United States and the world.

My family. We did much together. We attended a Ford company picnic. My father worked for Ford Motor Company in the mid-forties. (left to right, back row: Russell being held by our father, Burgess, me, and my mother, Viola; front row: Donald, Bernadine, and Duane)

My thoughts return to the time I entered Jones Elementary School. My family had just moved from Ypsilanti, Michigan, to the neighboring town of Ann Arbor. My new school was larger than the one I had previously attended because it housed both an elementary and a junior high school. I would attend school there until senior high, which started with tenth grade. Jones Elementary School was about four blocks from my home and a pleasant walk.

I remember going with my mother to enroll in the school. I was so excited; I was going to be in second grade. I already missed Miss Campbell, my first-grade teacher, but I knew there wasn't much I could do about that. I would have to get used to it. When we visited the school, the principal, an older white lady named Miss Gibbons, took me to be introduced to my new teacher. Miss Donnelly seemed like a nice enough person, but the fact that she was white made me a bit uncomfortable. I had not had a white teacher before. I tried not to let that bother me and decided I would do my best work for Miss Donnelly, just as I had for Miss Campbell. I also noticed that while Miss Donnelly was pleasant, she did not give me a warm hug like Miss Campbell did when I met her. It only took me a couple of days to realize that this teacher was never going to give me a hug. She wasn't going to be very nice either.

On the third morning at Jones Elementary, I left for school with a heavy heart. I heard my mother and father arguing. I didn't know what they were arguing about, but they were both very angry. When I left the house, they were still verbally abusing each other. There were times when my father used words with my mother that were not very nice. When he did this, I felt very sad. Once at school, as I was settling down, I learned we would begin the day with painting. Easels and large jars of different shades of paint lined up along the window in the back of the room. Two days before, Miss Donnelly had shown me where the paintbrushes were and told me to wash each one in the large sink in the back of the classroom. I brought an old shirt to school that Mother had bought at the Thrift Shop. I folded it carefully and put it away in the corner of my desk to use as a smock when we painted. My father didn't wear shirts like the ones most of my classmates brought to school for painting. The Thrift Shop was three or four blocks from the school and soon became the Sears Roebuck of my family and several other families in our neighborhood. For years, even after I was married and raising children, we often shopped at the Thrift Shop for things we could not afford to buy new, like gym suits, and Girl Scout and Boy Scout uniforms.

The space reserved for painting in class was in the back of the room. I was finishing my masterpiece when I felt my teacher's hand on my shoulder. With her strong bony fingers pressing hard on my shoulder, she turned me around and appeared to be in shock at what she saw. I had somehow managed to get paint on my smock. She pulled me in front of the class and said, "Look class, the new girl has paint all over her smock." Some of the students just looked at me, others smiled weakly. I was mortified! Here it was only the first or second day in my new school, and my teacher had embarrassed me in front of my classmates. At first I didn't think the teacher had singled me out because I was not only new, but also a Negro. But after the incident with the sundae, almost everything that had happened to me before, and certainly after, took on a different dimension. Were things happening to me because I was me, or because I was me with dark skin? Whatever the reason, it is now some sixty years later and I have never forgotten that morning in second grade.

Most of the other memories of my days in elementary school were pleasant. All of my teachers in elementary and secondary school were white. I never thought much about this, because other than my second-grade teacher, they all treated me with respect.

I remember with fondness my third-grade teacher, Miss Lane, a short, robust lady with short dark hair. We became friends almost as soon as I entered her classroom on the first day. She seemed to have decided to take me under her wing and give me a bit of special attention. It wasn't long into the school year when I learned Miss Lane was not married and lived in the big white apartment house on the corner opposite the school's front entrance. Although her apartment's location wasn't significant to me, I later learned that the people who looked like me lived on the streets *behind* the school. Miss Lane lived where the white people lived, in front of the school. The school entrances determined where people lived.

One day, Miss Lane approached me and asked if I would like to have lunch with her in her apartment. I was so excited I nearly exploded as I belted out a "Yes!" accompanied by a full grin. Miss Lane explained that she would send a note home with me to my parents asking for their permission. I knew my mother would agree and allow me to accept. I was right. My mother gave me the note to return. At the bottom she had written the words "OK with me," and signed her name, Viola Calvert. I proudly returned the note to Miss Lane and we made the arrangements.

I didn't say anything to my classmates because I wanted this to be our secret. I think Miss Lane knew that I would not spread the word, because she never asked me not to mention it to the other boys and girls in the class. On the appointed day, I waited in the back of the room until the other students had left for lunch. Then Miss Lane and I walked out of the front door of the school and across the street to her apartment building.

I will never forget that day or that walk. I felt like I was walking toward and into a mansion. It was the biggest building other than the school that I had ever been in. Miss Lane lived on the top floor. We climbed three flights of stairs, but it didn't matter at all. I felt I was climbing to heaven. I took in as much as I could. The stairs were carpeted so our footsteps were silent. I clung to the banister and noticed how brown and shiny the wood was. Even the smell in this building was different, like a mixture of cleanliness, newspapers, and furniture polish.

We finally got to Miss Lane's apartment. When she opened the door I thought I was in heaven. One whole side of the large front room was lined with books. Except for the school library, I had never seen so many books in one place in my life. The rest of the front room was filled with interesting things. Most of the pictures and little objects that I learned to call "artifacts" were souvenirs from trips Miss Lane had taken to Europe and other exotic places. She showed me the kitchen, the bathroom, and her small bedroom. Everything had its place. It was oh so comfortable and simply lovely. Miss Lane had set the table before she left for school. Instead of an oilcloth covering the table, like ours at home, I noticed two small pieces of cloth under the silverware and the glass, with a napkin on the left. My mother told me later when I described the luncheon that the cloth was called a placemat.

Lunch was delicious. I had a choice of sandwiches, peanut butter and jelly or egg salad. I knew what peanut butter tasted like but I wasn't quite sure about egg salad. To be safe, I decided to have half of each. The egg salad was on brown bread, which I had tasted when I had the tiny tea sandwiches at church. We had milk for our beverage, and pieces of apple and small vanilla cookies for desert. Perfect! I was so happy. I liked what I saw. Everything was so attractive, neat, and warm. From that day forward I was determined to live like Miss Lane. I couldn't thank her enough. I remember taking the time to write her a one-sentence thank-you note on a piece of penmanship paper. She must have enjoyed being with me that day too, because there was more to come.

Later in the spring, when flower bushes around the school were blooming and the fragrance of forsythia and lilacs filled the air, some of our fifth- and sixth-graders went to "the campus" with other fifth- and sixth-graders to practice songs for the May Festival. One afternoon near the end of the school day, Miss Lane asked me to stay after school. I wondered if I had done something wrong, but after thinking about it, I was sure that wasn't it. After my lunch with Miss Lane, I had become her best and most faithful student. After the other students left, Miss Lane asked if I would like to go to the May Festival, which was on a Saturday afternoon at the Hill Auditorium on campus. (We rarely referred to the University of Michigan as anything other than "the campus.") Of course I needed my parents' permission, but we both knew this would not be a problem. By the end of my third-grade year, my mother was involved in the Parent Teacher Organization and supported anything I did relating to school. I could hardly wait until my parents approved and the particulars were planned. I would meet Miss Lane at her apartment and we would walk the short distance to the campus, which was almost on the grounds of the high school I would later attend.

I had thought Miss Lane's apartment building looked like a mansion, but it was nothing like the Hill Auditorium. The Auditorium was so big and had so many doors across the front. When we entered the building, someone gave Miss Lane two folded sheets of paper and took us to our seats. Miss Lane handed me one of the programs and explained that this person was called the usher. I was somewhat familiar with this because we had ushers in our church and our church had bulletins that looked something like the programs we were given.

Once we were seated, I could hardly take my eyes off the stage, which had huge golden-looking pipes in the back and a lot of steps. The fifth- and sixth-grade chorus would stand on the steps. In front were chairs where the orchestra would sit. Once I had the stage under my belt, I glanced around at the audience. I saw many more white faces than black. In fact, I saw only a very few people who looked like me. This discovery of more whites than blacks in such settings happened more often the older I grew. The casual awareness of such an absence of black faces in public spaces didn't have the impact when I was in third grade that it had on me after my "hot fudge" incident.

The concert was oh so lovely. I was almost overwhelmed by the sight of several hundred boys and girls all dressed in white and standing on that stage. I looked to see if I saw anyone I knew. There were several students from our school in the choir; in fact all of the black boys and girls in the choir were from Jones. Again, that fact did not mean much to me at the time, except that I knew either them or their younger brothers and sisters. By the time the concert ended, all I was sure of was wanting to know how I could join the chorus when I reached fifth grade. Miss Lane assured me that I would have an opportunity to "try out" for it. I had to wait almost two years, but I was in the May Festival Chorus in both fifth and sixth grades.

I still remember the fun we had leaving school early twice a week to attend practice sessions on campus. We started rehearsing in our individual schools and in music classes very early in the year. The combined chorus did not practice together until closer to the May Festival, in the spring. The other fun part about being in the chorus was that we all had to wear white. Our shoes could be black, but the rest of the outfit had to be white. Once again, the Thrift Shop played an important role in my life. I was growing at a rapid rate so I couldn't wear the same dress for two years. While the dress from the Thrift Shop wasn't new, it was new to me. I did manage to wear the same pair of black patent leather shoes for both performances. The shoes were a bit tight the second year, but the joy of being in the chorus took my attention off my feet. Little did I know then that one day I would sit on that very stage as a tenured faculty member of the University of Michigan when my daughter JoAnn received her bachelor's degree.

In the sixth grade, our curriculum became more interesting. An effort to prepare us for junior high began in seventh grade, when we had a sprinkling of more advanced and different types of classes. I enrolled in my first sewing class, which was in the same room as the incident with my second-grade teacher. It was also where my sewing career began. After I began a family and had taken several sewing and tailoring classes, I made most of the clothes for myself and for my three children.

Next to the sewing classroom was a small cafeteria. It was almost impossible not to become absorbed by the wonderful smells coming from that room. My class was just before lunch, when I was already starving to death, or so I thought. One day I asked if I could go to the restroom as an excuse to wander by the cafeteria. When I peeked in, the cook, Mrs. Detwilder, spotted me immediately. She gave me a big smile and asked if I was hungry. I told her yes, but that I was on my way to the restroom. She told me to hurry, take care of what I needed to, and come back to her. She promised to have a surprise for me. I ran to the restroom, did what I didn't really need to do, and hurried back to the cafeteria.

Mrs. Detwilder beckoned me in. She handed me a slice of wheat bread covered with peanut butter and strawberry jam. She told me to go quickly to the cloakroom and eat it as fast as I could. I was famished, so it didn't take me long to eat the entire slice of bread. It was so delicious. I didn't have anything to drink but as I hurried back to my classroom, I stopped for a quick drink from the water fountain at the end of the hall and returned to my project in class. The slice of bread with the peanut butter and jam not only tasted good, but the thoughtfulness of Mrs. Detwilder meant so much to me. I needed her kindness. I love peanut butter and jam on wheat bread to this very day. And every time I have a chance to eat it, I think of Mrs. Detwilder and feel very warm inside.

The rest of my elementary school days were quite pleasant. I was a good student and continued to develop good relationships with my teachers. I had lots of friends and liked everything about school except the gym classes. For some reason, I was quite clumsy athletically and was always the last one chosen to join a volleyball or basketball team. I couldn't turn a somersault or do most of the simple gymnastic feats that other girls my age could do.

Somewhere and sometime between the sixth and seventh grades, I grew up. I had entered the realm of womanhood at ten and shortly after that, at about the age of eleven, I started to earn my own money. I was tall for my age and could easily pass for fourteen. I wanted to buy and do things that cost money, and my meager allowance of twenty-five cents a week was not enough. I wanted to work, but even if I had been old enough to obtain working papers, girls who looked like me could not work in grocery stores or other retail places where young girls worked. Some of my friends told me that if I could pass for fourteen, there were white women who would hire Negro girls to help them in their homes. A few of my close friends had discovered this, and some had more opportunities for this kind of work than they could manage. They were generous enough to give me the names of white women who would hire me. Once again with my need to work in one hand and my nerve in the other, I started to contact these women. It didn't take long before I had found myself two jobs.

At my first one, the family wanted me to come to their home every day after school. I was so proud. I was going to earn my own money. My parents didn't object. In fact, they encouraged me. I was to work two hours each weekday and four hours on Saturday for the Cook family. Mr. Cook was in the insurance business and Mrs. Cook took care of the family and the house. We worked out all the arrangements, including my pay, which was forty cents an hour, in cash, at the end of each week. My responsibilities included helping Mrs. Cook prepare dinner. Because I had often accompanied my grandmother when she went to homes to cook dinner or to prepare for parties, I was familiar with how to set a table. I scrubbed the potatoes for baking, washed other vegetables, and did different chores. I never stayed for dinner, so cleaning up after the meal was not my job. There were times I wished I could have stayed because by the time I had to leave, the dinner in the oven was making me very hungry.

On Saturdays I helped clean the house. I dusted, and cleaned the venetian blinds often enough to make a promise to myself never to put them in any house of my own. I learned how to scrub a kitchen floor properly and how to clean silver. After I completed my four hours at the Cooks' residence, I went across the street to the Schwabs' and worked a few more hours. There were times when I was tired, and I didn't want to do a second job on Saturday. However, I never tired of collecting my pay. My earnings made it possible for me to buy things for myself and to buy Christmas presents for my family.

Working in these homes exposed me to more than just how to prepare a potato for baking or how to clean a venetian blind. The experience exposed me to a lifestyle. The houses that I worked in were lovely. They were in a part of the city where only whites lived. I learned more about racism and housing discrimination. I saw how these homes were decorated and how good it felt to be in an environment that was attractive, warm, and inviting. I was reminded of how I felt when I had lunch in my third-grade teacher's apartment. There was something different about these homes from most of the homes in my part of town. There was carpet on the floors and tile in the bathrooms. These homes did not have linoleum rugs in the living room and oilcloth on their dining room tables. Why were these homes so different? I didn't really have the answers at that time, but I knew it had to do with people being white or black. What I gained from all of this was the desire to have the same lifestyle as an adult that these white people had. I didn't realize at the time how difficult this would be.

One of the things that impressed me about these homes was the fact that the dishes I set the tables with all matched. The dishes in my home did not match. All of our dishes were different. I liked the way the table looked when the dishes were the same. One day when I was walking in the downtown shopping district, I passed a store that had a display of dishes in the window. I stopped and looked at those lovely blue-and-white dishes, and I got the bright idea of buying a set of them for my mother for Christmas. (This was during the time when our family still celebrated Christmas. Soon after I entered high school my mother became a Jehovah's Witness and that put an end to the holiday celebrations in our home.) I decided to go into the store and inquire about the price of the dishes. The entire set was $4.95, which was a lot of money. In fact, it was almost as much as I made in a week. I thanked the clerk and slowly began to walk out of the store. I think the clerk knew I wanted those dishes. She told me I could put them on layaway, but I didn't know what that meant. She explained that I could put fifty cents down and come in each week to pay more until the entire amount had been paid. I was very interested in this layaway plan. When I left the store I couldn't stop thinking about buying the dishes for my mother.

The following Saturday, after I received my pay from both jobs, I returned to the store and put a deposit on the dishes. I made a payment each week until I had paid the entire amount. I also planned to carry the dishes home and hide them somehow until Christmas Day. After I had paid for them, the clerk asked me where I wanted the dishes delivered. Delivered? I didn't want the dishes delivered. I wanted to take them home all by myself. I think the clerk thought I was a bit naive. She explained to me that the dishes came in a large box and were heavy. I told her I didn't care how heavy they were, I wanted to carry them home by myself. The clerk didn't realize how proud I was. This was the most expensive purchase I had ever made. I was going to be able to give my mother this set of dishes so our table could look more like the one I set at the Cooks'. How I managed to carry that large heavy box all the way home I don't know. I think my pride gave me the strength to do it. I still remember how proud I felt as I struggled to carry that big heavy box down Main Street. I wanted everyone who saw me to know that I had bought something very big.

The concept of layaway became very much a part of my reality for many years to come. When I started making my own money, my desire to buy things my parents couldn't afford to buy me increased. I didn't have many clothes, and had to wear most of what I had over and over again. When I saw a beautiful blue coat in the window of a department store downtown, I knew I couldn't afford to buy it. However, I remembered the layaway plan. I went into the store and asked about the possibility of putting the coat on layaway. Before many weeks had passed, I had a new winter coat! I also realized I could get other things I wanted that my parents couldn't afford. I was learning, very early in life, how to be independent.

My ability to take care of myself and become more independent grew during this period in my young life. I learned one evening at dinner that my mother had gone to the doctor that day and discovered she had tuberculosis. I wasn't sure what tuberculosis was, but she had to go to a sanitarium. My brothers and my sister and I were all crying because we didn't know what that would mean for us. Who would take care of us? My father worked every day and we were too young to be left by ourselves. I was the oldest, but I couldn't take care of everyone. And then Grandma Thomas, my father's mother who lived across the street, came to our rescue. My father would stay in our house, while my brothers Don and Duane, my sister Bernadine, and I would move across the street and live with my Grandma Thomas. We lived this way for about a year.

Because I had a special relationship with Grandma Thomas, I enjoyed living in her house. Her lifestyle was different from ours but I liked that too. Things that I had come to like about the homes I worked in were in some ways reflected in the way my grandma lived. She had white linen tablecloths on her big round dining room table where we ate every night. She insisted that we use the large white linen napkins that were folded neatly in silver holders. We each had a napkin with initials on it that bore no relationship to our name. She taught us how to scrape the crumbs off the table with a small brush and use a little silver tray that caught the crumbs. This was different from eating on the oilcloth in our house. I liked eating this way. I liked living the way Grandma Thomas lived.

Every other weekend and usually on Sundays, my father would take us to visit my mother. However, because of our ages, we were not allowed into the sanitarium. The only way we could see our mother was to stand outside on the side of the building where her room was. My mother would come to the window and wave at us. We would throw her a kiss or two and my brothers would perform little stunts for her like a cartwheel or a somersault. These were joyous times, but also very sad, because we could not actually be with her. After our appearance we had to wait in the car until my father visited with her, which he did more often than we did. I will never forget how much I looked forward to driving out to the sanitarium to visit my mother.

By the time she returned home I was quite the lady. I still worked after school but found time for my activities in church and at the community center. I even managed to pay for piano lessons from Virginia Wilson, a single woman who worked at the Dunbar Community Center. After I learned to play one or two songs in my red beginner's piano book, I found a new teacher. At first I was hired by Mrs. Seeback to help her with light housekeeping. Her husband died and left her to care for their sons, Dale and Terry. When I learned that Mrs. Seeback earned part of her income by giving piano lessons, I immediately made a deal with her. Part of my pay would be in the form of lessons. I always wanted to play the piano well, but my schedule eventually became too much to manage. Something had to go, and it was the piano lessons.

There were so many things I wanted to learn, to do, and to have. I realize that over scheduling myself became part of my personality. Even in my retirement I still want to do more than I have time and energy to accomplish. No day is ever long enough.

THREE

The World Around Me

Before the hot fudge sundae incident, my view of the world did not provide me with a true picture of what it was really like. At that time, I realized people looked different and were different, but it never occurred to me that, for these reasons alone, people would or should be treated differently. While my early observations produced a distorted view of the real world, I'm glad I had that distorted introduction to the world I lived in. I think the experience, as distorted as it was, provided me with some of what helped me make the transition into the real world.

My transition into the real world, where people are treated differently for all kinds of reasons, but especially because of skin color, was difficult. The difficulty came because it wasn't easy for me to accept the experiences I was having as truly honest happenings. For example, did my third-grade teacher invite me to lunch and to the concert because I was Gwen Baker or because I was Gwen Baker who was black?

If it was because I was black, then was it also because she thought I needed these opportunities? My thinking on these questions was complicated. Was it all right for her to have invited me because I was black? What made her think I needed these experiences? How did she know what I needed? Did she have some magic mirror that she looked through that told her that inviting me to lunch might in some way contribute to expanding my world? Or did she invite me because she liked me? What did she know about what

I attended James Baker's junior prom at Ann Arbor High School. This was the first of many dances I attended with James, my future husband and the father of my three children.

I needed as a young black girl? I had these questions and many more that I could not answer.

My work environment also gave me great concerns. While I relished the opportunity to earn a few dollars each week, I was never comfortable with what I did. I wasn't comfortable taking a bus into an all-white neighborhood. I felt a twinge of jealousy as I walked down the clean and attractive streets with houses that were all in fine repair with nice-looking cars in the driveway. Why were there these differences? Why was what I was seeing and experiencing in my little work world so different from where I lived? There were no junkyards anywhere near these houses. These neighborhoods were a long way from railroad tracks and slaughterhouses. Why did I have to enter the houses I worked in through the back door? Why were there no black people, except those working in the houses, living in the neighborhood? The only answer I could come up with was because of skin color. I told myself this was exactly the reason I was served a hot fudge sundae in a white paper cup. My skin was black. The girl with the white skin was served out of a glass dish.

There was not much I could do about what I was observing other than think about it. It didn't take me long to come to the same conclusion I had made about the venetian blinds. I hated to wash and dust them so much that I made myself a promise never to have them in any house I would own. I also made myself another promise: I would do whatever I could to make sure that in my future I would be able to live like the people I was working for. And, of course, I also realized I would not be doing this kind of work the rest of my life. How would I get around this situation? Most of the black people I knew, except for our minister and the people who ran the community center, were domestic workers. Some of them, like my father, worked at factories in Detroit. My father worked for the Ford Motor Company until he was able to start his own business.

For years my father ran his own rubbish pickup company. He developed his business with my youngest brother Russell's help. In 1980 my father sold Russell the business for over a quarter of a million dollars. My brother and his wife, Doris, grew the business into well over a million-dollar company over a ten-year period. I once suggested to Russell that they change the name of the business from Calvert's Rubbish Company to something more acceptable. My brother immediately replied that if Calvert Rubbish Company netted him in excess of a million dollars a year, he wasn't going to change the name. There was no further discussion. To this day I am extremely proud of what Russell and Doris have accomplished. They have the lifestyle I thought about when I was cleaning houses after school. I'm sure if they told their story it wouldn't be surprising to learn of the racial barriers they had crossed to build that kind of success.

When I wasn't working, I was quite involved in church activities. I was very comfortable in church because my grandmother had introduced me to the Second Baptist Church when I was very young. I was baptized into the church when I was nine years old. I shall never forget the day when my grandmother decided I would join the church. She had discussed this with my parents and evidently they did not object.

The Sunday I "gave myself to the Lord" was quite a day. Evidently, there had been some planning going on with several families in the church who had children my age. When I marched up to the front of the church as the "church doors were opened," several of my friends were behind me. When the doors of the church are opened, the minister welcomes "sinners" to join the church. I didn't feel like a sinner. I just did what I was told to do. After that Sunday, my grandmother began to plan for my baptism.

The process of being baptized took a lot of planning. I had to wear a long robe. I needed rubber beach slippers, and most importantly, something to keep the water from getting to my hair. How we looked was critical, because the baptism was done inside the church. There was a large font called a baptismal that was filled the day before the ceremony to take the chill off the water. In those days, no one thought about making sure the font had a heater. I guess we were lucky to have a font. It was also important for girls to keep the water out of their hair because we had to dress for the Welcoming In Reception that was held immediately after the service. In those days, long before there were products that protected our hair from moisture, we did whatever we could to keep out the moisture. Water was our enemy. Once our hair was wet, there was no curl. I guess I should explain that none of the curls from the hot curlers would endure the water. When water came into contact with our hair, the result was coarser-looking curls that females especially were not fond of. So we used bathing caps and shower caps for such occasions.

Those of us who would be baptized that morning met before the service for prayer and to change into our baptismal clothes. We heard the choir and the congregation upstairs singing and making sure all was done to create the right spiritual environment. When the time came to line up on the stairs that led to the font, my heart started beating very hard. I had watched others being baptized before. But I hadn't taken in the fact that the person being baptized was pushed all the way under the water. I heard my name called. I was usually first at everything because my last name started with a C.

My grandmother was by my side and pulled me up the steps. There was no turning back. I wanted to cry, but I saw the warm friendly face of our minister, Reverend Carpenter, as he extended his hand to me and suddenly I was okay. It all happened so fast. He took my hand, called my name, and as he pushed me into the water, I heard him say, "In the name of the Father . . ." I thought I was drowning, but when I came up from the water he was finishing his blessing, ". . . and of the Son and of the Holy Ghost." Water was dripping everywhere. I was choking because I had let go of my nose even after I'd been told to hold it until it was over.

The singing got louder and my grandmother reached for me with tears in her eyes. She helped me down the steps and made sure I wouldn't slip in my rubber beach shoes, purchased from my favorite store, the Thrift Shop. I was shaking from the chill of the water. My grandmother helped dry me off and change my clothes to prepare for the reception. One by one I heard the other children being baptized. We were greatly relieved when it was over. I didn't realized then that my baptism was just the beginning of my life in the church.

The church was almost a second home to me for many years to come. I became a favorite of our minister and his wife, as I had become a favorite of many of my teachers. Sometimes I had to pay a price for this. My peers didn't always appreciate my being favored.

I became a member of the Blue Crown Choir, made up of young boys and girls who had joined the church. Being a member of the choir meant meeting for practice at least once a week and for a short Sunday session between Sunday school and the church service. We also had to wear choir robes. Our robes were consistent with our name. We had long royal-blue cotton robes with long sleeves, topped with a very full short white overblouse. On our heads we actually wore a blue-and-white crown. I'm not so sure we looked as special as we thought we did, but being a member of the Blue Crown Choir was an honor. The choir was organized and directed by the minister's wife, Mrs. Carpenter. She was a tough lady, strict and demanding. Everything had to be perfect. And perfect it was. Our robes were spotless and starched to the minute. Our crowns had to sit exactly so the point of the crown was above our nose. And of course, the singing was rehearsed to sound as good as we could make it. One of the members of the choir was Willis Patterson, who later became dean of the School of Music at the University of Michigan.

There was only one problem. My father's sister, Aunt Jewell, was the pianist. Aunt Jewell usually came late to rehearsals no matter what time they were held. This always meant a few sharp words to her from Mrs. Carpenter. During our rehearsals or performances, my aunt would hit a wrong note or two. This threw us off-key and Mrs. Carpenter into a tantrum. Some choir members had better voices than others. I'm not sure if my voice was one of the better ones, but Mrs. Carpenter liked me and would always assign me a song to sing either as a soloist or in a duet. She decided that the Christmas gospel song "Go Tell It on the Mountain" would be my song to sing whenever the choir performed during the holidays. I learned to like this song, and because I liked its message, I put my all into it. My other favorite was "I Come to the Garden Alone." Everyone enjoyed hearing me sing this song. Of course, the person who enjoyed it most was Grandma Thomas. Becoming a choir member was my introduction to a long association with the Second Baptist Church.

The choir was not my only activity in the church. I attended Sunday school and often received the award for not having missed one Sunday in an entire year. My relationship with Sunday school continued for many years. I became a Sunday school teacher after I had my own children.

Church was an important part of my life before and after baptism. I remember reciting the Easter verses for the Easter Sunday service. I was usually Mary in the Christmas pageant and held the lead in most of the other pageants and plays that were so much a part of my life in the church. My warm relationship with the Carpenters continued until their deaths.

There was something very special about the Second Baptist Church. The church was a black church located in the black neighborhood. There were only three black churches in the city at the time. The other two were the African Methodist church and the Church of God and Christ, a sanctified church. Most people who attended the Baptist church seemed a little more reserved than those who attended the AME church, and certainly a great deal more reserved than those who attended the sanctified church.

The church was a haven for me and probably for most of the other members. It provided the support I needed while struggling with a world I was trying to understand. Everyone in the church looked like me, and I was accepted for who I was. The church was filled with wonderful people who had many talents and skills. Some of them had terrific voices, and when they sang the hairs on the back of my neck almost came to attention. Others were especially good at organizing events. Still others, men and women, came together and cooked delicious meals that were sold by the plate for takeout at fund-raisers. Almost everyone came to church dressed in his or her finest clothes, and each one wore a smile. I looked forward to going to church. It made me feel good.

Some of the leaders in the church held professional or semiprofessional jobs in the community. One man in particular, the executive director of the Dunbar Community Center, seemed to have the respect of everyone in the congregation, including the minister. Douglas Williams and his wife lived with their three children on the second floor of the Dunbar Community Center. Whenever Mr. Williams came to church, he was really dressed. I had never seen a black man look as good as Mr. Williams did when he strolled down the aisle. The ushers escorted him to the front row where he always sat. For a long time I actually thought his name was on the seat. When he came to church, he came alone. His wife did not come with him. She had joined a white Episcopal church. I was told the members did not object to Mrs. Williams joining because of who her husband was. At that time, the minister, Reverend Carpenter, and Mr. Williams appeared to be the representatives of the black community. Almost anything that needed to be done for blacks or anyone who wanted anything from the white world, like a job, found it necessary to go through these two men. They were the liaisons between the black and the white communities.

The community center was named after the black poet Paul Laurence Dunbar. The Dunbar, as we called it, was located two blocks from the church and two blocks from my home. When I was not working or in the church, I was attending a meeting or hanging out with my peers at the Dunbar. It had several clubs, all of which I joined. We had a choir led by Mrs. Virginia

Wilson, one of the leaders at the Dunbar. She was single then and we depended on her for most of our activities. She could really play the piano, and in addition to all my other activities, I took piano lessons from her. I don't know how I managed to do all these things, but I enjoyed every minute of the time I spent in my black world.

And, oh yes, there was a volunteer, Mrs. Roberta Britt, who held special classes for the girls. Mrs. Britt was an elegant lady. She and her husband owned and managed a house on the campus that provided housing for young black women who could attend the University of Michigan but could not stay in the dormitories. I really liked Mrs. Britt. She was open and frank with us about things young girls needed to know. She told us how important it was for us to keep clean in body, mind, and spirit. She often demonstrated where and how we should give an extra scrub or two. Later in my life, I became friends with Mrs. Britt's family, the Ellises. I am still in touch with several of her great-nephews and great-nieces. This family has had a tremendous impact on my life.

Because I hung out at the Dunbar so much, I became friendly with Mr. and Mrs. Williams. They invited me to their apartment for a cold drink or to chat and play with their children. They soon asked if I would like to babysit for them. This opportunity came about the time I was in the ninth grade and was getting ready to make the big transition to Ann Arbor Senior High School. My after-school work was interfering with my social activities, and I no longer wanted to wash potatoes and clean venetian blinds. The appeal of my friendship with the Williamses went way beyond the opportunity to earn a few dollars. These two individuals were very special. They had both gone to college in the South. They had graduated from predominately black colleges and received master's degrees in social work. They were offspring of black professionals who had done very well for themselves. They were the only black family at that time who were living like some of the white people I had met.

The Williamses' apartment was similar to Ms. Lane's. It was warm, attractive, and filled with books and all kinds of exciting pictures and things. I felt good being around them. My association with this lovely family convinced me that I could dream about living the way I wanted to live. It further convinced me that one sure way to do this was to make certain I went to college. It wasn't long before Mr. and Mrs. Williams asked me to call them "Ma" and "Pa" instead of Mr. and Mrs. Williams. They became my surrogate parents until they died very late in life. Their sons were a part of this union and I'm still in touch with the two younger ones today.

Once I gave up my after-school job, I spent even more time at the Dunbar. I shared many of the challenges I faced at school with Ma and Pa Williams. They were so proud of me in seventh grade when I joined the chorus. And when I became one of the editors of the yearbook, we had a party with cookies and punch. I shared these things with my mother and father, but they were not as excited about my achievements as Ma and Pa Williams seemed to be.

The Dunbar Community Center served as the center for all the activities available to black children. While there was a YWCA and a YMCA in the city, black youngsters were not allowed to participate in their programs. However, the Girl Reserves movement, which later became the Y-Teen movement in the YWCA, was very strong across the nation. Arrangements had been made with the YWCA and the Dunbar Center to organize a Girl Reserves Club at the Dunbar. The Girl Scout movement was also active, but it did not extend its reach into the black community until several years later. The establishment of a Girl Reserves Club in our neighborhood brought a few opportunities for the girls to join some activities with white girls in the Girl Reserves at the YWCA. But nothing at this time even hinted that the YWCA would play a major role in my future life.

The Girl Reserves uniform was a navy skirt and a white blouse. Most of our club members had some difficulty getting our uniforms together, but once again the Thrift Shop came to my rescue. There was almost nothing that could not be found there. Our club was not large, but was made up of girls who lived in the neighborhood and wanted to do the kinds of activities the Girl Reserves were known for. One such activity was weekend retreats, most often held at a nearby camp. I still have the Memory Book from 1946 that some of the participants signed when I represented our club. The retreat was held in June, when school was out for the summer, at Clear Lake Camp in Dowling, Michigan, and lasted several days. Dowling wasn't far from my home, but it was far enough to make the trip exciting. I was excited to have a cabin with a really nice view of the waterfront. There were girls from Kalamazoo, Flint, Lansing, and other Michigan cities. Although there were only a handful of black girls in the group, I was used to being in the minority. The sponsors wanted everyone to enjoy the experiences, so our differences never became a topic of discussion. The retreat provided me with my first opportunity to learn how to swim. I learned how to float on my back, which is about all I can do today. But there is more to the swimming story later.

The activities available through the Dunbar Community Center and the YWCA gave me opportunities to develop a fine network of young girls like myself. It was also a way for me to share my ideas with others and to learn how other young girls felt about growing up. Unfortunately, there were almost no opportunities to talk about our differences. It was as though any discussion about race was taboo. I found the same experience at the conference I attended a year or so later in Grinnell, Iowa.

Being selected to represent the Girl Reserves at a national YWCA-YMCA High School Conference at Grinnell College in Grinnell, Iowa, was a real honor. I was almost beside myself when I was told I would join this group and travel by train to Grinnell. I had never been on a train before. The excitement of taking a trip by train, going to Grinnell College, and participating in this National Conference was so exciting, and the opportunity could not have come at a better time in my life. I was finishing ninth grade and getting ready to enter high school. I completed ninth grade in the summer of 1947. I had achieved many honors, but best of all I'd been elected president of my ninth-grade class. Of the forty-seven students in the class, nine of us were black, five were Greek, and the rest were white. By this time, I had already established myself as a leader. The conference took place in June, so there wasn't much time to prepare once school was out. The excitement was unreal. With help from the trusty Thrift Shop, my mother, and Grandma Thomas, I was able to get my clothes together and pack. Around a thousand students attended the conference. Again, the black students were in the minority: probably no more than 2 or 3 percent were black. The meetings were well organized, with topics kept to fairly general themes, mostly issues important to young teens. I met a lot of people and enjoyed it all. I think this group of young people got along so well because the YWCA and the Dunbar Community Center were again the sponsors. As I look back at these two experiences, I realize that in the late thirties and early forties, racial issues were not openly discussed. Schools and colleges avoided these issues, and the leadership in those days were not prepared to think about or to encourage discussions about racism. The purpose of these experiences was simply to bring the two groups together.

We were given time to shop for souvenirs in the small shopping section of Grinnell. The town was small and we could reach almost everything by walking. I went shopping with some of the new friends I had met. We chose to do most of our shopping in the five-and-dime. I had about three dollars to spend and decided to buy my mother and father a souvenir. I knew the layout of the five-and-dime because I'd spent a lot of time in the store at home.

I wanted to buy my mother of box of chocolates, which was a dollar. I didn't want to spend all my money on souvenirs, so I decided to buy my father something that would not cost more than twenty-five cents. The relationship I had with my father was not all that great. I was closer to my mother. I felt that spending less on him was enough. I bought him a small notebook, something so he would know I had thought of him. I never dreamed that the difference I spent for the two gifts would be so obvious, or would produce the response I received.

When I returned home, bubbling over with enthusiasm from the week's experiences at the conference, I proudly presented my parents with their gifts. My mother was very gracious in accepting her box of candy. My father was not as gracious. He was angry. So angry, that after he said a few very unkind words to me, he threw the notebook at me. It landed on the floor in my bedroom. At that moment, it seemed as if my world was coming to an end. I'd had no idea he would react the way he did. All I could do was to fall on my bed and sob.

I cried for a long time, and the crying has never stopped. Since that day I always give second thoughts to what I spend on gifts.

I learned a lot about my expanding world at that conference. I learned even more about the world I had to live in when I returned home.

Finally finishing ninth grade was a "big deal." This was important for most of us because we left the school building we had been in for nine years, Jones Elementary, and moved to a different and larger building. It also meant we would have to walk several more blocks to high school. The high school's location was important to us because it was on the edge of the University of Michigan's campus. My friends and I felt like we were growing up.

Part of my growing up included interest in the opposite sex. I mentioned earlier that we did a lot of socializing in our neighborhood when we went ice-skating in the park. Part of the fun of ice-skating was being asked to skate around the park with a young man. Sometimes after skating a few times around the pond, my skating partner and I would retreat to the "shack" where we would sit, talk, and warm up. The first few evenings of skating with the young man I had an eye on led to a monopoly. James Baker, the young man who was to become my future husband, first became my ice-skating partner. I made it to the park as often as I could just to skate with James Baker. Before long, we were not only warming up together, but walking home together.

Our friendship began about the time I stopped going to the park in the evenings. I decided to eliminate ice-skating because my extracurricular activities, including the Dunbar Community Center and the church, were taking up a lot of time. Also, I was making extra money babysitting. All of this had to fit into my ninth-grade schedule. So James and I continued our friendship by walking to school together. He was in eleventh grade. I remember the day he asked me to go to the movies on Sunday afternoon. I was so excited. When I asked my mother if I could go, she agreed, but she said I was not to think about going steady until I was at least sixteen. I hadn't thought about going steady at all. I just wanted to be with James Baker whenever possible.

We continued to walk to school together every day. In the evenings he called me on the phone and we talked as long as we could without parental interference. The telephone in my house was on a small table near a window from which I could see James talking to me a few houses away. We thought this was such great fun. After the Sunday afternoon movie date, there were more. Then James asked me to his junior prom. I sat on the invitation for as long as I could before sharing it with my mother. She said she had to think about it, which meant she would talk to my father. To my surprise, they allowed me to accept the invitation. My mother and I began to plan for my formal attire. I prayed the Thrift Shop would not play a part in my wardrobe for the prom. Again to my surprise, my mother suggested we go shopping in Detroit. What a wonderful shopping trip! We went into several stores on the avenue in Detroit where they sold mostly wedding dresses. We finally found one that I liked, and that fit both my figure and my mother's pocketbook. This beautiful white taffeta and chiffon creation cost all of fifteen dollars, a lot of money in those days. Then my mother announced that I would need a coat, because the dance was in early spring and the evenings were chilly. I couldn't believe my ears. We continued shopping and found a gray pinstriped three-quarter-length coat that completed the outfit. I was in seventh heaven.

James's mother wanted us to have our picture taken by a photographer that evening. She made all of the arrangements. We had to be dressed two hours before the prom so we could go to the photographer's house. Mr. Jewett was the father of three friends—Ruth, Iva, and Coleman—and took the official and important photographs that came out of our neighborhood. Because we were important, at least to our parents and especially to Mrs. Baker, who was paying for all of this, we made the trip to Mr. Jewett's home studio. The evening was grand. Ms. Baker drove us to the prom, picked us up, and took me home, only a few houses from the Bakers. We never thought a thing about being driven to the prom by James's mother. No one in our neighborhood drove. Many families didn't have cars, and those who did had only one. Young people, even if they could drive, were not allowed to drive the family car alone, and certainly not in the evening on a date.

A year later, James invited me to his Senior Frolic. By then we were going steady. There wasn't any further discussion about this with my mother. In one short year much had changed. I was in tenth grade. I made my dress for the dance. James had his driver's license, and he had the car for the evening. We were growing up in fine style.

Going to high school presented me with a new problem. Our lunch break was less than an hour long. Some students had enough money to eat in the cafeteria or at one of the drugstore counters on campus. I was not that fortunate. I had to go home for lunch. I didn't question this, I just did it. It was a fast trip. Several of my friends had to go home for lunch as well. Actually, this was a blessing in disguise. That year all of my siblings came home for lunch. Our mother didn't work, and she always had a hot lunch waiting. We all sat down together and gulped down our hot soup and peanut butter sandwiches. My mother could make soup out of anything. I remember trying to enjoy my potato or carrot soup. Those lunches prepared me for the food I would have to eat later in life to maintain my health and my weight.

I adjusted to high school very well. I was one of two black students in my homeroom class. Homeroom was exactly what the name implied. It was our home in school for the three years we were there. We had a great teacher, Miss Zoller. Once again, I developed a good relationship with my teacher. I still have the lovely silver pin Miss Zoller gave me for graduation. I'm not sure if she did this for all of her students, but I was surprised and pleased when she presented me with the gift.

I liked high school. It was easy for me to make friends with other students who had transferred from smaller elementary or junior high schools. I took part in several extracurricular activities. I joined the a capella choir, was elected to the student council, and was on a college curriculum. Willis Patterson, who as I noted before became dean of the School of Music at the University of Michigan, was also a member of this choir.

I enjoyed most of my classes, except Latin. I had taken my first year of Latin in ninth grade. It was obvious from the beginning that foreign languages would not be one of my strengths. I needed at least four years of a foreign language to graduate on a college curriculum, so I managed to do the best I could. Sitting in Latin class, I was scared to the bone that I'd be called on to answer the teacher's question. I was most afraid when I hadn't studied properly. And, of course, those were the times Miss Reiger, the Latin teacher, called on me.

The classes I liked best were the ones where I could participate in discussions. Social issues were of particular interest to me, as they are today. In the Social Democracy class I think I shocked everyone, including the teacher, when we discussed racial issues. For some reason a student had asked why black people always drove big cars. Well, I wasn't going to let that question go without my input.

By the time I finished explaining how racism was the cause of some blacks driving big cars, I felt I had gained the respect of my classmates and my teacher. I clearly explained how racist behavior in the housing market forced blacks to buy things that whites allowed them to buy. They were limited in the kinds of houses they could buy. They were often refused mortgage loans. So they bought what they could buy without a lot of opposition. However, whites did not fail to extend their racism when it came to charging interest rates on the money lent to finance the cars. We also talked about how nice black people dressed, especially when they went to church. First of all, it was part of the culture to present oneself in fine style whenever blacks went to worship. It showed respect for the Lord. And we were not stopped from buying clothes. In some cities, the stores would not allow blacks to try on clothes before making a purchase. This was not the case in our city.

However, this did not stop blacks from buying clothes that were presentable for wearing to church. I had learned a lot about racism after my hot fudge sundae incident.

I constantly looked for reasons for racist behavior. Some of what I learned about racism came from long discussions with Ma and Pa Williams. Because they had lived in the South, they had experienced a different kind of racism. It was much more overt in the South than in the North. Also, because they were social workers, they were able to explain some of the racist behavior from a sociological perspective. But what I was learning and trying to understand about racism was not enough to totally prepare me for what was to come later.

By the time I reached eleventh grade, I needed to make more money than I was making at babysitting. I discovered the work-study program at school. This program would give me credit for working if I could find a job that met its requirements. Through my network of friends, I learned that the Mademoiselle Shop on State Street, a major thoroughfare that extended from my high school through the center of the University's campus, was looking for a stock girl. Once I made sure this job would be approved for the work-study program, I went to the shop to apply. The Mademoiselle Shop specialized in clothing for women and was situated in a most desirable location on State Street. It was less than five minutes from school to the shop. Because what little shopping I did was on Main Street or in the Thrift Shop, I had no reason or opportunity to go into the shops on State Street, where wealthy students and families shopped.

I was a bit nervous the day of my interview. I wasn't sure if I would be refused because I was black. Once again, with my application in one hand and my nerve in the other, I approached the shop with as much self-confidence as I could muster. The shop was lovely. The clothes on display in the window were absolutely beautiful. As I opened the heavy glass door to the shop, I noticed immediately that the display cases and counter tops were also glass. Thick carpeting covered the floor. I had never been in a shop like this before.

The clerk who greeted me was very friendly. I told her I was there to see the owner, Mrs. Sadacca, and she invited me to follow her to the office at the rear of the store. The remaining section of the shop was lovely. I couldn't keep my eyes off the clothes and the people looking at themselves in the mirrors.

The office door was ajar. An attractive lady with blonde hair sat at a desk. The clerk escorting me knocked gently on the door. Mrs. Sadacca immediately got up from her chair and came to the door. She was expecting me. She thanked the clerk for bringing me to her office and invited me in. She called me by my name and offered me a seat. I gave her my application. She took a minute to glance at it, then the questions started. Actually there were only a few questions and these focused on my availability for working in the shop. She indicated that although I would be released from school to work during the week, she also wanted me on Saturdays. This delighted me to no end because it meant I would make more money. She also explained that after working a few months I would be entitled to a discount on any clothes I might want to buy. This was so exciting. I couldn't imagine wearing the clothes I saw in the store. Once we settled everything, I signed the papers and agreed to report for work the following week. I was so happy I wanted to run to the front door, but I managed to smile at two clerks and walk slowly to the exit. I wondered what they were thinking as I passed by and smiled. I knew I would be working with these two women in the coming week. Once I left the shop, I did run. I ran almost all the way home. I was so excited, I could hardly wait to tell my mother I had an honest-to-goodness real job.

I worked at the Mademoiselle Shop until I graduated from high school. Some of my happiest moments were spent in that shop. I started as a stock girl, and was given a great deal of responsibility for organizing the stock. Almost right away I noticed there was no system for identifying specific types of clothing on the sales ticket. This presented problems in keeping track of stock. I developed a system that Mrs. Sadacca accepted immediately. Within a few months, I was asked to fill in for the regular clerks when they were at lunch or on vacation. I soon learned the art of selling clothes to wealthy people.

No one seemed to mind that I was black. It didn't take me long to identify clothing items I wanted and thought I should be wearing in the shop. My purchases were charged to me and deducted from my weekly pay. Some weeks I didn't take much cash home. But that didn't matter. I was able to wear cashmere sweaters to school and work, just like the white girls in my classes did. Occasionally someone made a nasty remark about what I was wearing. Being as sensitive as I was, this did not sit well with me. One day after a negative comment, I shared my feelings with Ma and Pa. At the conclusion of our discussion Pa asked me how much a cashmere sweater cost. I told him the sweater with tax and my discount came to $7.30. I didn't think any more about his inquiry. The next day, as I usually did after work, I stopped by to visit them at their home in the Dunbar Center. They were having dinner and invited me to join them, but I declined. I didn't visit long, but before I left Pa said he had something for me and got up from the table. He handed me an envelope and said this was from the two of them. Then he added, "Go buy yourself another cashmere sweater." I was dumbfounded. I almost cried right there on the spot. No one had ever given me anything like this. I hugged them both, thanked them profusely, and cried all the way home. To this day, when I look at a cashmere sweater or buy one, I relive the memory of that gift, that day, and that moment.

I learned much from working at the Mademoiselle Shop, and the experience netted me two wonderful friends. The shop had its own seamstress, Mary Otterbein. I tried to call her Mrs. Otterbein, but she insisted I call her Mary. Mary and I took to each other like ducks to water. We became very good friends. Mary often invited me to her home, where I had milk and cookies with her and her husband, Charlie. Mary and I exchanged favors. I did errands for her and she altered some of the clothes I bought. We worked together in the stockroom upstairs. The design of our workspace provided us with plenty of opportunities to visit and discuss shop gossip.

During my senior year in high school, my uncle, who was a captain in the army, was stationed in Japan. He was the same uncle whose room I had cleaned weekly for twenty-five cents when I was in elementary school. I mentioned earlier that he and his wife often sent me gifts from Japan and from other countries. One of the gifts they sent me during my senior year was several yards of beautiful brocaded silk. I showed Mary this material. She knew that my senior prom was coming soon and that I needed a wrap to wear. She offered to make me an evening jacket out of the silk. The results were stunning. Some fifty years later, the jacket is hanging in my oldest daughter's closet. It is still stunning.

One day Mrs. Sadacca announced that she wouldn't be coming to the shop every day. She had hired a manager to take her place. We were all very sad about her decision but soon learned to respect and like her replacement, Mrs. Kroter.

Mrs. Kroter was very different from Mrs. Sadacca in both style and looks. However, she was just as kind as Mrs. Sadacca and we got off to a good start working together. Actually, I was working for her, but it was a pleasure. I found myself spending more time on the floor selling. Mrs. Kroter's husband was also a nice person and we often spent a few minutes talking about one thing or another whenever he was in the shop.

One day Mr. Kroter and his wife were in the office discussing a wedding gift they were going to purchase for a friend's wedding. They were talking about silver patterns. Mrs. Kroter asked me if I had selected a silver pattern. I didn't understand what she meant. I tried not to look dumb but it was obvious that this was a new concept for me. Mrs. Kroter took the time to explain sterling silver and how nice it was to select a pattern. If I had a pattern, my friends could buy me a piece for my birthday or a holiday. If I didn't have all of my set by the time I got married, friends could buy me pieces or a place setting as a wedding gift. I really liked the idea, but for a person who had been eating on matching dishware, much less china, only for a few years, this was not yet a part of my lifestyle. To my surprise, a few days later Mrs. Kroter asked me to go with her to the department store a few doors down. She took me to the department where they sold china and silver. I had no idea why she took me with her. I thought perhaps she wanted me to carry a package for her. When we were waited on, she asked the clerk to show us samples of sterling silver flatware. I'd never seen such beautiful pieces in my life. The forks and knives looked too shiny too use.

After looking at a few silver patterns, Mrs. Kroter asked me which one I liked. I liked them all, but had a particular fancy for the pattern with a rose. I chose Damask Rose by Heirloom. Mrs. Kroter thought I'd made a good decision. She thanked the clerk and we left the store. It never occurred to me that I had just selected my graduation gift. Mr. and Mrs. Kroter presented me with my first piece of sterling silver, a beautiful spoon, Damask Rose by Heirloom Sterling, for graduation. Before I left my job at the Mademoiselle Shop, I was the proud owner of two more pieces of sterling flatware, a knife and a fork, compliments of the Kroters.

My senior year was not as pleasant as I would have liked. My best friend, James Baker, was away at college and I missed him a great deal. We stayed in touch mostly through the mail; long-distance phone calls were not as common as they are today. He came home to visit as often as he could. On several occasions I rode with his family to Ohio, where he was in school, for a short visit. We went mostly to homecoming or special events. Although I missed James, I was still doing well in my studies and my job provided me with a lot of pleasure.

At a senior assembly one day, it was announced that the senior trip would be to Washington, DC, and New York. We all had known there would be a trip, we just hadn't known where. I bought a few clothes over the course of the next few months and set aside the money I would need for the class trip. By this time I realized I could not depend on my parents for anything other than a place to sleep and food to eat. I was responsible for everything else, including school fees and books. I learned very early in life that the one person I could depend on was me.

My best friend, Elaine Henderson, and I were planning to be roommates. We were excited about the trip. We put the deposit down and planned our wardrobes and all the exciting things we would do during the trip. Shortly after I had made my deposit, my homeroom teacher, Miss Zoller, asked me to speak with her after school. I never had one thought that our conversation would be about the senior trip, but it was. Miss Zoller was such a nice woman, and I couldn't understand why she was having trouble looking at me while she spoke. She told me I could go on the class trip, but I would need friends or relatives to stay with in Washington. She told me that hotels there would not accept me as a guest because I was black. However, there would be no problem in New York. My bubble burst. Here it was again. First it was a paper cup because I wasn't good enough to enjoy my sundae in a glass dish like the white girl. Now I wasn't good enough to stay with my white classmates at a hotel in the nation's capital.

I guess I was surprised because I was attending an integrated school, and until that moment I had felt no discrimination there, at least nothing I couldn't handle. I couldn't say much to Miss Zoller except that I had no friends or relatives in Washington. The result was clear. I could not join my classmates on our senior trip. The most devastating part of the situation was that my anger turned to embarrassment. I was embarrassed because my blackness kept me from going on the trip.

In 1949, years before the civil rights movement and the legislation that grew out of that movement, there was no one I could turn to for help. There was no organization that had the clout to change things. The church could not help. The Dunbar Center, Ma and Pa Williams, could not help. Not even my parents could help. All I could do was cry. Why was this happening to me and to other people who looked like me? I knew it was racism, but why did racism have to exist?

The hardest part of this experience was telling my white friends and classmates that I wasn't going. What could I tell them? I finally came up with a reason. I would tell them it was too expensive. They would accept that. This is what I did. I took the blame because I was too embarrassed to tell them the reason I wasn't going was because I was black and blacks couldn't stay at hotels in the nation's capital. This incident added fuel to my fire.

The hot fudge sundae lesson was being absorbed and translated into a spirited black woman in a white world. The overall result became a bigger part of my daily life than I'd ever thought it would or could be.

At the end of my senior year I was voted best-dressed girl in the senior class. This was due to my employment at the Mademoiselle Shop. But it also pleased me, largely because I had graduated from the Thrift Shop all by myself.

I was also awarded the Michigan Honorary Society Award at graduation and received a scholarship from the Rotary Club to attend the University of Michigan. The scholarship was announced in the local paper, the *Ann Arbor News*, which noted: "Miss Calvert, a Negress, was graduated in June from Ann Arbor High School." It was the first time I was referred to as a Negress. And the last.

FOUR

Mixing Education and Marriage

I spent most of the summer of 1949 working, dating, and preparing for my freshman year at the University of Michigan. James was home for the summer and we spent a lot of time together. Most of it was spent at Wild Goose Lake in Chelsea, Michigan, where his parents were building a summer home. James was from a large family, and many of them came together on weekends for waterskiing, fishing, and picnics at the lake. There were only about a dozen families living on this small lake, and most of the families were related.

The history of Wild Goose Lake is an interesting one. I was told that in the early 1900s, Mr. Baker and several of his friends and relatives bought property there for the purpose of designing and constructing a golf course. This group of black men all played golf but could not play on any white golf courses. Although the initial work on the course was completed, for mainly financial reasons the dream of a nine-hole golf course was never realized. The investors divided up the land and many of them built cottages or small houses on their parcels. By the time Mr. Baker built his summer home, his children were grown, and several had contributed to his flock of grandchildren. The Baker cottage was a five-bedroom summerhouse. After the cottage, as we called it, was finished, there was rarely a weekend when it wasn't filled to capacity.

Because the family was large, the weekend gatherings often included many family members and friends. Ms. Baker was an excellent cook, as were her daughters. They spent a great deal of time cooking and baking for the weekend meals. When the menus required trips to surrounding farms to purchase corn and other vegetables, James volunteered to drive, and I was right next to him in the front seat of the family car. Often the weekends included a trip to pick strawberries or other fruits to make sauces for ice cream, preserves, or jellies. I always looked forward to our times at the lake. It was fun being with the Baker family.

I continued my job at the Mademoiselle Shop and had no problem planning my college wardrobe. However, it soon became clear that even with my Rotary Scholarship of $70 per semester I needed to save money for my books. Things were tight financially, but I felt I could handle my expenses. Living at home meant I wouldn't have to worry about room and board. However, living at home was not an option for me.

Black students were not allowed to stay in the dormitories at the University of Michigan. Students whose families did not live in Ann Arbor had to live in private homes. These were maintained by black families who had an extra room or two, or in houses reserved exclusively for blacks. Most of the black female students lived in the Britt House. The Britts were my friends. Mrs. Britt volunteered at the Dunbar Center and worked with us girls. The Britt House was very large and could house about a dozen students. The main house for black males was referred to as the Lewis House. It was owned and operated by Mr. and Mrs. Edward Lewis, who were members of our church.

From the late forties to the early fifties there were only about two hundred black students at the University of Michigan. This was out of a student body of approximately 35,000. The housing situation was yet another racist slap in the face, but there was nothing at that time that could be done. Not only was the housing situation terrible, but for many years the black student enrollment was limited to two hundred. This was easy for the University to manage because in addition to labeling ourselves on an application, we had to submit a photograph.

The day of freshman orientation and registration had finally arrived. James was preparing to return to Central State College in Wilberforce, Ohio, and I was getting ready to enter the University of Michigan. I was excited, but I regretted the fact that I had to stay in Ann Arbor. My friends and I had dreamed of going away to school. Although most of my white friends did go away, my black friends did not. It was either the University of Michigan in Ann Arbor, or Eastern Michigan University just a few miles away in Ypsilanti.

My first choice for college was Smith College in Massachusetts. I never knew anyone who attended Smith. I'm not sure why this was my first choice. I must have indicated my interest in Smith on a form or two in high school, because I was invited to attend teas given by the women of Smith at the Michigan League. When I attended these teas I was always the only black student present. The women and the few men there were kind. No one ever indicated any interest in my attending Smith. They introduced themselves to me as we sipped our tea, asked one or two questions, and moved on to someone else. I wasn't sure how to apply for a scholarship, but there didn't seem to be anyone I could ask. After discovering how much it would cost to attend Smith, I knew better than to ask my parents if they could either send me to Smith or help with the tuition.

My second choice for college was Talladega College in Alabama. This too was a college for girls, only this college was for black girls. I had read about Talladega in the material on colleges I had received. I had also heard about it from Ma and Pa Williams. Most of my information about predominately black colleges came from them.

Where I wanted to go to college didn't seem to matter to anyone but me. Gradually I resigned myself to staying in Ann Arbor and attending the University of Michigan. Receiving the Rotary Scholarship marked the end of my giving any consideration to another school. It took me several years after graduating from Michigan to realize what a fine institution it was, and still is. Once I entered the professional world, I realized it had been a privilege to attend the University of Michigan.

After receiving my bachelor of arts degree, I planned to complete a master of arts degree. I would never have thought I would also receive a PhD. And not in a million years would I have imagined receiving an honorary doctorate of law degree from the University of Michigan. This happened in 1996, the year I retired.

The entire process of enrolling as a freshman at Michigan was an overwhelming experience. Trying to figure out where to go and what to do was monumental. Yet in spite of the confusion, I enjoyed every minute of being part of the University. For eighteen years I had lived on the edge of this campus and now I was finally a part of it.

I remembered the days I went with my grandmother to check coats at the J-Hop on campus. I must have been in ninth or tenth grade. My grandmother was in charge of hiring a crew of women to check coats for the hundreds of university students attending their junior ball, which they called the J-Hop. I was thrilled at the opportunity to make extra money, but also because I was actually on campus. Once or twice I was able to peek into the ballroom and watch the sea of beautiful women in gorgeous long formals dancing with men in black tuxedos. What a wonderful sight. A well-known dance band provided the music, and listening to a live band in the intramural building was a real treat. The students had decorated the gym to look special. When I was checking coats for the ball, I knew I would go to college—somewhere, somehow—but I never thought it would be the University of Michigan. I never dreamed that one day I might actually attend the J-Hop in that same building. But eventually I did attend, and someone checked *my* coat in the same place I had checked others' coats several years before.

Because there were not many black students on campus, I functioned mainly in a predominately white world. There were a few social activities given by black fraternities and sororities, and those functions allowed me to meet black students. However, because there were no special places for black students to hold social affairs in those days, they were usually held at the Michigan League. Sometimes we gathered at the homes of blacks in the community who had large basements or family rooms.

It didn't take me long to meet several male and female students with whom I became friendly. Most of the students were from Michigan, a few from New Jersey, and one or two from southern states. In 1949 there was a flood of men returning from World War II and going to school on the GI Bill. They were a few years older than most of the male freshmen who had just completed high school. This made it possible for freshmen and upperclasswomen to have a dating pool. I met several women who became lifelong friends. One of these, Barbara Crane, lived off campus in my neighborhood with her grandmother. Barbara and I were able to walk to school, study, and go to social functions together. James was away at school, and I was so caught up in my relationship with him that I did very little dating.

Toward the end of my first semester, I wasn't feeling as well as I usually did. This was in December 1949. I soon discovered the reason for my lightheadedness and my upset stomach. I was pregnant. The discovery brought my world to an end, or so I thought. The world in which I lived then was very different from today. For a young woman to become pregnant out of wedlock was a disgrace. I was so ashamed I didn't know what to do.

I knew the first person I had to discuss this with was James. When I told him, he suggested we get married immediately. I was grateful for his warm response. We both realized we needed to tell our parents. This was something we didn't want to do, but there was no choice. He told his mother and I told my mother. I simply couldn't tell my father, nor did James tell his father. We let our mothers tell our fathers. Neither James nor I had close relationships with our fathers, so this was the easy way out.

Over the next few weeks I cried many tears. I was so ashamed. Fortunately I had James to lean on. He insisted on marriage. I didn't object because I didn't want an abortion. My father sent me a message through my mother that he didn't want me to have an abortion. This comforted me because I didn't think my father cared enough to offer his thoughts on what I should do. The way my mother delivered his message told me that she agreed with him.

The Bakers encouraged marriage. In fact Mrs. Baker and one of her daughters, Elizabeth Hill, said they would take care of the baby so I could return to school after the delivery. Mrs. Baker also said that if I wanted to have an abortion they would cover the expense.

Breaking the news to our parents was only the first of many painful steps we had to take. How would I tell Ma and Pa Williams? They were next in line. To my surprise, they did not condemn me, as I had expected. In fact, they were most supportive. Getting pregnant in that day and age was clear evidence that I had fallen in the gutter, but their response was that just because I had fallen in the gutter, I didn't have to stay there.

James and I decided to marry as soon as possible. We agreed that he would remain in college. He had a year and a half to go. I would drop out of school. As soon as possible after I had the baby I would return to the University. We married quietly in January 1950.

The days of my pregnancy were not pleasant. Physically I did quite well. I exercised, watched my diet, and tried to keep my spirits up. However, I constantly felt as though I had literally fallen in the gutter. I was embarrassed and very angry that I had allowed myself to become pregnant. To this day I am not sure how it happened.

I moved in with the Baker family. James was in school. He didn't work, so we had no income. The Bakers were more than able to cover James's tuition and college expenses, but there was nothing for us, or for me, to live on. The Baker family always appeared to have a firmer financial base than other families in the neighborhood. They had a big house in town as well as the lake house they had built. They had a new car every two or three years. Their car made all of the other cars on Fourth Avenue look very much out-of-date. I had no idea what kind of work Mr. Baker did until I moved in with them. It seems that Mr. Baker was born in Canada and married Ms. Baker in her early twenties. Mr. Baker worked in the Ann Arbor Foundry when they first married. They had children early in their marriage and bought the house they were living in when I moved in with them.

Mr. Baker was a frugal man and saved as much money as he could without penalizing his family. One day, as the story goes, there came an opportunity for Mr. Baker to invest in the foundry. Mr. Baker was eager to participate in this investment. His frugality had paid off: he had saved fifteen hundred dollars in a cigar box he'd kept hidden under his bed. He solidified the investment along with nine other men, only two of whom were black. It didn't take long for their investment to pay off. The Ann Arbor Foundry was one of two foundries in the state of Michigan that made parts for automobile factories. They also had the contract for making manhole covers for Ann Arbor and for other Michigan cities.

Although the Baker family had a very good income, they lived modestly and enjoyed their wealth. Unfortunately, the Bakers did not continue their pattern of investment. They were comfortable, but by the time James had graduated from college, the original pool of investors had dwindled to two, Mr. Baker and Mr. Thomas Cook. The need for the equipment the foundry made was also dwindling. However, the two men continued to work every day. The property was sold some years later, after celebrating fifty years of business.

This was perhaps one of very few businesses in the country where blacks and whites shared ownership. Mr. Cook was a Russian Jew. This was significant to me in light of the many facets of racism I had already discovered in my short life. One of the exciting aspects of their relationship was that the two families shared special cultural events and celebrations. The Cooks learned much about the black experience from the Bakers and the Bakers learned a great deal about Jewish culture from the Cooks. Mr. Baker invested in Jewish bonds to a limited extent, and gifts to members of the

Cook family included money for trees to be planted in Israel. In return, the Cooks made contributions to the AME church, the Baker family's church.

James's and my financial situation at that time was a disaster. I had no income and couldn't work because I was pregnant. I simply could not ask my parents or his parents for financial assistance. So I began to think of ways to make money while I was pregnant. One of my best friends, Betty Williams, lived a few doors from us. Betty was still in high school and had not found work for the summer. We put our heads together and decided we could take in laundry. Because Betty's mother worked she was not home during the day. Ms. Williams agreed to let us use her home for our laundry project. We put an ad in the newspaper with borrowed money and waited for our project to unfold. Unfold it did. During the two or three months we worked, we took in more laundry than we had bargained for. We not only earned money, but it gave us something to do. Washing and ironing every day, all day long, reinforced my desire to return to school and complete a degree. Cleaning venetian blinds, washing and ironing clothes, and being on welfare were not going to be part of *my* future.

In September 1950, James and I were blessed with a beautiful baby girl. We named her JoAnn Elizabeth: JoAnn after a friend, and Elizabeth after one of James's sisters. I remained part of the Baker household during James's senior year. Ms. Baker and Elizabeth kept their promise to help me with the baby. I knew I would need to find work for at least a year while James finished school. I think it was more important to me than to him that James finish school. I was determined not to marry a man who didn't have a college degree. Because of this, I didn't mind working while he completed his studies. We didn't have to pay rent or buy food, but I still needed an income.

It was not easy for blacks to find anything but domestic work in the small town of Ann Arbor. I had had my share of cleaning and doing laundry. What was I to do? I discussed my dilemma with Ma and Pa Williams. They in turn discussed it with our minister, Reverend C. W. Carpenter. They eventually told me about a bookkeeper/secretarial position the Ann Arbor YWCA was trying to fill with a minority, for the YWCA had no minorities on the staff except a part-time cook. The three of us were aware that I had no experience for this position. However, I had taken a typing course in high school at my mother's insistence. My mother always felt that if I found a job as a secretary it would be good enough for me. I was now glad she had insisted: the fact that I could type was a plus.

There was another positive factor in my favor. While this position focused on bookkeeping and secretarial work, the person also had to function as the receptionist. The three of us knew that I had what it took to be a good receptionist. So with my typing skills and confidence in one hand and my nerve in the other, I went for an interview. I landed the job. After months of feeling depressed over my pregnancy, once I was hired for this responsible position in the YWCA, I began to have hope for what was come.

I enjoyed my work, though it was all a challenge. I knew very little about accounting, but because the amounts of money I had to keep track of were not great, I willingly accepted the responsibility of developing a bookkeeping system. My work at the Mademoiselle Shop had occasionally included keeping track of the accounts, which gave me some of the knowledge I needed in my position at the YWCA. I thought I could type, but I really couldn't. My high school typing class had taught me the keyboard, but the rest I had to learn. I'm sure no one at the YWCA knew how many sheets of paper I discarded with typing errors. Sometimes I took paper home with me to keep from sharing my mistakes with the janitor. The one position I excelled in was as the receptionist. I liked people, and I soon found that this was the basis for developing the skills I needed to be effective.

James graduated and received his bachelor of arts degree from Central State University in Wilberforce, Ohio. I was thrilled that we could now live together. The only drawback was that we were also living with his parents. This was a comfortable arrangement for a while because I didn't have to take JoAnn to a babysitter when I went to work each day. However, living with his parents made me feel too much like a guest. I had no responsibilities for preparing meals or keeping house. It was somewhat awkward for everyone, but mostly for me.

I realized almost immediately that James needed to find a job. His degree did not prepare him to do much other than teach. We found out that he lacked some of the courses required to be a certified teacher in Michigan. Because Central State College was in Ohio, it prepared its students only for what was required to teach in that state. So we faced two dilemmas. James didn't have the necessary credentials to teach in Michigan, and we needed to find a place to live.

In the early fifties, in Ann Arbor, Michigan, it wasn't easy to find an apartment if one was black. There were a few makeshift apartments that some black owners rented to blacks, but these apartments were very scarce.

Once again racism was standing in the way. We thought about trying to buy a house but the same situation prevailed. Blacks could not buy in white neighborhoods, and the number of houses available in black neighborhoods was limited. Besides, we had no money to buy a house even if we could have found one. These obstacles did not deter us from looking for a place we could call our own. James's parents, especially his mother, were aware of our desire. One day Mrs. Baker offered to help us with a down payment if we could find a house. She told us she had helped two of her older children by lending them the down payment. We were thrilled with her offer. We continued to look.

In the meantime James tried to find a teaching job. It was next to impossible to obtain a teaching position without the necessary credentials. What were we going to do? James needed a job. Mine at the YWCA was ending because the property was being sold; the Ann Arbor YWCA would merge with the YMCA. I had no idea what this merger meant in the world of the YWCA. Little did I know that my future would soon be influenced not only by the merger, but also by the existence of the YWCA as a women-only organization.

The answer to our problem of finding a job for James was the foundry. James and I discussed this possibility; although we both preferred that he teach, we didn't have much of a choice. If we were going to find a house, James needed a job. We also needed a car. There was no problem being hired by the Ann Arbor Foundry. It wasn't the cleanest job in the world, but James would have a job and a weekly paycheck. He started work almost immediately.

We made a joint decision that James would complete the courses for state teaching certification. Neither of us overlooked the fact that, when possible, I would start taking classes again. We also agreed that since we had one child it might make sense to have our second child before I returned full time to the University. Because my first pregnancy had surprised us and seemed to come quickly, we decided to start trying to have our second child, a boy. We were so young and innocent. We just knew the second child would be a boy, and that my second pregnancy would come quickly. However, it took us five years to accomplish our plan of having a second child.

One day when we were driving through a neighborhood blacks were moving to, we saw a for sale sign on a small, white, attractive Cape Cod bungalow. I wrote down the phone number and called when we returned home to see how much the seller was asking. The price seemed right. It was $4,500. The owner was asking $2,000 down and would accept a land contract. I didn't understand what a land contract was, but felt whatever it was we could handle it. James and I made an appointment to see the house.

The house was empty when we went inside. It had two bedrooms, a living room, dining area, bath, and cellar. The one-car garage was all we needed. The large backyard had an extra lot on one side. It was just right for us, and to our surprise, the salesman didn't seem at all concerned that we were black. We later learned the house was being sold on a land contract partly because this form of financing was much easier for a black couple to get than a bank mortgage. It never occurred to me that one day I would be a board member of a savings and loan association and participate in making decisions about mortgages in general and minorities in particular. All went well. We borrowed the down payment from the Bakers and prepared to move into our own house.

James and I were thrilled with the house. We spent as much time as we could looking for used furniture. We didn't need much. I remember the day we went to Sears Roebuck to look for a stove. We were so grateful to that store for allowing us to charge the $98 for a four-burner gas stove. We also picked up a secondhand icebox. Not a refrigerator, but an icebox. For almost two years we purchased ice from a truck that went through the neighborhood selling blocks of ice to those who still used an icebox. We also had to heat the house with a space heater. We didn't complain at all. We were so happy that we had a place of our own, a car, and a weekly paycheck.

For the next four or five years we focused on getting used to being husband and wife. We hadn't really lived together during the first two years of our marriage except for short periods of time. Living together in our own house required many adjustments. In addition to being husband and wife, we were also full-time parents. Things were not easy, but I was determined to make our marriage a happy one. We both wanted to be good parents and we gave our all to this responsibility.

One of our major problems was money. James was working, but the paychecks never seemed large enough to cover all our expenses. There were weeks when there was hardly any money left for us to enjoy. We felt we had done very well when we had enough money to buy a six-pack of beer for a weekend's relaxation. I had always been good at managing my own small bits of money, so managing our budget soon became my responsibility. I said I could rub two pennies together and make a third, which I did throughout our marriage. However, I soon felt the need to find a way to bring in extra income.

Our minister, Reverend Carpenter, called me one day. He had heard I was no longer working at the YWCA and asked me to come to his office to discuss an idea he had. I didn't know what to expect. He was familiar with the responsibilities I had fulfilled at the YWCA; after all, he helped me get that position. He told me he needed someone to help manage and organize the church's finances, and offered me the part-time position of bookkeeper. I only needed to work a few hours a week. After discussing this with James and making sure that Mrs. Baker would help with JoAnn, I accepted his offer. This was perfect because it didn't require a lot of time and it gave us extra income.

I realized how fortunate I was to have this job, especially when I became pregnant with our second child. In the mid-fifties, many places would not allow women to work when they were obviously pregnant. My pregnancy didn't interfere with my work at the church, and I worked there until I delivered our second child.

We were blessed with another beautiful girl whom we named Claudia Jayne. Because it took five years for me to become pregnant with our second child, we thought it might take another five years to have a third child. So we decided to start as soon as possible and prayed for a boy. If our prayers weren't answered, then we would do whatever we could to not have any more children. To our surprise, I became pregnant a few months later. Seventeen months after the birth of our second child, James Grady Jr. a beautiful boy, was born. Our third and last child.

With three young children, I realized I needed to give up my work at the church. JoAnn was now in school. That left me with two children at home who needed my attention and care. For the next two years, I stayed home to take care of our family. However, there was still a need for extra income.

After I left school, several young women I'd met during my freshman year stayed in touch with me. On many occasions, Carol Watson, Eugenia Foree, and Edith Martin invited themselves for dinner or to spend an evening with us. They always contributed to the meal and we enjoyed their company. They often watched the children in the evenings when James and I went to a movie or an event. As I look back now, I think they realized we were short of finances but never mentioned it.

One evening when we were having dinner together, they presented me with a proposition. They told me how much they enjoyed my cooking. They wanted to have dinner with us five nights a week and would pay us ten dollars each to cover the expenses. I couldn't believe my ears. I always felt that the "good Lord" was looking out for us. Now I was sure. Thirty dollars extra a week was a godsend. It wouldn't amount to exactly thirty dollars, but I knew how to stretch the meals to feed everyone for an additional ten dollars a week. My budget for food at the time had been twenty-five dollars. Now it would be thirty-five. We ate a lot of casseroles! But my mother had taught me how to cook inexpensively. She had also taught me how to prepare balanced and nutritionally good meals. The situation provided us with extra income and added to our joy as a family. We all looked forward to having Carol, Genie, and Edith for dinner. For me it was a connection with a world I had missed so much. Until then it hadn't been possible for me to return to school, but I thought about it often. Sometimes I drove around the campus so I could feel vicariously what it was like to be a student.

Taking care of the kids, keeping house, and being a wife kept me pretty busy. JoAnn being in school demanded a different kind of attention. We made sure we were good, supportive parents. We attended the PTO meetings and parent-teacher conferences. We volunteered as much as we could. JoAnn attended an integrated school. This wasn't a problem for those of us who lived in Ann Arbor. While we were aware of the 1954 *Brown v. Board of Education* decision regarding integration, it had little meaning for us because our schools were already integrated. School integration, however, didn't mean there was no racism.

One day when JoAnn came home from school, she ran into the house crying hysterically. When I finally calmed her down to find out what was wrong, she said someone at school had called her a Negro. In that moment I realized we had not taken the time to explain this to her. We were raising our children the way we wanted them to grow up. Our family and friends were all different shades; that was a simple fact. I hadn't realized that perhaps this was something we should have explained to her. But why?

I tried to comfort her. I told her that yes, she was a Negro. She refused to accept it and said that Bobbie, her closest friend and playmate, was a Negro but she was not. When I asked her why, she told me that Bobbie had really dark skin and she did not. Therefore she was not a Negro. Still sobbing, she said she didn't want to be a Negro because people didn't like Negroes. As I hugged her and tried to explain what a Negro was, I knew we had a lot to do to help her understand in a way that would not permanently damage her. I don't think we were ever successful. For me it was the hot fudge sundae in a white paper cup. For my daughter JoAnn, it was being called a Negro in first grade. We both had discovered racism at a very early age, but JoAnn's discovery was made much earlier in her life than mine. To this day Bobbie and JoAnn are friends. They both share the fact that their lives continue to be impacted by racism.

Being a wife and a mother continued to present me with challenges. The lack of money seemed to control everything we did. After working at the Mademoiselle Shop, I thought I had given up visits to the Thrift Shop, but I discovered that those visits helped stretch our dollars. I never shopped with coupons but caught all the food sales I could. Nothing I seemed to do left us with discretionary funds. I was beginning to need clothes for myself. Some of what I needed could not be found in the Thrift Shop. I had to find a way to make extra money.

The day I found an Avon catalogue in my mailbox, my first thought was to discard it. After perusing the catalogue, I had an idea that perhaps I could become an Avon Lady. I immediately took the necessary steps and within two weeks I opened my first box of Avon "goodies." The first women to become my customers were my close friends, neighbors, and relatives. I was so excited. My first order did indeed bring us extra income. And not only did I have extra income, I was also able to use some of the products I couldn't possibly have bought prior to this venture. My only concern was whether I would have enough time. Caring for two children at home did not leave much time for door-to-door selling.

At this point I had another idea. I'd been invited to several Tupperware parties. Although I wasn't able to buy much, I enjoyed the outings. Avon wasn't organized around house parties but rather door-to-door, person-to-person selling. My idea was to organize my approach around parties. I contacted some of the wives who lived in married student housing. They were very interested in sponsoring parties because most of them also lacked the funds to buy the products they wanted. Sponsoring parties allowed them to receive products. This was a huge success. I made a lot of money; at least it was a great deal of money to me. I was able to buy the first new winter coat I had had in years. I still remember shopping for it in one of the nicest department stores in Ann Arbor. It was light beige and made me feel like a queen. With the extra funds I could also buy things for James and the children that we could not otherwise have afforded.

I think one of the reasons why having extra money to buy clothes meant so much to me was because of my earlier experience with clothing, when I discovered one could make purchases on a layaway plan. It had been through this plan that I'd bought my first winter coat. And I had put a down payment on the set of dishes I bought for my mother on layaway. Learning how to provide for myself was a lesson I had begun to learn early in life. Being married had not changed much. I still found it necessary to provide most things for myself and for others. A strong streak of independence can be an attribute, but with it comes a lot of responsibility for self and for others.

I sold Avon for several months, until my desire to return to school became overwhelming. My involvement with Avon proved to be more than I could have imagined; the experience with Avon gave me what I needed to approach this wonderful corporation for assistance when I was associated with the YWCA later in my career.

The children were growing and somewhat easier to manage. I knew I couldn't take classes during the day, but I began to think about taking one or two courses in the evening. I discussed this possibility with James and he agreed that I should try at least one course to become acclimated to studying again. I had managed to put aside the tuition needed for one night course. I enrolled in the university again, and this time I promised myself I wouldn't stop taking courses until I received a bachelor's degree. I didn't need motivation.

What proved to be most helpful was the encouragement I got from Carol, Genie, and Edith, my friends who at one point became my boarders. They were as excited as I was about my going back to school. Carol was especially supportive and still is. As I write this book, Carol is the only one of the three still living, and she remains as supportive of any of my endeavors as she has always been.

My first attempt at acquiring a college education was interrupted. So much had happened in my life since the day I enrolled at the University of Michigan. I had a few years of marriage behind me and three lovely children. So far I had been successful in integrating the role of wife and mother. Now I was embarking on adding still another variable to my life's equation.

FIVE

Balancing the Roles of Parent and Student

About the time I was organizing my thoughts to accommodate my status as a student again, we were sidetracked by the need for a larger house. Still plagued by lack of money and the limited options blacks had finding suitable housing in the city, we realized James would not be able to take courses for his teacher's certification. We didn't have the money for tuition and he couldn't take time from work to attend classes. He was the primary breadwinner; he needed to work. We had so much on our plate, we just didn't want to deal with the racism we would face if and when we looked for housing. By this time, I was convinced that while we didn't have much in the way of material things, we had much to be thankful for. I truly believed that the man or woman above was looking out for us.

Occasionally, when I had the time and Reverend Carpenter needed me at the church, I would go in to work for a couple of hours. One of the days I was in the church office, we received a call from a man who was selling his house. He identified himself as a white man who explained to Reverend Carpenter that he knew it was difficult for blacks to find housing. He lived in a predominately white neighborhood and on a block that was occupied by whites, but he was willing to sell to blacks. He called the church to see if the minister knew of any parishioners who might be looking for a house to buy. He invited Reverend Carpenter to see it.

I tried very hard to manage the roles of mother and student. At the invitation of the Ann Arbor newspaper, we are preparing for an article in its "Holiday Season Recipes" section. We are making a banana cake, one of our family's favorites.

Reverend Carpenter knew we wanted to move into a larger place. He invited me to go with him to look at this house. I took one look at the exterior, surrounded by beautiful trees and flowering bushes, and fell in love with it before we went through the front door. The house was just what we needed. It was fenced in and had an extra lot. It was perfect for a family of five and a dog that had recently joined our ranks. I was so excited.

The price seemed a great deal out of our range. However, once James saw the house, he was as thrilled at the possibility of owning it as I was. We reviewed our income thousands of times and always came up short. Finally we developed a plan that allowed us to purchase it. The plan included more income from a better-paying job for James and part-time work for me. Of course we would first need to sell the house we were living in. We had just put in new kitchen cabinets, and we had replaced the space heater with a furnace.

After juggling of our finances and consulting with our parents and one of the banks, we were able to sell our house for the amount we needed to purchase the other one. The transaction actually went more smoothly than we had expected. Because Reverend Carpenter and the owners who were selling the house were well known in the community and by the bank, we were saved from what might have been a negative experience. Being a black couple buying a house in a predominately white neighborhood did not prevent us from completing the transaction. However, it didn't take long for the neighborhood to become 99 percent black. The white people couldn't move out fast enough.

I had never been happier in my life. We had enough space to accommodate our needs. We were living in a lovely neighborhood with good schools. The house and its surroundings would satisfy our needs for years to come.

By the time we moved into our new house on Miner Street, Claudia was old enough to go to school. Jim, our youngest, was mature enough for nursery school, and I was ready to take classes again. Having the children taken care of for most of the morning allowed me to take morning classes. I set aside at least one morning a week to work in the nursery school, which was my contribution toward the fee. At this point in my life, I was so well organized I could have written the book on organization. I was up early, getting James off to work and dressing and feeding the kids. I dropped them off at their respective schools and drove to campus for a 9:00 a.m. class. I also had time to take an 11:00 a.m. class. Until James Jr. was old enough for first grade, which meant all three of the kids would be in school most of the day, I could take two morning classes. My afternoons were spent with household chores and community involvement.

We also scraped together the tuition for my husband to take one course a semester toward his certification requirements. I obtained an NDEA (National Defense Education Act) loan to help me through my undergraduate work. Yet we still needed ways to meet our financial needs. James found work through a friend cleaning offices in the evenings and on weekends. When we ran short on time I left the kids with a relative and helped him with these jobs. We both knew this was very temporary. Cleaning offices motivated me to finish my coursework as soon as possible and get a teaching job. James was also determined to complete his requirements for the Michigan teaching certificate. We wanted no part of having to do this work for a living.

We were surprised at how much it cost to support a family of five. By the time I returned to school full-time, our need for additional income became even greater. I was very good at managing our budget. James was willing to turn over his income to the household budget but would not become involved in managing our meager income. This irritated me at times, but it was easier for me to simply do it and avoid an argument. Arguing was becoming more prevalent in our daily lives. I think the shortage of money, time, and energy contributed to most of our disagreements. I spent more time trying to be a good parent and student than I did being a wife. There just didn't seem to be enough of me.

To complicate matters, I felt I had to participate in church activities. I taught Sunday school, and James became a deacon. We both wanted to be involved in church work and managed to add this to our busy schedules. I was also approached to accept an appointment on the Ann Arbor Human Relations Commission. I did this for about a year but had to resign when my coursework required more time. While all of this was going on, I had the desire for social contact with black women. Some of these needs were met through church activities, but even though the women in the church were wonderful, we had little in common. In fact, I often felt like a bump on a log. I was in my late twenties, married, and attending the university. There was no other woman in our church doing what I was doing. Most of the women my age were raising families, and if they worked, they were working in jobs I had decided not to do. The women I had met when I first attended the University had all graduated and had professional work in cities other than Ann Arbor. Most all of the students in my classes were quite young, and to them I was an old lady. Besides, there were very few black female students at Michigan.

By the time I was taking junior- and senior-level coursework, the classes were smaller and provided more individual interaction. It was almost impossible to establish contact with fellow students in large lecture sessions. Smaller classes presented more opportunities to become acquainted with students whose course of study was usually similar to mine. This helped establish contact with someone if only to share notes or books.

In one class I happened to sit next to a woman who looked older than the other students. I extended a greeting to her and she responded very warmly. I knew almost immediately she was the kind of woman I wanted to know. We had coffee together after class, exchanged phone numbers, and decided we would meet each week to review our readings and help each other when we could. Julia Shea and I became good friends. Julia knew three other women students about our ages, and arranged for me to meet them. I soon had four women on campus who gave me the support I needed; we supported each other. They all had children. One woman was divorced but the others were married. We were all short on money and shared many of the same problems with our children, husbands, and coursework. We started studying together at the library. Occasionally we met at someone's home for a social outing. We involved our husbands when we met socially, although it wasn't often. None of us had a lot of time to socialize. Some of our children became friends. My oldest daughter, JoAnn, exchanged sleepovers with Julia's oldest daughter. Our contact with each other continued after we graduated. In fact, I recently had a note from Julia thanking me for a sympathy note I had sent her for the passing of her husband.

While I sought companionship from women I had something in common with, I assumed I would find it from black women. But at this time there were no black women my age at Michigan working on an undergraduate degree. The women I had met and supplied me with what I needed at the time were white. In fact, it was not common to find married women of any color working on an undergraduate degree in most colleges and universities in those days. Today it is very common, but this was not the case in the late fifties and early sixties.

My student life was coming together nicely. I received good grades and enjoyed the learning process. There were times when I had to play student for both James and myself. He was completing his teaching certificate requirements, and toward the end of his courses he had to write several papers. James was not a writer, so I did most of his writing. Not only did this put an extra burden on me, it also irritated me.

While we managed to hold our marriage together, there was more than enough to cause friction in our relationship. The need for more income was always there. I finally decided that with a night job, I could still attend classes during the day. And I could study at night if I found the right job. I applied as a nurse's aide at the University of Michigan hospital. I hoped I could find time to study when patients didn't need my services. The man I interviewed with in the personnel office said that with my background I might find nighttime office support more interesting. I almost fell out of the chair. I applied for the nurse's aide position because I'd never seen blacks doing anything in the hospital other than maintenance or nurse's aide work. To my surprise, this suggestion came from a white man. I was getting different signals about what I should expect because of my blackness. I was so conditioned to racist behavior it surprised me when what I expected didn't happen.

I accepted the office support position on the night shift. This was perfect because we had only one car and going to work when James came home from the foundry meant that he could take me to work, watch the children, and pick me up at midnight. Also, there were many more opportunities to study on the night business force than there would have been working as an aide. I remained at the hospital until I finished the requirements for my bachelor's degree. It was about the time I graduated that James found a teaching position at one of the Michigan state training centers for delinquent boys, a position he held until he retired.

During the time I was working on my degree, I constantly checked my transcript with the office of certification in the School of Education to make sure I would have the courses necessary for state certification and for the courses required by the Ann Arbor public schools. Because I lived in the city and had a family to take care of, it was important for me to teach here. At that time, one could count the number of black teachers in Ann Arbor on one hand. Racism was very active in the school system. However, I was determined to teach in that system, not simply because it was convenient, but also because I was a graduate of the system.

I took more courses than were necessary to ensure my appointment. At one point, I tried to satisfy the requirements for two different assignments to make sure I would have a position in Ann Arbor. My first choice of positions was a speech therapist. I enjoyed the course work and wanted to help small children with their speech problems. My grades in the required courses were very good. However, I discovered that there were only five speech therapists in the system and turnover was not great. This information convinced me to prepare for elementary teaching. I knew this would be a challenge because I needed two semesters of student teaching, one for speech and one for elementary teaching. By the time I reached my senior year, I was more than exhausted. The pressures of trying to be an A student, a good mother, and a wife were beginning to wear me down.

One cold winter day as I was walking across the campus to one of my classes, I fell apart. I felt like the entire world was on my shoulders and I couldn't bear another moment of that burden. I started to cry and could not stop. I found myself walking in the direction of the Student Health Center. It was as if someone had taken me by the hand and was leading me to the Center. I was still crying when I arrived at the receiving station. I was in such a state that I could hardly give the receptionist my name or describe my problem.

I was taken to a room and told to take off my clothes and get in bed; someone would be with me shortly. I remember looking out the window as I cried, seeing the snowflakes fall. Knowing how very cold it was made me cry even more. I was so tired. I was tired of studying, tired of caring for my children, tired of being a wife, and tired of all the other things I was doing. I was tired of everything.

Once I climbed into bed, it didn't take long for me to fall asleep. I guess the personnel at the Student Health Center had a pretty good idea of what my problem was. They let me sleep several hours before someone came in to talk to me. The doctors paraded in and out for the next few hours and scheduled a series of tests. They notified my husband and told him I would be confined for a few days. I was too weak to object to any of the decisions people around me were making on my behalf. I felt warm and safe from everything external to the Health Center. The food was delicious. I did what I was told and slept when I was not being examined or was not under an X-ray machine. I was in such a state that I didn't want to see my children or James. Before this attack, I had had no idea of what exhaustion could do. By the end of the week, with the help of the counselors, I knew I had to revamp my schedule and reduce my load both at home and at school.

Once released from the Health Center, I had second thoughts about trying to obtain double certification. I decided to satisfy the necessary coursework for elementary school teaching only. This meant I would do only one semester of student teaching my senior year. As much as I enjoyed the preparation for speech therapy, I knew I couldn't physically or mentally handle the requirements for double certification with all of my other responsibilities.

I reorganized my work schedule at home. James assumed more of the responsibilities with the children and the house. We hired a housekeeper a few hours a week. Even hiring a part-time housekeeper became a problem, because most domestic workers in the city were black, and many of them were friends or people we knew. In the early sixties, at least in our small northern town, blacks generally did not work for blacks, and certainly not for someone they knew. We finally found a young white woman who was slightly mentally retarded but could do the work, and who could not have cared less about the color of our skin. Once again racism added to our concerns, and to the burden of simply trying to live day by day.

It is difficult for me to describe how I felt when I graduated from the University of Michigan in 1964. Lyndon B. Johnson gave the commencement address that year. I sat with thousands of students in the U of M stadium, and yet I felt like the commencement was just for me. I had finally achieved my goal. I had graduated from the university! I laughed and I cried. My thoughts raced from having "falling into the gutter" by becoming pregnant my freshman year, to picking myself up and out of the gutter, to receiving a degree from the University of Michigan. No one but God knows how wonderful I felt.

These feelings stayed with me and were more than evident when I walked into my very own fourth-grade classroom. I was thirty-three years old. I had been married for fifteen years. I had three children and a husband. Sometimes it felt like I had four children and no husband.

Before the commencement exercises I had submitted my application for a teaching position in the Ann Arbor public school system. I felt pretty good about my transcript. I had taken more courses than were required. By the time I graduated, I'd been invited for an interview. Prior to the interview, I discovered that the director of personnel for the school district was Thad Carr, who had been my high school Social Studies teacher. He was one of the teachers I liked, but I never understood why he gave me only a B-plus when I took his course. I felt I had earned an A, but I didn't challenge him. I made the appointment for an interview. My letter confirming my appointment informed me that Thad Carr would interview me.

I was as nervous as I could be. However, once again, with my nerve in one hand and my transcript in the other, I went to the interview. To my surprise, once I sat across the desk from Mr. Carr my nervousness left me. We talked about Ann Arbor High School and finally got around to my preparation for teaching elementary school. Within less than forty-five minutes I was told that I would have an assignment at Wines Elementary School and I would be teaching fourth grade. I almost fell out of my seat. I could not believe my ears. I had completed my student teaching assignment at Wines for third grade. I knew the principal well and most of the teachers. I was so excited I could hardly drive home fast enough to share my good news. Now James and I were both going to be teachers.

My assignment to Wines Elementary School could not have been more perfect. The principal, Mr. Emerson Powrie, was a wonderful person and a wonderful principal. We got along extremely well. He knew my mother because she had served as president of Jones School PTA when he was the principal there. Wines Elementary was just a few years old, with wide halls, windows along one side of every classroom, bathrooms in each class, lots of supplies, and current textbooks in the storage room. It was a perfect setting in which to teach. And to top this off, the school was located five minutes from my house. This meant I could meet my children at home for lunch. The man or woman up above was certainly looking out for me.

My classroom was situated directly across from the room I did my student teaching in. Alma Cooper, my former supervising teacher, was delighted that I had been assigned to Wines. There was nothing she wouldn't do for me and she did so much. Other teachers were also very helpful. Sally Canfield and I had started a friendship when I was student teaching and she was a teacher. When I was assigned to Wines, we were both delighted. My friendship with Sally began in 1965 and continues to this day. She married one of our teacher friends, Ronald Jaworowski. They are still married and live together in retirement in Ann Arbor. (Note: Ron died as I was working on this manuscript.)

Throughout the summer, prior to actually performing as a fourth-grade teacher, I was totally involved in preparation. Whenever I could find a couple of hours, I spent the time planning my teaching units. I designed the bulletin boards, complete with color coordination. I used the school library during the summer and selected the collection of books for my room. I reviewed films and tapes so I could choose the ones I wanted to use. This was also a good way for me to freshen up on the background I felt I needed to teach certain units.

That summer my mother, my oldest daughter, and I traveled by car to California to visit my brother Russell. Whenever we stopped for gas or relaxation, I combed the small shops in the area for something to use in my classroom. The stops in the Painted Desert and the Grand Canyon were wonderful resources for my unit on rocks and minerals. I was bubbling all over.

Finally, the first day of school arrived. I couldn't have been happier. I had twenty-six children in class. Because I had student-taught third grade, I knew several children in the class. The children appeared to be as excited as I was. The number of boys and girls in the class was about the same. However, out of the twenty-six children, only two were black. I was the only black teacher at the school. All of us, including the children, lived in the neighborhood. About ninety were children of professors who taught at the University of Michigan. Two of my own children were about the same ages as these fourth-grade children. Jim was in third grade and Claudia was in fourth. However, they were not in the Wines school district. They attended Mack School, which was more diverse than Wines because the neighborhood was changing. Many white people responded to blacks moving into the neighborhood by selling as quickly as possible.

Because I had children in the same age group as my students, I had a pretty good idea of what to expect in terms of interests, skills, and behavior. Also, because I was older than most beginning teachers and had children of my own, control and management of the classroom environment was easy and comfortable for the children and me. As I write, I can still feel how excited and happy I was at that time in my life. I had gone from being a student to a wife to a mother, and now I was also a teacher.

Most of the children in class were above average in almost all subjects. This allowed me ample time to work with the few children who needed extra help. One of the most interesting aspects of teaching in that school system was that the required curriculum appeared to be compatible with the needs and experiences of the students. I think because the University of Michigan was located in the city, it influenced all aspects of the system. Also, at that time in the early to mid-sixties, there were more than adequate funds to support the curriculum, school facilities, teacher salaries, and extracurricular activities. This meant there were funds for providing up-to-date textbooks. Teachers had more than one series of readers to choose from.

The fourth grade was when students began learning a foreign language. French was the language taught at Wines. A special French-speaking teacher provided instruction for each class. My classroom's French teacher, Marilyn Cogan, and I became friends. We did a lot of things together in and out of school. I still remember when, years later, James and I met Marilyn for dinner at a restaurant in Paris.

The stockroom at school was filled with all kinds of material for art and music classes. There was a full-blown physical activities program, including equipment. The library was extensive and had a full-time librarian. The facilities were well organized, and teachers had a lovely planning room. There was a good-sized auditorium. The well-kept playground was designed for all age groups. The school setting was ideal. And to complete this picture, we had funds available for taking the children on trips. I used all of the funds allotted for field trips for each teacher per year, and then some. In my first year we took seven field trips. They were such fun and a great learning tool.

There was never enough time in any one day or school year to do all the things I wanted to do with my class. Whenever I planned a unit, I always planned a field trip to support the concepts I wanted the children to explore and learn. For example, when we studied rocks and minerals we went to the museum on the University's campus to expand our knowledge. A trip to the famous art museum in Toledo, Ohio, was part of our learning experience when the children studied the great artists. We traveled across the border to Windsor, Canada, to help teach the children about the geography of Michigan. Our Canadian trip also gave the class an opportunity to learn about traveling to a different country, although a very large percentage of my students had already experienced international travel.

When we studied the development of transportation we made a trip to the Ford Motor Company, including a visit to the Ford museum and the assembly line. Ann Arbor is very close to Battle Creek, Michigan, the home of the Kellogg Company. We couldn't imagine studying any aspect of food without a visit to Kellogg's.

The children and I had a great time in the classroom. I enjoyed teaching. While the students were the center of my attention, I discovered how important it was to have good interactions with the teachers, the office staff, and most importantly the janitor. I had a habit of rearranging the classroom several times a year and I needed the janitor's assistance. Sometimes I brought the janitor cookies I had baked. I soon discovered that a smile and a pleasant greeting was all I needed to have the janitor come to my aid.

I was not the only new teacher that first year at Wines Elementary. Several other teachers were either new to teaching or new to the school system. I was older than most beginning teachers. I was very impressed by one of the new teachers who had decided in her mid-forties to go to college so she could receive a degree and teach. She was fifty-two years of age, and an excellent teacher.

Most of the teachers found time to meet in the teacher's lounge during their planning time or during lunch. Because I generally went home to be with my children during lunch and spent most of my planning time in the library, I had to make a special effort to interact with my colleagues at other times. I found that recess was a great time to have conversations and to share classroom experiences with other teachers.

It didn't take long before I had identified three or four teachers other than Sally Canfield that I wanted to know better. We formed a dinner group that met once a month in each other's homes. These dinners included our spouses, and for several years our social life revolved around these gatherings.

The dinners each month gave us all an opportunity to share our classroom experiences. We discussed our likes and dislikes with the system and the school. In general, these opportunities allowed us to vent. Besides having a place to vent, we often exchanged ideas about teaching.

Each couple spent a lot of time planning the dinner menu and took special care to make sure the evening was tasteful and elegant. I learned a lot about entertaining. While James and I had been married the longest, we had not had the resources to buy the silver, china, and crystal that most of the others had acquired. Planning for our turn to entertain also gave us the motivation to buy what we needed to continue entertaining in the style the group had established.

Many of our conversations during these evenings centered on the travels most of the group had taken. James and I listened and learned a lot about traveling abroad. Our appetite for taking a trip to Europe was developing. Most of the students in my class had traveled more internationally than I had. Because of this, James and I decided to expand our horizons and plan a trip to Europe. We found a five-week tour that fit our interests, needs, and pocketbook. Our major problem was finding someone who would take care of our children. One evening when we were visiting our neighbors, we mentioned wanting to take a trip to Europe but not knowing what to do with the children. Although we wanted to take them with us, our budget would allow only the two of us to go. There would be no problem asking relatives to take one or two, but three children for five weeks was a bit much. James and I had no thoughts about our neighbors coming to our aid. For one thing, they were close to our parents' age, and they hadn't had the responsibility of caring for young children in many years. To our surprise, they volunteered to be our babysitters. JoAnn was in junior high school and could help a great deal. Without a moment's hesitation, we accepted their offer and began to make plans for traveling to Europe.

There were times during our planning when I got cold feet. We didn't have much money in our savings account and I wasn't so sure we should spend what little we had on this trip. We needed new furniture and weren't sure whether to buy a few pieces of furniture or take this trip. I discussed this with my mother. She was a Jehovah's Witness by then and had traveled around the world a great deal attending their conventions. My mother convinced me to take the trip. She said that a fire, a tornado, or something beyond our control could destroy the furniture, but the experience and memories of Europe would last forever. She elaborated on the value of travel, saying that if we were confined to wheelchairs, or lost our sight or hearing, we would always have our European experience. She didn't need to say anymore. For two young married people in our neighborhood in the black community, traveling to Europe was quite an event.

The days leading up to our departure were filled with visits from friends and relatives, who brought gifts of all kinds. When my mother came to say good-bye, she noticed a coffeepot in my suitcase and asked why I was taking a coffeepot. I told her I didn't want to miss my morning coffee, and I didn't know what the coffee would taste like in the seven countries we would visit. "If you want everything to be like it is at home, then stay home," she said. "When you travel, the joy of the experience is tasting and smelling different foods, hearing different languages, and meeting people who are different." I left the coffeepot behind.

My mother gave us good advice. That trip to Europe was the first in a lifetime of travel. Two of my later professional appointments were filled with travel. Today, if I had a choice of putting money in the bank or going on a trip, I would choose the trip, remembering the wise advice my mother gave me years ago, and remembering how each of my trips contributed to my knowledge of other people and other cultures.

I returned to my teaching in the fall, full of excitement from five weeks of travel to seven countries in Europe. James and shared our travel experiences with family and friends. We felt more comfortable with our dining group from school because we could also share our travel experiences with them.

I enjoyed entertaining as much as I did teaching. For me the two went hand in hand. The second year I taught, I invited each student in my class to have lunch with my family. I scheduled the invitations for Friday and invited two or three students at a time. The menu was always the same: hot dogs, potato chips, lemonade, and cookies and fruit for dessert. One Friday, as I prepared to serve the food, Gladys, one of my students, said she could not have hot dogs because she was Catholic and did not eat meat on Friday. I never stopped to think that on Friday the Catholic students might not be able to eat meat. My sensitivity to diversity had not yet developed to that extent. I always had peanut butter and jelly, and offered that as a substitute. Gladys was happy with that. I called her parents that evening to tell them how gracious she had been, and that she'd explained to me why she couldn't eat hot dogs. Her parents said they were well aware of my luncheon menu. They decided not to say anything to Gladys or me but to see how their daughter handled the situation. They were very pleased at how Gladys had managed this. Gladys and I both learned something. She learned how to protect what was important to her. I learned to be more sensitive to diversity. This lesson was the first in a series of lessons that helped shape and influence my awareness of cultural differences. Little did I realize the importance this would have on my future.

Parent-teacher conferences were held once a year at Wines Elementary School. These conferences were scheduled midyear. The timing was essential because it provided several months for the students and the teacher to become acquainted. Involving parents in the educational process of their child was critical to each student's success. I looked forward to these conferences. For most of the children in the class, I had met at least one of the parents prior to the conferences. The families of the students attending this school were middle or upper middle class. Generally speaking, children from these families had parents who were very interested in the schools their children attended. They participated in meetings of the Parent Teacher Organization, which provided interaction between parents and teachers. There were also other activities and reasons for at least one parent from most of the families to visit the school or their children's classrooms.

My conferences were almost over for the 1964 school year. While most of the conferences were held in the afternoons on designated days, a few families required evening meetings so both parents could participate. One family needed special consideration for an evening appointment, for it had an unusual set of circumstances. The father, Rudolf Schmerl, was a professor at the University of Michigan. He was also involved in a professor exchange program between the University of Michigan and Tuskegee University in Alabama. He wanted to attend the conference for his children. Although he couldn't make an afternoon appointment, he could meet in the evening when he was in Ann Arbor on a break.

I scheduled an evening conference. I was anxious to meet this father, primarily because he was involved in an exchange with a professor from a predominately black university. That evening, as I waited for the parents to arrive, I took a long look at my bulletin boards and the classroom in general. I spent a lot of time making the classroom warm and attractive. I liked to have the bulletin boards reflect the work the children had done. And I wanted the room to reflect the science or social studies unit we were studying. As my eyes moved around the room, I could feel a smile cross my face. I liked what I saw, and I hoped that Professor and Mrs. Schmerl would be impressed.

The Schmerls finally arrived. Their son was an exceptional student and the conference went very well. Just before they were ready to leave, Professor Schmerl left our threesome and slowly moved around the room, examining the bulletin boards. I was pleased that he was interested and expected him to say something very positive about what he saw. The class was studying a unit on Michigan. The students and I had made a time line with paper doll-like figures, all with white faces, imposed on the geographical representations of the state.

When Professor Schmerl cleared his throat and spoke, I could not believe what this man, this father, said to me. He acknowledged what we were studying and then asked me why there were no black explorers in the time line. "Why, there were no black explorers in Michigan," I replied. "Are you sure?" he asked. I conjured up some feeble response. When we said good night I was in a state of shock. I sat at my desk for quite some time trying to understand his question and my answer.

The more I thought about this incident that evening and over the next several days, the more confused I became. If there had been black explorers in Michigan why hadn't I known about them? My concern became more encompassing. I thought about the readers we were using. I took the time to go through all three sets of our books to see if there were any people other than white people in the readers. There were none. I spent more time looking at the mathematics text we were using, and again, all the pictorial representations were of whites.

Why were there no pictures in these books of children who looked like me? I spent time in the library on several occasions trying to find books that were either about blacks or included pictures of blacks. The only books available that offered any suggestion to the reader that we were living in a city, country, and world that was not all white were those whose contents focused on a specific nation. Books on Africa, Mexico, and other non-white countries were the only ones that offered any diversity at all. I even checked the filmstrips and the picture file. Nothing.

My concern about the lack of inclusion of any kind in almost all of the available teaching material grew. I kept reviewing the question Professor

Schmerl had asked me. "Are you sure?" How could I be sure if I could find no evidence or even the smallest suggestion that perhaps the explorers of Michigan might have been a diverse group? I tried to analyze the situation. I thought beyond the explorers of Michigan. The very fact that I found little if any diversity in all the materials I reviewed brought me to some conclusions.

As I write, I am reminded of what was happening in the nation during the sixties. I had begun my teaching career in the mid-sixties. The civil rights legislation was signed in 1964. I had attended predominately white elementary schools. My high school was predominately white. I graduated from a university that was predominately white. The city in which I lived was less than 5 percent black. I was raised and taught in a predominately white world. All of my teachers had been white. I had been taught from a curriculum that included little or no diversity. If there had been people other than whites, how was I to know? Of course we heard from time to time about Booker T. Washington, Marian Anderson, Paul Robeson, and a few other well-known historical figures, but very few others.

What was I to do? Where could I go to find anything about the contributions of blacks and others to the development of the United States? The answer to my first question was that I must explain to my students that this world was not all white. How to do this, what method I would use, took some time for me to decide. The answer to my second question didn't come so quickly, but it came. I would do research in libraries other than the Wines school library. I would also talk with other teachers to see if they knew of possible resources. My research would focus on the involvement of blacks, and once I had a better understanding of their involvement in this country and its history, I could expand my research.

I also came to the conclusion that perhaps the most effective way for me to expose my students to diversity would be to begin integrating concepts and material about diversity into subject matter that was familiar to them. I spent time reviewing guidelines for the various areas of study I was required to teach in fourth grade. I decided to begin with a subject area that the children enjoyed. My first attempt would be music and literature. We had a music teacher named Geraldine Wilson who was very cooperative.

I developed a unit on Greek mythology. Who could object to this focus? I could include musical and literary concepts in this unit. One of the reasons

I selected Greek mythology was that I had discovered a book on African mythology in the school library. It had only been checked out twice, several years prior to when I checked it out. I felt that once we had spent time learning about Greek culture and the role mythology played in that culture, I could introduce African mythology and do a comparison. This would open the eyes of the children to more than one world culture.

The class became so excited about mythology that we decided to do our version of Pandora's box and put on a production for the school and the parents. What a success this was! While the production focused on Greek mythology, I created several writing opportunities for students either to react to the African mythology they had studied or to put themselves in the place of an African child and create a story. The students were being exposed to diversity in a subtle way and through a method that was legitimate and successful. They were learning about diversity as they developed their skills. And I was learning how to teach what was referred to in the late sixties as a multiethnic approach to a curriculum.

Teaching fourth-graders at Wines School during the next three years, I developed other units of study in which I integrated information about or by other ethnic groups. My information base was largely black because it was easier to find more on black history. Also, after passage of the Civil Rights Act of 1964, more information and resources about various ethnic groups appeared in educational materials. About that time Ezra Jack Keats, a well-known author of children's literature, published a book entitled *The Snowy Day*. All of the characters were black. This was such a big step in the development of multiethnic literature that *Time* magazine featured the cover of this book on one of the magazine covers.

I continued my research and became a collector of any materials I could find on different ethnic groups. Once I had the material, it was easy for me to develop a strategy to integrate aspects of my discoveries into the required curriculum. I was preparing for my future.

The death of Martin Luther King in 1968 brought the eyes of this country and the world to the attention of the black experience. The work of this wonderful human being and the passage of civil rights legislation provided opportunities to develop approaches to multiethnic education that were unheard of. During the years that followed, many new audiovisual materials appeared. Scholars and researchers found opportunities to study and research the history of black Americans. It didn't take long for Hispanics, Native Americans, and Asians to embrace the interest and the need for sharing information about the involvement of their own ethnic groups in the history and development of the United States.

After my first year of teaching, I was eligible to apply for a student teacher. I had two student teachers. They were both excellent and helped me continue to develop ways to integrate aspects of ethnic diversity into the all-white curriculum.

I spent a great deal of time researching information to develop my teaching units. I was eager to discover as much as I could about my ethnic background. The more familiar I was with my own history and the black experience in America, the easier it would be to integrate what I was learning into other aspects of the curriculum. My student teachers understood what I was trying to do and often contributed material and ideas. Working with young teachers who were learning how to teach was of great interest to me. I never dreamed that my experience as a supervising teacher would have such an impact on my future as both a teacher and an educator.

In 1967, at the end of my third year of teaching fourth grade, my principal, Emerson Powrie, informed me that I had been selected to receive the Ann Arbor Teacher Award. It was such a surprise! One of my student teachers, Normie Frances, had nominated me for this award. I was totally unaware of her nomination. The award consisted of an invitation to join the faculty of the School of Education at the University of Michigan. My assignment would be to supervise student teachers throughout several schools in the area. In addition to observing the students in their assigned classrooms, I would conduct weekly seminars for them. This meant that I would leave my current teaching assignment at Wines for a year. The University of Michigan would pay my salary for that year, after which I would return to the Ann Arbor school system for another teaching assignment.

This award served as a catalyst for what was to happen in my future. I was more than happy, for the experience would allow me to have the time and opportunity to do the research and planning necessary to develop a multicultural curriculum. It would introduce me to a variety of teaching styles and teacher behaviors. It would also allow me to work on a master's degree in education administration. I had already begun taking classes during the two previous years. If I planned well, perhaps with a year at the

School of Education plus a summer or two of classes, I could complete the requirements for a master's.

The summer was filled with organizing and planning for the coming year. Everyone in my family and all of my friends were excited for me. The school year would not be easy. I needed to plan carefully so I would not shirk my duties as mother and wife. The children appeared to be doing well in school, and James was enjoying his teaching duties at the Maxey Boy's Training School in Whitmore Lake.

I was in my mid-thirties but already going on fifty. I felt I had lived a lifetime. So much energy had gone into trying to prove to myself and to the world that I could make something of myself. I had not shaken the shame of becoming pregnant at eighteen. I was determined to be a good mother to my children, a good wife to my husband, and a good member of my profession.

SIX

Student and Professor

It's difficult to describe how I felt returning to the campus of the University of Michigan as a faculty member. My title was that of lecturer and was only for one year. I had plans for that one year, and I was willing and ready to roll up my sleeves and take advantage of everything that came my way. Even though I had an overload of responsibilities as mother and wife, I was convinced that I could handle my new set of tasks. I was in a state of euphoria. With my nerve in one hand and lots of energy in the other, I was ready to go.

I had decided to work on my master's degree during my assignment as lecturer for the year. I organized my schedule for observing my student teachers around the courses I wanted to take toward completion of my degree. If all went well, I could complete the thirty hours necessary for a master's before I returned to the Ann Arbor public school system. I knew it wouldn't be easy, but I had made it through the requirements for my bachelor's degree, so I was confident I could make it through my master's program.

I wanted to obtain a master's degree for two reasons. First of all, my salary would increase once I completed the requirements. Second, after having taught a few years, I realized the importance of leadership in the public school arena. Until now, all my efforts toward integrating multiethnic material and concepts into a curriculum were conducted only in my classrooms. Because I felt so dedicated to infusing these concepts into the school-wide curriculum, I knew I needed to convince those responsible for changing the status quo of its value. I also felt I could be more effective if I were in a position of leadership. For example, if I were the principal of a school, I could work with the faculty to achieve integration of this concept. And with a master's degree it would be much easier for me to apply for positions that could eventually encourage school-wide participation. A master's degree in school administration could provide me with the necessary tools to achieve my goals. While I enjoyed teaching, I wanted to be in positions of leadership where I could make a difference in what children were taught. This approach could prepare more effective teachers as well as individuals who might willingly embrace diversity.

As a lecturer in the School of Education, I was not in a position to ask students to do more than what was required. I was responsible for helping student teachers become more effective with their teaching strategies and techniques. However, when I had the students together in their weekly seminars, I would occasionally explain how they might become more effective in the classroom by using examples that reflected diversity of some kind. The more I became involved in the value of teaching from a multiethnic perspective, the more I realized that a great deal of sexism also existed in textbooks and other student materials. My thinking about what to integrate into teacher education began to expand to include more positive attitudes about girls and women.

After passage of the Civil Rights Act in 1964, there was an interest throughout the country in developing educational materials that embraced the concepts behind multiethnic education. Most of what was being published and circulated had to do with black Americans. Toward the end of the sixties, materials that reflected the history and contributions of Hispanics, Native Americans, and Asians were becoming available. However, it wasn't until the early to mid-seventies that a definite attempt was made by publishers, professional organizations, school systems, and state boards of education to move in the direction of even acknowledging cultural diversity. This was also the beginning of activities across the nation and throughout colleges and universities that reflected the concerns and issues of ethnic diversity.

As I plunged into the assignments for my graduate courses, I was always thinking about how to enhance the assignments and gain further insight into the history and experiences of ethnic groups. While my focus was primarily on the black experience, I was interested in what I could learn about the other ethnic groups that had begun to surface.

I was on top of most everything to do with education and diversity. I combed the research and the literature looking for anything that would expand my knowledge base. As a result, I structured all of the topics of my assigned term papers around the basic topic of diversity. I soon found myself an advocate for the integration of multiethnic material and concepts into almost everything I did.

In 1964 I completed a wonderful and exciting year as lecturer in the School of Education at the University of Michigan. I also completed work on my master's degree that same year. The 1963–64 school year had seemed the most incredible year of my life. My family remained intact. My children and my husband were most cooperative. There were times when schedules and fatigue resulted in flare-ups, but we worked hard to maintain our togetherness.

When I returned to the Ann Arbor public school system in the fall of 1964, I was assigned to a different school. Although I really wanted to return to Wines, my assignment was second grade at Lawton School. I convinced myself that going from fourth to second grade would give me an opportunity to tailor my approach to multiethnic education to a different grade level. Also, the school was in an all-white school district. I knew too that what I was trying to do would be needed. The socioeconomic level of this school district was a little higher than that of Wines: many of the parents were either professors or successful business people. All of the students lived in the area; busing for the sake of integration had not yet begun.

Once again I was the only black teacher in the school. By now, being the only black in many situations at the University of Michigan and in the local school district was no longer an oddity for me. In fact, these situations reinforced my rationale for a multiethnic approach to a curriculum. I was truly becoming a "spirited black woman in a white world." The experience behind the title of this book, *A Hot Fudge Sundae in a White Paper Cup*, served as the catalyst for how my professional life was developing.

I took advantage of my environment and made it work for me. I remember when I went to Lawton, references to people who looked like me was changing from "Negro" to "black." It was difficult for some people, both white and black, to make the transition. It was especially hard for older blacks, who had already found it difficult to adjust from "colored" to "Negro." Now they had to get used to being called "black." Because black was a color, people who were being referred to as blacks, including many children, could not understand the reason for this new term. The children in my second-grade class were no exception.

The next four years of teaching second grade were uneventful, until I returned from lunch one day in the fall of 1968 to find an unusually quiet classroom. Normally second graders were all around the room, talking and making noise until the bell rang. The bell had not rung. The class was much too quiet. I knew something had happened. I soon discovered that one of the children in another classroom had told one of the students in my classroom that they had a "black" teacher. Because I was the only person of color on the faculty in the school, I was highly visible. Once the situation was described by the students who witnessed this, I realized that while the reference to me as a black teacher by the student in another class was accurate, it was said in such a tone as to make it more like a slur than a description of what I was. The student involved started sobbing when he called out, "I told him you are not black. You are brown. You are the color of your car." In those days, a teacher could console a child by putting his or her arm around a child, which I did. Finally when everything had quieted down and I had admitted to being black, the class accepted my pronouncement, but reluctantly. I knew I had my work cut out for me. I also felt more than ever that my assignment had been appropriate for the school and for me.

Until then, I thought I had done a great deal toward creating approaches to the curriculum that were multiethnic. A very important aspect of this approach was that concepts and information had to be subtle as well as integrated. What could I do to help these young children feel comfortable about using the term "black" in reference to people, and especially to their teacher? I had an idea.

In some of the literature that was being published, I had come across books for children entitled *Black Is Beautiful*. I knew these were written primarily for young black children, but I decided to use this concept and integrate it into art activities in my white classroom. I talked with the art teacher and gained her support for what I wanted to do. Together we developed an entire unit on Black Is Beautiful. The purpose was to involve the children in the creation of beautiful works of art that used a black medium. What a project! To this day, I'm not sure where all the creativity came from. The art teacher and I never seemed to run out of ideas. The children were most creative and responsive. We created black mobiles and hung them in the classroom. We worked with clay and painted their beautiful work with black paint. We also painted with black paint on different colored papers. We made three-dimensional figures out of black construction paper. After several works of art in media that were black and beautiful, the children became much more comfortable using the term "black" with people, and especially with their teacher.

Throughout the year I continued to infuse the second-grade curriculum with multiethnic information and strategies. When I read to the children, I read stories about blacks like Booker T. Washington. I included stories about individuals from other ethnic groups when I came across suitable material. Their language art lessons developed out of appropriate reading materials. We rewrote some of the mathematics stories to include girls, or to change a derogatory description, or to include an ethnic group.

Our inclusion soon took an international flavor. We became involved in an art exchange with a school in Japan. This exchange opened up another world for most of the children. Simple concepts were explored. Geography was involved. The children learned the difference between a Japanese and a Chinese restaurant. When we invited a policeman or a fireman to class, I requested persons representing two different ethnic groups, or a male and a female. The children and I were having fun, and their parents approved of what we were doing. By the end of the first semester, other classes, and even a school assembly, imitated much of what we were doing.

During that year I was very much attuned to activity on the U of M campus. I was especially interested in the development of the Black Action Movement (BAM). Before I returned to the school system, I had been invited to meetings of some of the black students who were creating a list of concerns they had and planned to present to the president and the board of trustees at the University of Michigan. I listened with great interest because much of what they were dissatisfied with seemed to run parallel to my reasons for feeling so strongly about the benefits of a multiethnic approach to the curriculum. The BAM movement, however, focused on more than curriculum. They wanted integration and involvement throughout all aspects of the University. One of their concerns was the lack of black faculty.

Much of what was happening on the U of M campus was happening in some form on other campuses throughout the nation. I closely watched what was developing on campus. I continued to weigh the expected outcomes of the approach I was advocating for curricula and courses of study. The student demands were often akin to possible outcomes of multiculturalism. It occurred to me that one of the benefits of exposing students to diversity would be the opening of doors to positions that had previously been closed to ethnic minorities. I felt that what I was proposing and thinking was developing at a most opportune time.

While I enjoyed my teaching at Lawton School and certainly valued my opportunity to help shape the minds and thoughts of young people, I had a great need to make an impact on teacher training and teacher education. I had benefited so much from working with students who were in the pre-service arena that I really wanted an opportunity to return to the University setting. If I could help young students preparing to teach understand the need to involve the history and contributions of ethnic groups in the development of our nation and world, then the kind of activity that BAM was invoking would no longer be needed. I wanted to return to the university and work with student teachers. It didn't take long for me, once again, to take my pen in one hand and my nerve in the other. I wrote a letter to Dean Wilbur Cohen, dean of the School of Education at the University of Michigan. I asked the dean if I could return to the School of Education to work with student teachers. I did not have a PhD, but they had allowed me to work with student teachers as the result of my award, and they had known that I did not have a master's degree.

While I waited for a response from Dean Cohen, I continued to hope I could return to work with student teachers. I also knew they might be looking for people of color to bring onto the faculty because of the BAM concerns. I felt I had done a good job the year I was at the School of Education, fulfilling the requirements of the Ann Arbor Teacher Award. I wanted the appointment not just because I was a person of color but also because I had performed well when I was in the position of lecturer. It did not take long to receive a response. I was invited to return to the University to serve as an instructor in the School of Education. I would do exactly the same kind of work I had done as a lecturer the year before. My luck was still with me. I resigned from my position as teacher in the Ann Arbor public school system and prepared for my position at the University.

I was very happy and excited about returning to the University. However, I had made good friends at Lawton School and I was sad about leaving. In fact, some thirty-five years later, I still correspond with students and parents who were so supportive of my work at Lawton School.

I thought I had made it clear to the dean of the School of Education that I wanted no part of a PhD. I was happy with the idea of being an instructor. I guess I had convinced everyone but myself. When one doesn't have tenure or full faculty status, certain fringe benefits do not apply. Being an instructor did not give me enough points to have an office all to myself. I was privileged when I was on the award status, but that privilege was no longer extended to me. I shared an office with two PhD students. In a way this was a blessing because I met two very fine individuals. One of these students was Dolores Cross, who is now a retired college president. Dolores and I became very good friends, and I helped her collect some of the data for her doctoral research. The trips with her to Detroit schools gave me experiences I shall never forget. Schools and conditions in large urban school districts were very different from schools in small cities like Ann Arbor and Chelsea, Michigan. Given my exposure to Dolores Cross and her research, it didn't take her long to convince me to enroll in a PhD program.

My commitment to influence teacher education through the inclusion of multiethnic concepts and information helped me make the decision to apply for admission to the doctoral program at U of M.

I had no difficulty being admitted. My only difficulty was, once again, trying to meld my responsibilities as mother and wife with my assignment in the teacher education program at the University. By now I was almost an expert at planning and organizing my work and responsibilities for survival, and I was determined that this would not be my Waterloo. Working while attending classes on the same site allowed me to take graduate classes in the morning and hold seminars and office hours for students in the afternoon.

For the most part, graduate coursework was not difficult, except for statistics, which gave me a run for my money. I believe it was the only course in which I received a B grade. The professor of this course was a friend, Betty Morrison. While I expected this to help me, it did not. I didn't want her to know how much trouble I was having with the coursework. She assumed I was smarter than I was. I did learn enough to get me through my doctoral research. We had become good friends, and spoke at length on the phone throughout the years. I was very sad when she died in 2007.

I had reviewed a great deal of literature for the term papers I was required to do. Because I had focused all of my work for the master's degree on some aspect of ethnicity and diversity, my recorded review of the literature required for my dissertation was about half completed when I started the doctoral program.

With my course work in good shape, I prepared for my preliminary exams. I had a lot to read and even more to put to memory. I had to find time and ways to accomplish my tasks at home, and to maintain balance with my children and husband. I had little time for activities other than those at home and school.

While I didn't quite fall apart as I had when I was working on my bachelor's degree, I started having problems with aches and pains throughout my body. When I went to an orthopedist for an examination, the doctor concluded that my aches and pains were from fatigue and overwork. I was in the midst of my graduate program and did not want to stop, so I rearranged much of what I was doing at home. I tried hard not to reduce my activities and involvement with the children. I put our social life on hold. James went along with what I had rearranged. At that time he was very supportive of me in pursuing my PhD; he felt my having that was better than an insurance policy. He pointed out that he might not always be around to help support me. If something happened to him, like an early death, at least I would be able to take care of myself.

How many times I ironed clothes with a book on the ironing board, reviewing material I needed to memorize. I kept a book with me at all times, especially when I was compiling bibliographies for a course of study on multiethnic education. Some of the material was appropriate for children, and my children served as my audience. I read books to them in the evening that satisfied my role as parent and student. I was prepared for my examinations and I did very well.

From the time Professor Schmerl asked me about the ethnic composition of the explorers of the state of Michigan until I began my doctoral work, that question that kept coming into my thoughts. I wondered if the reason

I became so caught up in trying to find information and materials about ethnicity was partly because I was black. And was it also because I had been reared in an environment that supported diversity even though it was not discussed or thought of in the way I'd been considering it at the time? Would the degree to which a teacher perceives diversity have any impact on whether or not the teacher would develop or teach a multiethnic curriculum? These were some thoughts and questions that formed the foundation of my doctoral research.

Each semester I taught an elementary methods course. I designed the course to expose my students to the concept of ethnic diversity. I was the only instructor who was teaching the methods course in this manner. Therefore I felt I could design a study that would compare what my students learned and felt about ethnic diversity to a course taught by another professor who did not include any aspect of ethnic diversity in his or her course.

The title of my dissertation was "The Effects of Training in Multi-Ethnic Education on Pre-Service Teachers' Perceptions." The purpose of the study was to determine whether a change could be made in the perception of ethnic groups held by students enrolled in a course in elementary school methods that emphasized a multiethnic approach to teaching.

I passed all the requirements for the PhD, defended my research, and completed my dissertation. I took a deep breath and breathed a long sigh of relief once I received the beautiful maize-and-blue hood during the commencement in August 1972.

I was to return to the University of Michigan as assistant professor of education in September. I was so proud of what I had achieved, yet I was more than exhausted. I could still hear the words spoken by Ma and Pa Williams when they learned about my pregnancy. "Just because you have fallen into the gutter doesn't mean you have to stay there." They were so right. It had taken me a long time to get to the point where where I felt I had paid for my mistake. I was clearly no longer in the gutter.

Between the late sixties and early seventies, the nation was more aware of ethnic diversity than perhaps at any other time in its past. Civil rights legislation was nearing a decade in age. Busing was something most people were either reading about or involved in. Although the Ann Arbor public schools were not involved in busing, there was much discussion about what the schools needed to do to encourage positive attitudes among students and teachers. There were incidents in the schools and especially the high schools—name-calling between whites and blacks often led to physical confrontations—that suggested something needed to be done.

At that time I was involved in the Parent Teacher Association (PTA). James and I were also involved in discussions and meetings of black parents to encourage the school administration to do something that would help students, teachers, and parents understand the need to recognize and understand ethnic diversity. We met. We discussed. We picketed the administration building to help those in power respond to our requests. Finally, the PTA and the Ann Arbor School Board concluded that the schools needed what was then being referred to as a multiethnic curriculum. They also decided not to allow student teachers in the Ann Arbor public school system from universities that did not require some coursework reflecting a multiethnic content or experience. Because I had been involved as a parent in many of the discussions with the school board and the PTA, I was well aware of what these requirements would mean for the placement of University of Michigan student teachers.

My advocacy for multiethnic education had not gone unnoticed at the School of Education. The focus of my work on my master's degree had certainly brought the subject to the attention of my professors and to many students in my graduate courses. Also, my dissertation was on this subject. Therefore, when the School of Education became aware of the new requirement from the Ann Arbor public schools, I was invited to participate in discussions about how we, the School of Education, might satisfy the requirement. I was no longer on the outside looking in. I was in now on the inside looking out, and forward.

The years I had spent studying and teaching a multiethnic approach placed me in a position to make a real difference. No longer would my attempts to sensitize students and student teachers be confined to the classes I taught. With the background I had in multiethnic education, I was equipped to help plan and organize ways in which this approach would be more widespread. I readily accepted the assignment to help the School of Education satisfy the requirement of educating and training student teachers in multiethnic education. I worked closely with a small committee. The professors in the School of Education would help compile a list of courses offered throughout the University that had some aspects that would expose students to diversity. Our students would be required to take three courses from the multicultural course list the committee had compiled.

By this time, the term "multiethnic" had become "multicultural." The concepts behind the term "multicultural" were more encompassing. Multicultural included a much wider scope of diversity, taking into account gender and socioeconomic status. In order to give students an additional opportunity to focus on methodology for the classroom, I developed a course called Methods in Multicultural Instruction. There was no other teacher education program in the country at that time that had such a requirement. It didn't take long for the need for instruction in multiethnic education to penetrate the requirements for teacher certification throughout most of the nation.

During this same period, teacher education and related professional organizations began to demonstrate their commitment to diversity in various ways. Boards of directors in most of these organizations realized the need to include individuals from different ethnic groups into the governing structures as members of boards and committees. When I was elected to serve on the board of directors for the American Educational Research Association (AERA), I was one of the first blacks to do so. Other associations followed: the Association for Supervision and Curriculum and Development (ASCD), the National Council for Social Studies (NCSS), the American Association for Colleges of Teacher Education (AACTE), and the National Education Association (NEA), to name a few.

Soon most of these associations had ethnic representation on their boards. No longer were the speakers at the annual meetings and conferences of these and other groups all white and male. Their conference programs reflected their sensitivity to the need to involve people from all ethnic groups, and their publications reflected their commitment to diversity. Most professional organizations now had committees or caucuses to assist their attempts to be inclusive. As a very active professional educator, I was a member of most of the associations that interfaced with education. As a result, I served on boards and committees when and where I felt I could be helpful.

In 1973 I joined two of my colleagues and a friend on a trip to West Africa. This experience was extremely important to me for at least two reasons.

First, I had had very little exposure to my own ethnic background. A trip to West Africa would help me fill in the blanks with a historical perspective on my ancestry. Second, it would be a wonderful experience for the collection of facts, information, and artifacts that would augment my teaching.

Finally, at this stage of our marriage, James and I were feeling the strain my new interests and responsibilities had placed on me. This trip held the possibility of giving our marriage some breathing space. Time away from one another could give us both time to think about our future together.

The African Association in New York City planned the trip. We were scheduled to visit Ghana, the Ivory Coast, Nigeria, and Liberia. The trip would take several weeks, and we were allowed to deviate somewhat from the schedule. For example, because of my status as a professor at the University of Michigan, I was able to arrange accommodations for my companions and myself at the faculty guest quarters at the University of Ghana. This meant that we didn't have to stay in the dormitories on campus. We were treated like guests and we thoroughly enjoyed our private and separate guesthouse.

One member of our small group, Carol Watson, had parents who traveled a great deal. Carol's parents put us in touch with a family they had met in Ghana and with whom they had become friends. The Quashi family received us as long-lost relatives. The husband and wife were both involved in businesses in Ghana and served as our hosts. We saw and experienced much more than we might have with the larger group. We traveled in and around Ghana as though we lived there. This was truly a fine experience, and we all stayed in touch with the Quashi family. I visited them again on another trip about ten years later. One of the daughters, Constance Quashi, spent a summer with my family and me. Later, when I lived in New York, the Quashis contacted me whenever they were in the city on business or visiting two of their children who had settled in Brooklyn.

The trip to the Ivory Coast was fabulous. We stayed in the famous Hotel Ivoire, which was newly built. It was a lovely facility, complete with supermarket and ice-skating rink. Our travel included a great deal of preparation, both for our comfort and our craving to learn about the history of these countries. We could not read enough or ask enough questions. We visited families, schools, and places of worship.

Nigeria was different from the previous two countries. In Ghana, we could see and feel the economic and political progress. The same was true for the Ivory Coast. In Nigeria, we saw less of the progress and more of the struggle this country was going through to achieve economic and political freedom. The day we walked through the main section of Lagos, the capital city, we saw piles of rubbish on the streets. The gutters were filled with debris, including dead animals. It was hard to look at. The more I learned about the history of this country and of West Africa, the more I understood the causes of what we witnessed. Much of what I learned I could not accept. My experience with racism in the United States had not prepared me for what had happened to black Africa, and to what was still happening. The colonization of many of the countries in West Africa had left an indelible mark on their future development.

Our African experience ended with a trip to Liberia. This was the country I was most interested in. I had met a young woman from Liberia at the University of Michigan named Adriana Stewart. Carol Watson, Eugenia Foree, Edith Watson, and I had all become friends with her. Even when I was not in school and raising a family, Adriana (Addie) kept in touch with me. She often joined my student boarders for dinner with my family and me. A trip to Liberia meant a visit with Addie. It also meant seeing our friend Gus Dundas again. Gus had been a guest of my family when the University had extended us an opportunity to invite foreign students into the homes of faculty members. All of my expectations were met. We had a great reunion, and we met new friends. Some of the people we met stayed in our home years later. Some never made it through one revolution or another. (As I write this, Liberia has just elected its first black female as president.)

The trip to Africa helped me better understand my blackness. I had a heritage I could acknowledge. What I experienced and learned greatly contributed to my ability to share information with my colleagues and students. The experience helped me broaden my approach to multiculturalism and include the impact of international cultures on the many diverse cultures of the United States. On a personal note, the separation from James quieted the storm that had begun.

Shortly after my African experience, James and I decided to build a new house. We both felt this might provide the glue that we needed in our relationship. The new house captured our attention for a while. We enjoyed the new space and it served nicely as a place to entertain our friends and my students. By this time, JoAnn was in college and was not living at home.

Claudia and Jim both enjoyed the new house and the new neighborhood. We had moved into the neighborhood of Lawton School, the last elementary school where I had taught. Some of our neighbors were parents of children I had taught. The wife of our neighbor next door had gone to elementary and junior high school with me. They were the only Greek family, and we were the only black family, in our neighborhood. Much had happened to me since the day I'd been served a hot fudge sundae in a white paper cup.

At this point in my life, however, I was struggling to keep my marriage intact. It was not an easy task. Trying to balance all that needed to be done was a strain on my nerves and energy. Because I was excited and happy with what I was trying to do professionally didn't mean that my children and my husband were satisfied. Sometimes there was just not enough of me to go around.

As a new assistant professor, I was well aware of the requirement to complete postdoctoral research and publication within six years to be considered for tenure. Because I was on the faculty of the School of Education when the school was developing a multicultural component for teacher training, I was able to take advantage of several opportunities to complete my postdoctoral research. Once the research was done, I published my first article in the *Journal for Teacher Education*, published by the American Association of Colleges of Teacher Education. The article led to invitations from several other publications to contribute articles on multicultural education. I was elated.

My professional career was off to a good start. However, I was spending many evening and weekends in the office studying and writing. In addition to writing articles trying to satisfy tenure requirements, I was organizing opportunities to expose the students to diversity, including a workshop in the School of Education. I had the support of the Dean's Office to invite several outstanding individuals to participate. I had met James Banks at one of the conferences I attended. He was becoming a well-known educator whose interest was multiethnic education. I invited James Banks and Geneva Gay, another professor who wrote on multiethnic education at that time, to participate. This workshop was scheduled to cover several days. Organizing this took a great deal of time, but it was worth it. Students were interested, and the sessions were attended by students in the School of Education and beyond. Professor Al Loving helped me in several efforts to talk with students about multiethnic topics. At that time, Professor Loving was the only African American professor at the University of Michigan. By the time I left for Washington, DC, in 1977, there were approximately twenty minority members on the faculty.

I knew that to obtain tenure I needed to have more than one published article. My friend Dolores Cross and I had often attended education conferences together. Dolores was on the faculty at Northwestern University, and on several occasions we discussed the possibility of writing a book. The time had come for us to do more than talk about it. We decided on the title *Teaching in a Multicultural Society* and invited Lindley J. Stiles, who was also on the faculty at Northwestern, to join us in our endeavor.

Lindley had published many times and knew the turf. We organized a group of faculty members from Northwestern University and the University of Michigan to discuss issues involved in multiethnic education. We met several times at both universities to share ideas of what should be included. The professors who were interested were invited to contribute to the book. This turned out to be a great idea and after a lot of hard work our combined work was published by Free Press in 1977.

After a year or two on the faculty, I noticed the wear and tear on my family life. It was not so much with the children, because they were at the ages where they were becoming quite independent. JoAnn was in college and working. Claudia and Jim were in high school. Their lives were full and they were content with whatever time I had for them. Their father was not quite so content. I was so close to applying for my tenure three years after my appointment that I just had to continue my efforts.

At the end of my third year I received a call from the Office of the President of the University. It was one of the first in the country to establish an Affirmative Action Office. The president, Robben Fleming, called and asked me if I would accept the appointment as director of affirmative action for the University. This was a great honor, because at the University of Michigan, the director of affirmative action reported directly to the president. In other institutions, the person in charge of affirmative action reported to the head of Human Resources. This position was not only an honor for me, but the salary would double what I was making at the time. Yet I knew that if I left teaching for an administrative position before I received tenure, I would never receive tenure. Tenure was important to me because it would give me security. The pattern for most black professors at that time was to leave teaching for administration, which for some turned into a dead end. Black professors who did not also complete tenure requirements in six years often lost their job security. The saying among faculty was "publish or perish." I turned down the offer and told the president I would not leave my current position as assistant professor until I had received tenure.

The following year I submitted my requirements and made the tenure list in four years, not six. Soon my phone rang again. This time President Fleming said he had noticed my name on the tenure list, and offered me the director of affirmative action position again. I accepted the second offer and never regretted it.

In the early seventies more and more institutions of education across the nation were responding to issues of diversity. The University of Michigan had organized a Commission for Women to which I was appointed. There was also a Minority Commission. These two bodies represented the University's affirmative action efforts. In 1976, President Fleming appointed me to chair a committee whose task it was to reorganize the Affirmative Action Office. In a document dated May 5, 1977, the president announced the results of this committee's work, with his approval. In 1978, I became the second director of affirmative action, following Nellie Varner. Professor Varner then became the dean of the Rackham School for Graduate Studies.

One aspect of the director of affirmative action position at the University was made very clear to me from the beginning. President Fleming told me I should not plan to be in that position for more than two years. When I asked why, he said the pressure of working with the deans and the faculty would be onerous. Affirmative action was not easily accepted. We did not discuss this further because I clearly understood what he meant. It was the issue of racism all over again, but in a different setting.

The end results of the Black Action Movement (BAM) had caused the regents of the University, the administration, and the faculty to make some changes, which were beginning to take place. There were more students of color on campus. For years, the University held the black enrollment to two hundred students. It could do this rather easily because pictures were required with applications. Blacks and other minorities were slowly being hired as faculty members or administrators. Hiring was only one aspect of affirmative action. Policies and procedures were needed across the University to secure many of the changes that were occurring. The most difficult part of affirmative action had to do with attitudes and behaviors. Because of my previous academic work and my experiences with multiculturalism, I had developed the sensitivity I needed to tackle the job. Having received tenure certainly added to my professional profile. It also meant I would retain a position as a faculty member at U of M.

Because I reported to the president of the University as director of affirmative action, I had the respect and clout this position needed. Reporting directly to the president made me a member of his cabinet. I was required to attend the weekly meetings he held with his cabinet, at which I was the only woman around that table. The only other black person in the cabinet was William Cash, who served as secretary to the president.

At this point in my professional career I was feeling secure and confident about what I had achieved. Tenure was something to feel good about. Several colleagues at U of M and in other institutions had not completed the necessary requirements for tenure and were forced into administrative positions or dead-end jobs. I was also making more money in my new assignment than I had been as an associate professor.

While my career was moving along nicely, my marriage was stumbling. My husband no longer supported my career endeavors. There were times when I felt uncomfortable inviting students or colleagues into our home for fear of unwanted behavior from James. One evening when several students were at the house for dinner, one of them said to me, "Professor Baker, you have it all. You have a husband, children, and a wonderful career." Little did she know that what she saw was not real. I did not have it all. Yet in spite of the unsettling environment I was living in, I forced myself to focus on my new position and give it as much as I could. Before the end of my first year as director of affirmative action I had decided to seek an attorney to start my divorce proceedings.

I enjoyed my position because I now had a good overview of the administrative aspects of the University. At that time there were over 40,000 students. The faculty was unionized. The students were more involved in the affairs of the university than ever before. This was in the mid-seventies, only a decade after the passage of civil rights legislation. The University had responded to the Black Action Movement's demand for changes. The

Affirmative Action Office was one response to the civil rights movement and federal legislation, but even though there had been some movement toward incorporating diversity into this institution, there was still much to be done.

From my experiences with racism and sexism, I knew that the responsibilities of this position required extra efforts to change attitudes and behavior. I also realized that new policies and further legislation were needed. I gave serious thought to how I could help bring about change. I knew that to be successful I would need a great deal of support. The fact that I was located in and functioned out of the president's office was not something to be ignored.

By this time in my life I was in my mid-forties. I had experienced my share of racism and sexism. I thought about how my skin color had a negative effect on the way some people treated those who looked like me. It all started with how my hot fudge sundae had been served to me. This was a beginning, but it certainly was not the end. As I prepared for this position, I reviewed the intervening years to identify areas in which I had recognized racial discrimination of some kind. It was easier to identify racial discrimination than sex discrimination. When one is both black and female, the discriminating behavior is generally due more to skin color than sex. When individuals ask me whether I feel the need to be an advocate for one or the other, I reply that when I was born, people saw me first as a *black* child; the fact that I was a *girl* was secondary. However, this did not keep me from being concerned about sexist attitudes and behaviors. In fact, this kind of thinking had guided me to move from using the term "multiethnic" to "multicultural" when I was developing curricula for the classroom.

I was committed to helping people understand the value of diversity, regardless of the reasons for any differences. I was also committed to helping individuals understand and eliminate racist and sexist behaviors, no matter when they occurred.

I organized the Affirmative Action Office with great care. I made sure that my staff of six was diverse. Ann Schlitt, a young woman who headed up the women's unit, had completed her student teaching with me during the year I taught at Lawton School. Ann was very effective in the classroom and worked extremely well with me in developing a multiethnic/multicultural curriculum. To this day, Ann and I are still friends. She married Eric Kobell, one of the ministers at Riverside Church in New York City, which I joined after I moved to New York in 1981.

My staff and I worked to develop our goals and objectives, and found ways of sharing these with the entire University. I was pleased with the individuals I worked with. They not only reflected diversity, they were all committed to making sure the University was in compliance with all federal legislation and more. The "more" represented what we felt was needed to make the University a model of diversity. Even in 2004, as the University bravely defended its admission policies, the affirmative action program at the University some thirty years before planted some significant seeds in support of multiculturalism.

As I neared the end of two very successful years as director of affirmative action, I became convinced that James Baker and I could no longer live together as husband and wife. The arguments became a daily part of our existence. There were days when it was difficult. The children were grown, in and out of college. Our son Jim had decided to go into the navy. Claudia had dropped out of college and was working but living at home. JoAnn had completed one degree, was working and on her own. There was no real reason to stay in a marriage that was not bringing me any pleasure. I was becoming depressed and decided it would be best to get a divorce. I made the decision; James was against it. I'm sure he was partly reluctant because he had relied on me for so much, and it might have been somewhat scary for him to think of living alone. I was looking forward to being on my own because I anticipated some peace of mind. It took time and some courage to put a marriage of twenty-eight years behind me. James had been my first and only boyfriend. We had truly grown up together. But we had developed into two totally different individuals over the twenty-eight years. Actually it was thirty-three years, because we had gone steady for five years before we married.

One day during all of this turmoil, I received a letter from the National Institute of Education (NIE) in Washington, DC. The letter contained an invitation for me to apply for a position there, specifically chief of the Minorities and Women's Research Program. The focus of the program was to develop ways through which minorities and women could become more involved in educational research and dissemination. Once again, I felt the man or woman above was definitely looking out for me.

Every aspect of the job description ran parallel to my previous experiences. I was an educator. I had tenure at a research university. I had a PhD, which gave me some experience in research. I had already served on several of the national boards that this position would need to interface. My position as director of affirmative action had equipped me with a broad experience of administration. I remembered President Fleming telling me that after two years I would be ready to leave the position because of the stress. I needed to think of my future.

I knew this job had been created for me. I also learned that Lamar Miller, a colleague of mine, had been the main consultant for this program at NIE. I contacted Lamar to make sure I understood what was needed, and he encouraged me to apply. It took a while to set up interviews and appointments in Washington, but I was appointed chief of the Minorities and Women's Research Program at NIE in the spring of 1978. My salary doubled again. I filed for divorce and moved to Washington in June of that year. I was starting a new life. I never took the time to look back except to make sure that all the people and experiences that had contributed to my personal and professional life went with me in some way.

SEVEN

Taking on Washington

Leaving the University of Michigan, Ann Arbor, my family, and my friends was much more difficult than I had imagined. I think the only thing that got me through the good-byes was again having my nerve in one hand and my dreams of the future in the other. I was on the move once more. I had never lived in any city other than Ann Arbor, and now I was heading not to just any city, but to the nation's capital.

I was excited about going to Washington. I knew several people there and I leaned heavily on one friend especially to help me find an apartment. That friend was Evelyn K. Moore. Evelyn and I had become friends in Ann Arbor. In fact, Evelyn played a crucial role in helping the dean of the School of Education, Wilbur Cohen, decide to offer me a position. This was 1970, a year after I had received the Ann Arbor Teacher Award. Evelyn taught school in Ann Arbor and had taken a position as assistant to the dean before I became involved in the School of Education. She was in that position when I applied for an instructor position. After I returned to the School of Education, she shared with me the conversation she had with the dean about offering me an appointment. The dean was concerned about making appointments because of the Black Action Movement. He wanted to be sure the black community would look favorably upon my appointment. Evelyn assured him that my appointment as an instructor would be respected by those who were involved, and also by those who were concerned about ensuring diversity on the staff and within the faculty.

Not long after I joined the faculty as an instructor, Evelyn became executive director of the National Black Child Development Institute in Washington, DC. From time to time I traveled to Washington for a meeting or a conference, and would contact Evelyn. Almost always we met for dinner or a drink. At one of our dinner meetings Evelyn presented me with a gold charm of the Washington Memorial. She knew I had a gold charm bracelet and felt this would be a perfect addition, because she had a strong feeling that one day in the not-too-distant future I would be living in Washington.

After Evelyn left Ann Arbor and before I moved to Washington in 1978, I was asked to apply for the position of executive director for the National Council for the Accreditation of Teacher Education. This position interested me because the accreditation process was the logical means for encouraging teacher-training institutions to integrate aspects of multiethnic education into their training and education programs. By then, I had received my PhD and had several years of experience working with and training teachers at the U of M. I applied for the position and was one of two finalists.

The final interview was in Washington, where I stayed with Evelyn in her lovely townhouse. My competition was a white male who also had a substantial background in teacher education and training. We were interviewed separately, in different rooms in a local hotel. The entire process was nerve-racking.

After my interview I was asked to remain in the room until the search committee had made its decision. Sometime later, one of the committee members came and told me the committee could not make a decision, and we would each have another interview that day. I returned to my room following the second interview and was instructed to wait for the decision.

After a very long wait, they informed me that the position had gone to the other person. I was stunned. I had never been so disappointed in my life. I learned later that I had lost the position by a single vote, cast by the only black member of the selection committee. Somehow I maintained my composure and returned to Evelyn's. When I reached her townhouse I was in tears. Evelyn tried to comfort me, but it took a while before I could think of anything else. Her friendship helped, and yet this was something I had to learn how to deal with on my own. My mother also tried to help by saying that "when one door closes another one will open."

Another door did open: In the spring of 1978 I accepted the position of chief of the Minorities and Women's Research Program at the National Institute of Education. As I was planning my move to Washington, the first thing on my list of priorities was to find a place to live. I didn't want to rent; I preferred to buy. My divorce involved selling some real estate we owned, so I had funds to invest in housing. I was so fond of the townhouse that Evelyn lived in, I decided I wanted something similar. To my surprise, the first time I looked at the real estate section in the *Washington Post*, I found an ad for a townhouse in Beekman Place, where Evelyn lived. The size was perfect. It had two bedrooms, a bath and a half, and the price was within my range. It also meant I would be near a friend, five doors from Evelyn.

Because the townhouse was brand new, I wouldn't be able to complete the closing until a month or two later. I needed to live in temporary quarters for about two months. Fortunately during the interview process for this position, the Institute had housed me in a lovely place within walking distance of the office. The Tabbard Inn was a charming small inn with a wonderful restaurant. The Inn couldn't keep me for the entire period but recommended another slightly larger hotel next door. All of my housing needs were taken care of. My furniture would remain in storage until I could move to my townhouse. I needed to start work at the beginning of the summer to organize the proposal review process. This was for the first phase of grants to be awarded within four to six months.

As I look back over what I was experiencing at the time, I'm not sure how I got myself together to be in Washington by June 1978. I couldn't have made this physical transition without the help of another good friend, Catherine Baker. Catherine and I grew up in the same neighborhood. Her family lived two doors from my family's home. She was then Catherine Dixon, and was a few years younger than I. We were never close friends until she married into the Baker family. Catherine and her husband Leroy moved into a house up the street from where we lived on Miner Street. I'm not sure if it was because we married brothers or because our needs guided us, but we developed a very long and fine friendship. Catherine helped me move into my townhouse in Washington during the summer of 1978. Her son Timmy, who was about ten years old at the time, joyfully added two more hands as we put a lot of effort into getting me settled in DC. Catherine has since helped me move into all of the other cities I've lived in, including New York and Sarasota, Florida. Her son Tim, now a husband and father, is an internationally known disc jockey.

Making the physical move from my home in Ann Arbor to Washington at that time was overwhelming. I had to organize my life so I would be comfortable for a short stay in the temporary quarters in DC. I had never lived in anything but a house, so making an efficiency apartment my home for a few weeks was a challenge. And embedded and intertwined in all of this were all the feelings that separation brings, for during my move to Washington, I was involved in finalizing my divorce. The excitement of the move, combined with the challenges presented by my new responsibilities, contributed a great deal toward helping me put the separation from James, the children, my family, and friends into perspective. I was so busy doing new and different things that I had almost no time to fully experience the sadness that can come from separations. However, my children were as supportive as possible.

During this same period I lost one of my closest friends. This, and losing a husband of twenty-eight years, made the time very difficult emotionally.

Margot and Frank Ellis became friends of ours through mutual friends and relatives. Margot was an Alpha Kappa Alpha (AKA) sorority woman. She and Catherine Williams (Ma Williams), also an AKA, convinced me to become an AKA. Next to church affiliations, black sororities and fraternities are very important to the black experience. Frank Ellis was an Alpha Phi Alpha man, as was my husband James. Years later, our son became an APA man. Jim was proud that he and his father were in the same fraternity, and the fact that I was an AKA made him even prouder.

Margot was a librarian and worked in the Ann Arbor public school system. She shared my interest and enthusiasm for multiethnic education, and we shared newly discovered materials to add to our multiethnic bibliography. We often teamed up to do workshops on how to integrate these concepts into the curriculum. Margot was about ten years older than I. She was a good friend, colleague, and sorority sister. She was also a true mentor. She taught me many things about teaching, education, and family responsibilities. She developed cancer about five years before I divorced and moved to Washington, and died a few weeks after I made the physical move to DC.

Before I left the city, Margot and I had lunch together. We knew that her death was imminent. She knew I was divorcing James. In her very special way, she suggested that perhaps I could marry Frank, her husband. I almost fell out of my chair. I told her that I loved Frank like a brother, but I could never marry him. Margot continued the conversation with the thought that perhaps I would need *ten* men. Once again, I couldn't believe what I was hearing. I told her I couldn't sleep with ten men. She said you wouldn't sleep with ten men, you'd sleep with only one, but you would have a man to travel with, a man to play tennis with, and a man to go to the theater with. The list continued, based on my interests. I just listened. When she finished I put the idea of ten men on the top shelf in my closet of thoughts. Little did I know at the time that I would someday write a book entitled *It Takes Ten: Some Women Need More Than One Man*, for which I'm still trying to find a publisher.

I returned to Ann Arbor for Margot's funeral in July 1978, a month after I moved to Washington. I don't think I ever cried as much as I did that day at the funeral. Frank and I continued to be best friends. Unfortunately, Frank died while I was writing this book. Frank and Margot were highly unusual individuals, and I was truly blessed when they became our friends. James and I learned so much from them. They were inspiring, thoughtful, extremely warm and intelligent people. We did many things together, often with two other good friends, Josephine and Eddy Owens. Jo and Eddy, also deceased, contributed greatly to the joy I found in early friendships.

Each couple had two children. The Ellises had a daughter, Sylvia, and a son, Robert. They were like extended family. Frank Ellis's sister, Roberta Britt, taught the young girls who were part of the Girl Reserves at the Dunbar Center in Ann Arbor. Mrs. Britt and her husband owned the rooming house for black female students on the University of Michigan campus back then. This was important because blacks could not stay in the dormitories on campus. The Ellis family was large. They were from Oklahoma, and over the years I met all of them. We often traveled and socialized with Anne Ellis Chapman, one of Frank's younger sisters. One of Frank's brothers, Wade Ellis, was a professor at the University of Michigan. Years later, when I was with UNICEF, I ran into one of Anne Ellis's sons. Melvin Ellis Chapman, now retired from the State Department, continues to be a close family friend, especially of my brother Russell.

Jo and Eddy Owens were close friends and neighbors. I think the geographical closeness contributed to our friendship. During the time I taught at Wines Elementary, their youngest daughter, Kim, was in kindergarten there. Jo taught school and was not able to arrange for Kim to be picked up at lunchtime. Because I always went home for lunch with my children, I offered to give Kim a ride home each day. Kim is now married to Ricky Williams and they are raising a lovely family of two young men.

Jacque, the oldest Owen daughter, is probably the reason for much of my early travel abroad. The initial five-week trip to Europe with James was a catalyst for my interest in international travel. Jacque married Clyde Briggs, who worked for the U.S. State Department. They lived in several African countries and often extended invitations to me to visit them. Jacque told me that I was the only friend who would visit her. I think I almost wore out the carpet. I visited Jacque whenever I could, wherever she was assigned. I had visited several African countries with Carol Watson and friends earlier, and learned so much about the countries there, their histories, and their cultures from a different perspective. Jacque worked for the State Department. My earlier trips to Africa were made as a tourist, but my African visits and experiences contributed significantly to the international component of my multiethnic philosophy.

As I write, Haiti is recovering from the earthquake disaster of 2010. I listen to and watch the media coverage, reminded of the many times I visited Jacque in beautiful Haiti. The sun was always shining, which made the poverty seem less obvious. I enjoyed traveling in the mountains, trying to converse with the children along the wayside, and gathering artifacts that still decorate my home. At the time, we wondered about Haiti's future, but not as much as we do today. From visit to visit, the decline of the country became more evident. My last visit to Haiti was in 1995. I made this trip on behalf of UNICEF with Julia Roberts. I worry, along with many others, about how to provide what Haiti currently needs to survive, and about what the future will provide.

On one of my trips I was invited to take a tour of the schools. I had met an energetic young teacher working on her master's degree in New York at Bank Street College. She had married a Haitian and lived in Haiti. Marcia Gardere was interested in my multiethnic approach to education. Marcia was white, and I think because she was in an interracial marriage she understood what I was trying to accomplish. Although Paul was Haitian and an artist, his paintings did not have the traditional Haitian look. Fortunately I was able to purchase two of his paintings, which are still on my sitting room walls in Florida.

My friendship with Marcia was very pleasant. It was personally and professionally rewarding. She arranged for me to do a session or two on multicultural teaching with some of the teachers in the school where she taught.

My move to Washington meant that I would be leaving relatives and friends who had been so much a part of my life. Most of my family, the Calverts and the Bakers, continue to live in and around Ann Arbor. My social life, outside of friends I had met during my student and faculty days at the U of M, was confined to the friends I had from elementary and high school. Other friends, such as Mary Blakemore Scott and Hattie Howard, I met shortly after high school. Hattie and Mary were invited to Ann Arbor one summer by Hattie's aunt, Georgia Slueter.

Aunt Georgia, as I learned to call her, was the main cook for a white children's summer camp, Camp Davaja, located north of Ann Arbor. Aunt Georgia needed four or five helpers. I was invited to join Mary, Hattie, and another friend, Patsy McFadden, to work at the camp. Our responsibilities were to keep the dining room clean, set tables, help prepare vegetables, and do all of what helpers or assistants were supposed to do. Another friend, Betty Williams, was hired to care for the owner's grandchildren. For eight weeks we each earned a hundred dollars. We had our own living quarters, which were quite nice. We were given white uniforms. Our meals were provided at no cost. And to top it off, we had a day off each week. This day off was wonderful because I could spend time with James. We didn't have cars, but there was always someone going into the city for supplies who let us ride with them.

I am still in touch with Mary and Hattie. Aunt Georgia and Patsy McFadden are deceased. Our children are all friends. Our husbands and the fathers of our children are all deceased. A few of my other close friends include Ovilla Newman, Grace Rutledge, Betty Williams Everett, and Mayme Hall. We have cultivated long-lasting friendships that go back to elementary school. As I think of how fortunate I have been to have such close and wonderful friends throughout my life, I am reminded of a saying on a greeting card: Friends are the family one chooses. I have a very large and wonderful family throughout our nation and the world.

As chief of the Minorities and Women's Research Program, I was responsible for organizing the program to increase the involvement of minorities and women in educational research and development. What a challenge! During my orientation I discovered that in spite of all the grant programs, there was almost no attempt to involve minorities and women in the review of grants. While grants in some programs did fund minorities and women, very few minorities or women served as reviewers for grant applications.

Reviewing grants is one of the most valuable ways to learn how to write grants and to gain a clearer understanding of how research contributes to the development of the educational field. It made sense to me that we needed to design the review process so as to give a number of scholars and researchers the opportunity to be involved in the process. In this way, the reviewers would gain knowledge and expertise.

I knew I had to be careful about how I structured the review process. I was told that no other government program had involved as many minorities and women as I planned to do. We had to review hundreds of proposals in the first round. The process would need about one hundred reviewers. I knew I couldn't use all one hundred as first-time reviewers. However, I could put together a cadre of twenty seasoned, experienced reviewers who could help oversee the process. I would need help identifying eighty minorities and women to complete the review process. What a marvelous opportunity to integrate diversity into this process and at this level in the U.S. government.

To find the people I needed, I called my colleagues and friends. Word went out and in no time I had more individuals than I could involve. Participating in the process meant having an opportunity to learn how to read and evaluate proposals. It also meant a week in Washington, DC, meeting new colleagues and earning consulting fees. This was a wonderful opportunity for everyone involved.

As I write I can still feel the excitement of my world at that time. And yet I ask myself how I could have been excited just weeks after deciding to divorce my husband, a man I had been so close to for thirty-three years. And how could I have been excited after losing my good friend Margot Ellis? Looking back, I think the excitement, or at least some of it, came because I had *allowed* myself to get a divorce. I was able to rid myself of the extra load I carried because I had let myself down before completing my education. I was climbing out of the gutter and trying to find success in this world, and it felt good.

My children were not happy about the divorce but they were not openly defiant. They were in school or working and learning to grow up.

I fell in love with Washington for several reasons. The city is beautiful throughout the year. Each season has its own beauty. The flowering trees and shrubs adorn the magnificent national buildings, cathedrals, and monuments. The curving streets, roads, and bridges all contribute to the attractiveness of the capital. The city itself is not large, and it's easy to learn how to move around. In short, Washington is not only lovely, it's also manageable.

Here I was, learning how to live in the only other city I had ever lived in besides Ann Arbor, Michigan. It's hard to describe my excitement. Moving into my brand-new condo was like a dream come true. This lovely place was all mine, except for the mortgage, which was quite manageable. Some described my unit as an English basement apartment. I could park out front and walk down to the second floor of the townhouse. Once inside, there were two baths and two bedrooms on the upper level. The lower level had a large living space with a fireplace and powder room. Everything spilled out into a patio. I enjoyed buying furniture and decorating my new space so much I could hardly sleep.

The history of this area on the corner of U Street and Sixteenth Street suggests that the land on which Beekman Place was built had once boasted a grand castle with a surrounding moat. The moat on the Sixteenth Street side is still standing.

I wasn't only loving the city and my new condo, I was also enjoying my new job. My only thought about the program I was responsible for was to help as many individuals as possible with their research in ways that would lead to completing their doctoral degrees. The research projects would focus on the needs of the population we were designated to help.

The National Institute of Education was the federal unit for education prior to the establishment of the Department of Education. The Minorities and Women's Research unit was established approximately three years before President Jimmy Carter's term ended. We all knew, when Ronald Reagan was elected president, that the social problems my unit managed would no longer be a priority. Yet during the three years I served as chief of the Minorities and Women's Research Program, I was responsible for awarding approximately ten million dollars in grants.

I had a staff of five, all of whom had worked at the National Institute of Education. We worked well together, and each year we held proposal reviews as we had done the first year. I often traveled around the country with a staff member to visit projects we had funded. In the first year or so I spoke to groups at colleges and universities to describe the purpose of funding grants.

By the end of our second year we began to observe our successes. This program was referred to by some leaders in NIE as "the runaway train." I took this as a compliment because we were doing things that had never been done before. This was in part because it was the first time the federal government had set aside funding for this purpose. The program was important, but we knew things would take a more conservative turn when the Republicans took over. During the last phase of the third year of funding, I was unfortunately preparing to close down. We were packing boxes literally ten days after Ronald Reagan won the election.

Serving as chief of this program was professionally rewarding and satisfying. It was also personally rewarding. The professional gains were numerous. The position allowed me to use my creative ability to accomplish our goals in nontraditional ways. We engaged minorities and women in the review and awarding of grants, and supported the completion of doctoral degrees.

Because of our grants, the program's philosophy began to impact the institutions and students involved. For example, Hampton University and the University of Michigan were awarded sizable grants through the efforts of one of my former professors, Betty Morrison. This was one of the first grants that encouraged graduate students from a predominantly black institution and from a predominantly white university. I met Betty Morrison when I entered the University of Michigan as a freshman, at the time when U of M limited the admittance of black students to two hundred. After Betty received her PhD from Case Western Reserve, she was appointed assistant professor at the School of Education at U of M. She retired after over thirty years as a full professor. We were students and faculty members together at the School of Education. (Note: Betty died while I was completing my work on this manuscript.)

My professional growth was developing rapidly. I attended conferences and seminars, wrote articles, and enjoyed the publication of the book I did with Dolores Cross and Lindley Stiles, *Teaching in a Multicultural Society*. I now felt I could do a book by myself on the how-tos of multiethnic education. James Banks, a professor at the University of Washington, encouraged me. I had met Jim at a conference where he presented his first publication on black Americans. Over the years Jim and his wife Cherie became colleagues and friends. By the time I was in DC, Jim had published several books on multiethnic and multicultural education. We often talked about the differences between "multiethnic" and "multicultural."

The use of the term "multiethnic" was being challenged. Some of our colleagues felt that the "ethnic" part of the term was limiting—that it was primarily concerned with the acceptance and integration of the four federal groups: blacks, Hispanics, Native Americans, and Asians. The awakening, especially in the education community, was now asking, What about women? Also, how do we include the physically disabled? Do the aged need special attention? The poor?

I felt the term "multicultural" was much more inclusive, and advocated for this more inclusive description of what I believed. During any discussion about applying the broader term, my thoughts drifted back to the day my hot fudge sundae lost its taste and pleasure. I didn't want anyone to feel the way I had felt that day. As I grew in experience and broadened my exposure, my dislike for any kind of exclusiveness, discrimination, or racism increased.

As I thought about writing my book, I wanted to present material to help teachers integrate concepts that would inspire individuals to become more accepting and inclusive. I knew I needed to include history and a rationale. With this in mind, I wanted to develop specific and real-life lesson plans for teachers to use in the classroom for all subjects and grade levels.

Jim Banks was extremely helpful. He encouraged me to develop the book, and he took one more essential step: he connected me with a publisher. It was a good time for me to write. I could organize my work schedule to use one day a week to write, visit schools, and do research at libraries.

Once again, with my nerve in one hand and this time a portable typewriter before me, I began my task of writing *Planning and Organizing for Multicultural Instruction*. I reached out and connected to friends and colleagues who could help me in some way. I took the book project to Bank Street College, where it was published in 1983. (The second, revised edition was completed in 1993, during my tenure at the YWCA in New York.)

The book gave me a great deal of joy and has helped many teachers and professors teach a multicultural curriculum. Once convinced of the philosophy behind this approach, I found it became a way of life for me, and is useful in all aspects of life. I will always be grateful to Jim Banks for his encouragement and assistance. Whenever I look at a copy of this book, I'm reminded of those who helped in its development.

Because my work at NIE involved traveling extensively and giving speeches, not to mention my own work on the book, I don't know how I had time for a personal life. But I was enjoying my life in Washington. The social life there was full of opportunities. There was almost always a social event in the evenings and on weekends. And because I loved to entertain, when I wasn't going to an event I was giving one.

Another highlight of my life in DC involved sports. Evelyn Moore and I decided to learn how to play tennis. When she wasn't traveling for her work, we did our best to hit the ball across the net. We enjoyed the game, the exercise, and the socializing that came with it.

I had married James at eighteen. Most of my dating before we married was with him. In Washington I didn't know what was before me. I was single and independent, with a secure position, a lovely condo, and a car. What I felt I really wanted was companionship or company.

When my friend Margot Ellis suggested I might need ten men in my life, I thought she had lost her mind. After my experience in Washington, and even in New York years later, I realized what she had meant. I was almost never alone. I met some wonderful men, though the ones I met in DC were a great deal different from those I knew in Ann Arbor. They were sophisticated, well dressed, and traveled extensively. Maybe because of the political setting, they were also aware of what was occurring in the country and throughout the world. Conversation over dinner or a drink was fascinating.

After I divorced, I said I would be married in three years. I wasn't sure why I said this, unless it was because I had never lived by myself before. I enjoyed living alone for the first time, yet I didn't feel alone. I knew I'd find my second husband within three years. I dated several men and enjoyed most of them. While I didn't meet that special someone, I did meet several men who almost became number two.

Prior to my Washington move I had met a very fine gentleman at a conference I attended in DC. I later invited him to participate in the proposal review sessions we were conducting at NIE. He accepted and became very involved. He suggested that we have dinner one night. I was thrilled. I will not use this person's full name because he was and still is rather well known in the educational community, so I will refer to him simply as Andrew. We clicked immediately. In fact, we had several dinners together. Although he traveled a great deal, our times together didn't seem far apart because he called me daily, sometimes more than once. We did many things together when he was in the city: we took long walks, visited historical sites, and dined at excellent restaurants. He enjoyed dining, and as much as I enjoyed going out for lunch or dinner, I also enjoyed cooking. It was fun to cook for someone who appreciated my cooking skills and presentation. Sometimes his son joined us for a meal. He also introduced me to his daughters, who were as charming as he was.

We had fun together. He didn't smoke or drink. I didn't smoke, but enjoyed a glass or two of wine at times. He teased me about my fondness for wine, but didn't object to my having wine with our meals. I thought he would eventually become my second husband. We discussed getting married, and I was excited about the possibility. Andrew seemed almost too good to be true. We had similar thoughts and plans for our professional careers and for the future in general. Unfortunately, I soon had a rude awakening from my dream of having found a second husband.

This almost perfect man told me that although he and I each had three children, he wanted to adopt at least two more. When I heard this I almost had a heart attack. I collected my cool, as we used to say, and without trying to show my emotional reaction, I asked him numerous questions about why if we married he wanted to add two more children to our already existing six. He told me over and over that he loved children.

He also had an answer when I shared my concerns about the future. He said he wanted to adopt infants. We were nearing the age of grandparents and he wanted infants? Who would be responsible for these children? He had this well thought out. He planned to have his unmarried sister move from Boston and live with us to take care of the children and the house. This would allow us both to work.

I didn't need time to think this through. As much as I thought he really could become my second, I said no. We parted friends. I still hear from him occasionally. He did marry someone else shortly after we split up. It took me a while before I realized his proclaimed need to adopt children may have been his way of getting out of a situation that conflicted with an already established lifestyle. Several years later I learned I was right.

I began to wonder if finding my second husband might not be as easy as I had thought. I raised the bar a little higher as I continued to meet other men.

William (I will continue to use only first names) was not far behind. I'd been invited to a reception honoring someone I hadn't met before, but the person who invited me thought it would be a good opportunity to meet new and interesting people. Washingtonians are second to none in putting together lovely and elaborate receptions, and almost every occasion promised an exposure to outstanding men and women. I met several at this reception.

I noticed an attractive man, a bit my senior, glancing at me. He finally introduced himself and gave me his card before I left the reception. Two weeks later, while preparing for another event, I found William's card in the pocket of the suit I had planned to wear. It was a Saturday afternoon and I had a few hours before the evening's event. I decided to call. When he answered, he said, "Why have you taken so long?" I was stunned and stuttered a bit. After a few awkward words, he invited me to dinner the following evening.

What a gracious man he was. Now, I had recently met a man I described as "a very fine gentleman," and here I was meeting "a very gracious man." As he was somewhat older than I, I knew there would be no concern about either adopting or having children. This man already had a grandson I had met early in our relationship. His grandson had been raised well, and I could tell why. William had a wife of many years who had died the year before. Their daughter, the mother of his grandson, had attended private schools, graduated from a fine university, and was divorced and living with her father. Her mother was well respected and had taught at one of the local universities. Her father was known as a semi-diplomat, although I wasn't sure what that meant. He traveled often and proudly shared with me that he had visited Africa thirty times. His grandson had clearly been raised in an upper-middle-class black family, and the three of us often did interesting things together. Once we went to Martha's Vineyard and stayed at the prestigious Edgartown Inn. When we toured the area, I learned the history of the Vineyard, especially that of the blacks who not only had visited the island, but owned some of the beautiful gingerbread houses.

Early in our relationship William mentioned marriage. I'd been married twenty-eight years and had dated my husband for five years before we married, so I felt it was natural to want to marry again. I wasn't sure, however, whether I was the right woman for him, or whether he was the right man for me. He was handsome and intelligent, drove an expensive car, and always dressed in the latest styles. I'll never forget attending a formal affair with him; he wore black patent leather shoes with a bow tie. He wasn't out of step with fashion, though I was. He knew almost everyone at the social affairs we attended. He was a class act, and I was always proud to be with him.

Almost everyone who knows me is aware of my love for crystal. I don't remember my sharing information that with William. At that time I didn't own a single piece of crystal, but I still loved it. On our first Christmas Eve together, he carefully placed a lovely wrapped gift on my table. Throughout the evening I kept eying the package, wondering what it contained. Finally, when we were having a nightcap of his favorite scotch, he handed me the box and asked me to open it. As I picked up the box a light went on in my head: this box contains crystal. I sat down and placed the box on my lap, trying not to shake or become tearful. I opened the box. I was right. William had given me my first lovely pieces of crystal. How had he known how much I liked crystal? How could he tell?

Some years later a very wise woman connected my appreciation of crystal and my respect for its beauty and function with the title of this memoir.

I truly enjoyed William for all the reasons I've mentioned. But there was an aspect of his character I disliked and could not understand. If anything went wrong, it was my fault. And after he accused me more than once of being unable to do what Viagra did (and Viagra was either unknown or unavailable at the time), I chose not to deal with this aspect of his character. I simply bowed out of his life, knowing he would have no trouble finding another woman who enjoyed fine dining, entertainment, a beautiful car, and black patent shoes. I realized my second husband would need to have much more than that. Maybe a little Viagra would have helped. I'll never know. I learned of William's death a few years after I left Washington.

One evening during a dinner conversation with an old friend, after William and I had ended our relationship, a friend invited me to attend his church in the District. I'd always had a home church both before and after I took the dip in the baptismal font at Second Baptist Church, wearing a white bathing cap. He had nothing but glowing things to say about the pastor. I accepted my friend's invitation. Little did I know that attending church with this friend would impact my life and my search for husband number two.

On the Sunday we planned to attend the Church of the Redeemer, my friend offered to drive. By the time we entered the lovely little church, I knew many things about the minister, whom I will call Cameron. He was well educated and had served as pastor for several years. He also had three children and was in the process of a divorce. None of this made any impression on me until I heard him deliver the sermon that Sunday morning. What my friend had not told me was that this man was also extremely attractive in every aspect of his being. He was tall and thin, in good physical condition, spoke very well, and was easy on the eyes. My friend may have withheld all these things on purpose, having had, I suspected, an ulterior motive.

I didn't need any encouragement to continue visiting the Church of the Redeemer. After several Sunday morning services, I began attending services during the week, and soon decided to join the church. I met with the pastor to discuss my convictions as a Christian. The meeting lasted two hours, and I all but floated out of his office. There was something about this man that I liked. I had also met several church members who were friendly and welcoming. I left the meeting having set a date for my admission as a member.

I invited a few church members to a brunch following my induction service. I also invited my new pastor. It turned out to be a very pleasant occasion. I'd taken a lot of time planning a tasty and attractive menu. Normally a Baptist congregation would not serve alcohol. I did not say "drink" alcohol because outside of church events we did have alcohol, even if it was spiked punch. When I attended church services at Second Baptist I repeated the member's pledge but avoided the sentence that included abstinence from alcohol and tobacco.

Once I thought through this issue I decided to have a small bar at my brunch in case someone would like a drink. Several of my guests did accept a cocktail. When I asked my new pastor what he would like to drink, I assumed he would select something nonalcoholic. I was shocked when he asked for scotch on the rocks. My hands shook when I poured his drink and handed it to him. He noticed my discomfort and asked if anything was wrong. I smiled and said I was surprised he drank alcohol. He said he had forgotten I was a Baptist. We both laughed. After that, whenever I poured him a scotch, I remembered that first time. Later, he thanked me for including him in honoring my commitment as a member of Redeemer, and gave me a quick but warm embrace. I experienced such a nice feeling, and said, "I hope you will be my pastor as well as my friend."

Prospect number three knew I was aware of his personal situation. We had discussed his children. I also learned some of his likes and dislikes. He was a tennis enthusiast but had given it up because his former wife didn't like him spending so much time on the tennis court. This was of great interest to me because I enjoyed playing tennis but needed instruction and practice. It also reminded me of what my friend Margot had said about needing ten men. She said I would need someone to share my interest in tennis. So when Cameron called the following morning and suggested we go out to play tennis, I was delighted. I was also a bit embarrassed because even with all the instruction I'd had in DC, I was not a great player. But I put that aside and accepted his invitation, which was the beginning of more good things to come.

My new pastor had Mondays off. That became our special day of being together, in addition to many more. I was writing my multicultural text and had arranged my work week to have every Monday off. We spent the early part of Monday doing our personal tasks. I wrote and worked on my book, he did his administrative chores. We spent the rest of Monday and sometimes early Tuesday together. I think that because of my early marriage and not having dated many men, I was making up for what I had missed.

I was very happy during that time. Our lives were filled with each other. There was a twinge of thinking perhaps we should wait until his divorce was final, but we did not. We did keep our relationship out of the church activities until his divorce was final. By that time we felt we were ready for a life together.

We continued our tennis outings and I profited from his instruction. We enjoyed dining together and often shopped on Monday afternoons for our dinner that evening at my place. We enjoyed the same kind of music. Traveling during his vacation times, we went to concerts in and around Boston, his old stomping grounds. We had a wonderful time in New York, attending an exhibit at the Museum of Modern Art. Even today when I hear Pachelbel's *Canon*, my thoughts return to the many occasions we enjoyed listening to our favorite music.

He did not have a lot of money; in fact he had very little. I had worked for a church during the early days of my marriage and was well aware of what ministers were paid. That did not matter. We shared when we could and when that wasn't possible, I chipped in what was needed.

Cameron arranged for me to meet his children. We got along well, and although we didn't see them often, we had happy outings together. I enjoyed our relationship. After several months, however, I noticed that he was often having lunch or dinner with members of the church. At first I felt this was something he needed to do. Then it occurred to me that all of these engagements were with women. Not women in groups, but one on one.

When I asked him what restaurants he was enjoying, I learned these women were taking him to very expensive places. We didn't go to the most expensive restaurants together because I didn't feel I should pick up those expenses. We could do without those experiences until we could share the costs. He described the delicious meals he shared and the glasses of scotch that turned into martinis. The little I knew about martinis made me feel uncomfortable about his having expensive lunches and dinners that included heavy alcohol with women of the church. And all of these women were single. Sadly, I realized that his interest in other women went deeper than being a thoughtful minister.

My plans for my second husband were falling apart. I was miserable and didn't want to end our relationship. We had lots of telephone calls trying to work things out. I didn't realize how much I loved him, and went to bed crying many nights, not wanting to end it. I was disappointed and depressed, unsure of my future. This was in 1981.

It's interesting how things happen. During this difficult time, a friend's husband called to ask if he could bring someone by to meet me and see my condo. He said his friend wanted to see how blacks were living in DC. I thought this was a lame excuse to bring a man to my condo, but I agreed. He brought a lovely man, Reg Claytor, who lived in California. After a short visit, Reg gave me his card and invited me to contact him if I was ever in California. At the time I was traveling a great deal, but I was so emotionally involved I didn't intend to see Reg again, and if I did, I expected to be married. I took his card and put it away somewhere.

Soon after I had to fly to California. This was during the impending split with Cameron, and although I was in no condition to go anywhere, I thought I might schedule a session in California with a former psychiatrist. I was so emotionally confused and disappointed that I thought seeing Dr. Walter Shervington once or twice might relieve some of my pain. I hadn't felt such emotional discomfort when I divorced James. While I was packing for the trip, I discovered Reg's card from a few weeks before. I remembered him and learned he had been recently divorced. Even though I was an emotional mess, and Reg lived in Sacramento, I called and told him I would be in San Francisco in a few days. He immediately said he would meet me for dinner at my hotel. In spite of my depression, I looked forward to the visit.

Prior to my divorce I had reached a point in my marriage where I felt I needed professional help, especially someone who could understand the black experience. So much of what I was trying to manage had to do with my marriage, but it also had to do with being black and female. Unfortunately, I couldn't find a black psychologist in Ann Arbor. And then, as luck would have it, a young black psychiatrist joined the staff at the University of Michigan's Medical Center. My friend Carol Watson, who knew what I was going through, made it possible for me to meet Dr. Walter Shervington, who agreed to see me as a patient. We worked together until he left for another position in DC. His departure from Michigan at the time was a terrible shock to me. He referred me to a white psychiatrist. At that time in my life I was in such emotional pain I didn't care what color he or she was. To add to my distress, after a few sessions with the new doctor, he committed suicide.

I stayed in touch with Dr. Shervington through the mail. There was no email at the time, and I looked forward to letters from Dr. Shervington, although it seemed that the mail got even slower. I had become so attached to him that my feelings for him were mixed up with those for Cameron. Dr. Shervington had left Washington for San Francisco before I moved to DC, so I called him before I flew out there. As I expected, he was most accommodating, and agreed to meet me.

In spite of my emotional condition, when I met Reg Claytor in California we had a wonderful first date. Unfortunately I couldn't keep my breakup a secret. My depression was showing. I told Reg what I was going through. He offered to take me to my appointment with Dr. Shervington. I needed so much at that time. I poured myself all over him, not physically but emotionally. He nurtured me through that experience, and while he didn't become my second husband, he became one of the most wonderful men I've known. From the day I first met him in 1981, we talked or met daily until his death twenty years later. He did ask me to marry him, but while he was very special to me, he didn't want to leave Sacramento and I didn't want to move there. During our friendship he tried to bribe me to move west. Sometime in the mid-nineties his last offer was to build a studio over his garage so I could continue to write. But he did not pressure me into marriage.

After meeting and spending time with Reg and Dr. Shervington, I returned to Washington. I was still not prepared for my separation from Cameron, but I had a better understanding of why I couldn't cling to this man. During the week of Valentine's Day in 1981, Cameron and I finally said good-bye. As I look back over our relationship, I was needier than I thought. Or perhaps he was not as needy as I wanted him to be.

My three years were almost up and I hadn't found my second husband.

The program at NIE was ending. Luckily, I had been selected as the vice president for graduate and children's programs at Bank Street College in New York City. My appointment started July 1, 1981. My thoughts were now on ending the NIE program, preparing to move to New York, and finishing my textbook. I was no longer concerned with finding a second husband.

As luck would have it, I had another knock on the door, and was introduced to a most attractive man by my brother-in-law. The man I'll call Elmer was about to join the lineup.

My brother-in-law, Charles Snyder, was married to my former husband's sister, Mercedes Baker. He was the manager of low-income housing in Albion, Michigan. When Charles was in Washington attending a conference on housing, he met a man at one of the meetings and discovered he was recently divorced. Charles asked him if he would like to meet his sister-in-law, who was also single. Charles is a very light-skinned black. The man he was going to introduce me to was also a very light-skinned black. Charles knew this man was black and didn't give any thought to this. His new colleague thought Charles was white and assumed he was going to meet a white woman. When they arrived for cocktails and I opened the door, Elmer was surprised when he realized he was meeting a black woman. None of this was disclosed until much later in our relationship.

The introductory meeting was most pleasant. Some of the conversation centered on my upcoming trip to China. As I planned to leave Washington, I thought it might be time to take a trip on my own, by which I mean with a group of strangers. Because I had married so early in life, I had (with a few exceptions) always gone with my husband or with close female friends. I wanted to take a trip alone. My new friend was somewhat amazed at my proposed trip. He had never traveled abroad. His first trip to Europe and Africa with me came later in our relationship, and that was a trip!

Before the evening was over, Elmer said he would stay another day or two if I would go to dinner with him the next evening. I accepted his invitation. That date was the beginning of a new and different kind of relationship. Once again I was excited over meeting such an attractive and sophisticated man. From the day I had met Elmer, we were constantly in touch with each other on the phone. We lived in two different cities, yet in spite of our geographical split, it was a wonderful time for me.

The trip to China was quite an experience. I returned to Washington, closed up my office, and rented out my condo. And with my nerve in one hand and a contract for a new job in the other, I left for New York City.

EIGHT

The Big Apple

My friend and sister-in-law, Catherine Baker, helped me move to New York. I didn't like to drive but she did. Once in New York I discovered what a liability a car was. The annual parking fee for a car in New York was as much as I paid for my brand-new Pontiac. So I gave my car to my parents. Although I would live in New York for over twenty years, I never got accustomed to the city's high cost of living. One has to close one's eyes, open one's wallet or checkbook, and just do it.

During the time the minister and I were dating, we had gone to the Big Apple to visit a minister friend of his. This friend lived a block away from Bank Street College. In my wildest dreams I'd never thought of living in New York, and yet here I was doing just that, bidding farewell to our friends on the corner of 112th Street, which became my new address.

Prior to my leaving NIE, the president of Bank Street College, Richard Ruopp, had contacted my friend and neighbor, Evelyn Moore, about helping him fill a new position he had created at the college. Evelyn asked me if I was interested. I was. She arranged for me to meet President Ruopp at a conference he and I were attending in Los Angeles. We immediately formed a warm collegial relationship. I almost accepted the position before he offered it. The salary wasn't as much as at NIE, but he included an apartment and several other fringe benefits that I found attractive.

I didn't realize what having a rent-free apartment in Manhattan meant

My first meeting with President Richard Ruopp of Bank Street College after I was appointed vice president of graduate and children's programs in 1981.

until I moved there. I also discovered the college was one block from where I would live. My apartment would be next to President Ruopp's. From the interview, I also detected a concern about the fiscal status of the college. At this point in my career I'd had no fund-raising experience. Dick, as I soon learned to call him, hadn't listed fund-raising as one of my responsibilities, but I knew that as vice president for graduate and children's programs, raising money would come with the turf.

One of the positive aspects of this position was that the graduate school had a reputation for being one of the first to take a leading role in publishing multicultural textbooks. The Bank Street Readers were well known throughout schools of education, and they had a wonderful library to support their work. I had not yet finished the textbook I started in DC, but the library and location turned out to be an asset as I finished my book. It also gave me the support I needed to encourage teachers to respond to diversity in their classrooms. Many students who enrolled at Bank Street came from schools in the city or from urban schools with diverse populations. They were looking for direction and help. I was more than willing to be a part of this team.

I was very excited about taking the position at Bank Street College, and I spread the news to family members and close friends. Once my Uncle Mallory heard of my appointment, he immediately decided to give a reception in my honor in Ann Arbor, before I left for New York. Invitations were sent to over a hundred family members and friends. It was held at the Campus Inn, a very nice hotel near the U of M campus. The reception was well attended, and I felt like a queen.

I arrived in New York during the summer session, a few days before I was to report to the college. I'm not sure how Catherine and I found my new address—I should say Catherine because she was driving in that maze of traffic. I immediately recognized the area my minister friend and I had visited and was most surprised. I got an even bigger surprise when I entered the apartment building.

The building had a doorman, which was pleasant. But it also had a large, dark, dingy entrance hall and lobby. I was even more surprised when I saw my apartment. The longer I lived in New York, the more I realized that this was the norm. I even got used to the cockroaches, the makeshift kitchen, and the bathroom that barely had a shower. I swallowed hard, took one long look, leaned on my creativity, and soon turned that two-bedroom apartment into a lovely home.

I had a wonderful time traveling around the city in my time off looking for artifacts and pieces of odd furniture that could serve many functions. The furniture from my condo in DC fit quite well. The nice thing about the location was that I could walk to my office from my apartment in less than five minutes, and without a coat. The awful aspect of this location was the possibility of having to walk around someone sleeping on the street or people who had just died and remained on the sidewalk until the city picked them up. The first day I had to do this shook me up so much I was ready to leave. But I knew I could not. This was one of several things that I didn't like about the position or New York.

I had been so impressed by the reputation of Bank Street College that I'd failed to ask some of the questions I should have had answers to before accepting. The most important was more background information on the financial history and current budget. While I knew that development would be one of my responsibilities, if I had had more information, I might have thought more about my options, and I might not have taken the position.

I had no idea that raising funds for a graduate school of education would be so difficult. The main problem for schools of education was, and still is, that graduates from these schools do not receive salaries that allow them to be as generous as they might otherwise be. Also, the for-profit world is more interested in contributing to schools and colleges that will give their gift more visibility in terms of prestige and large enrollments. For example, a gift that might have taken the staff and me several months to cultivate was likely to end up at the $5,000 level. And yet gifts at this level were few and far between.

If I had taken the time to interview some of the faculty and learn more about their dedication to the school and their educational background, I might have better understood their needs. The staff and faculty appeared dedicated, and in most instances this would make for good staff morale. But to help an institution grow requires faculty and staff who see the need for change. I soon learned that although these individuals liked the school, they were extremely protective about the school's reputation. Many had been members of the staff and faculty early in the school's development. The geographical location of Bank Street College was originally on Bank Street in lower Manhattan. When it moved closer to Columbia University and Barnard, it grew in stature.

Most graduate schools have faculty and even staff who have doctoral degrees. Those with more than a master's degree were rare at Bank Street. When I arrived, some were working on completing their degrees. For this reason, the salaries weren't compatible with faculty in other schools, and also because Bank Street did not have the financial base to pay higher wages. Nor were they unionized. The school could not have existed if its staff had been eligible for higher salaries at other institutions. Also, staff members were so dedicated to the Bank Street reputation they provided what was needed on a minimal level.

Upon my arrival at the school, I detected not exactly an unfriendly attitude, but a chilly one. One day, without invitation, I joined a group of faculty members who were having coffee in the cafeteria. If I had known the topic of discussion, I would not have been so aggressive. Those around the table were responding to a letter they had received prior to my arrival in which they were informed there would be no raises for them this year. As I listened to the complaints, one faculty member who'd been there a long time turned to me and said, "You took away our raises. If your position had not been established, we would have had a raise." I was so stunned at his attitude and the apparent support of his position from the other members in the group that I'm not sure what I said as I prepared to leave. I realized at that moment I had a lot of hard work to do.

More delving into the financial history of this highly respected institution would have told me that the endowment was extremely low and would not be able to support the school far into the future without additional and much-needed income. Because of the high cost of maintaining a school in New York City—where almost everything, including a taxi ride, is expensive—more revenue was needed. Tuition increased every year, and even for a private school, the cost per credit was three to four times higher than tuition in surrounding schools. Private versus public was losing out.

The one steady stream of income was from enrollment fees for the Children's School. Middle- to upper-class families avoided sending their children to public schools in New York for several reasons. The most obvious was that public schools were declining in their ability to attract good and effective teachers. There was an overall change in the composition of the student body. Children of families who were moving to New York in droves had changed the look of the public school classrooms as well as the needs of these students. To avoid the changing New York public schools, parents who could afford private schools did so. Bank Street maintained a long list of students who wanted in. Some of these children went on the list as soon as they were born. This provided a solid income for Bank Street.

As I helped the Graduate School prepare for the fall registration of 1981, I soon realized the success of the enrollment would determine what classes would be offered and whose teaching load would be altered. It could mean the loss of a percentage of a faculty member's salary. This was not good. But it would have been more serious if the staff had been a younger staff with small children. Approximately 80 percent of the faculty members were married to working spouses. Most often the spouse was in a high-paying profession, and the position at Bank Street was supplementary. A few of the younger ones were finding supplemental work as consultants, teaching and working on funded projects in up-and-coming things like computers.

Registration lasted three days. The first day was filled with excitement. I observed the process, which was quite different from those I had participated in at the University of Michigan. At the end of the first day we were down in the student enrollment count. I tried to be a good coach, encouraging those who were assisting in the enrollment process. By the middle of the second day, even while I was engaged in conversation with students who were registering, I felt the tension over our projections for class offerings.

That evening was not a good one for me, or for anyone involved. As I sat behind my desk I heard the chatter of some faculty members who had gathered in the office next to mine. This office was occupied by a former dean whose responsibilities my appointment had absorbed. She was also one of the faculty working on a PhD at an institution outside the city. She was on a minor assignment at Bank Street and had returned for registration. This former dean had joined those on the faculty who were not happy with my appointment. I might mention that the few faculty members who welcomed my arrival were those who supported my advocacy for diversity. While I was trying to think through our lack of registrants and what we would need to reconfigure assignments, I was also feeling and hearing the resentment coming through the cardboard walls.

The next day did not bring me to tears, but the stress over the situation caused such stomach pain that I had to recline on the sofa in my office. I was in a fetal position, holding my stomach and trying not to let anyone know my reaction to what was happening. Eventually we did some reprogramming, and luckily one or two junior faculty members received grants to work on their advanced degrees. All of this helped us hold onto our plans for the fall.

As time went on, the attitude of my colleagues changed. I think they realized that I respected Bank Street as much as they did. I was also progressing in my professional involvement outside the college. They were quite proud when I was nominated for the position of president of the Association for Educational Research (AERA). AERA was and still is a major association in the field of education. I had served on its board of directors prior to my nomination and was one of the one or two blacks to do so. Although I didn't win the election, I did receive a lot of publicity, and so did Bank Street. They were as proud as I was when my book *Planning and Organizing for Multicultural Instruction* was published. I was still vice president and dean of Bank Street's Graduate and Children's Programs.

Little by little I made progress involving the faculty and staff in recognizing the need for the school to move toward developing a multicultural approach to our curriculum. I capitalized on the fact that the school had already established itself as a leader in the field after it published the integrated Bank Street Readers. Once the need to focus on diversity was identified, we were able to develop a plan for the total integration of a multicultural philosophy throughout the school. We worked the following year changing as much as we needed to throughout the college and the children's school. This included the marketing materials, the hiring process, admission forms, course outlines, and all that went into making the total institution multicultural.

During this process, which lasted more than a year, I had two very strong supporters who helped me and the process tremendously. One was Dorothy Carter, a wonderful faculty member who got along with almost everyone. She was instrumental in helping us rethink the content of our courses. Dorothy retired and lived in New York. She continued to write beautiful books for children about the experience of African Americans. (Dorothy Carter died as I was finishing this memoir in 2012.)

The other individual was a person I met the very first time I entered the president's suite. This young man, Eddy Bayardelle, was the director of a leadership program funded by the state of New York. Eddy was a gifted young man: he was bilingual and well known throughout New York state and the federal government. Eddy and I worked together to obtain additional funding through his contacts. I appointed him assistant vice president. After I resigned my position at Bank Street, Eddy and I worked together on the New York City Board of Education. He was one of my assistants when I served as a member of the Board of Education and also as president. Eddy was the chief operating officer of UNICEF when I became the president and CEO.

By the time I entered my third year at Bank Street we were not over our financial problems but we were slowly making progress. There was not a time that my thoughts were not on how to increase our revenue. When a student completed the master's degree requirements, the State of New York awarded the college $1,500 for each degree. One day when I had my thinking cap on, I asked for the number of unfinished degrees.

After I did the math, I realized that if we awarded even 50 percent of the degrees that were still labeled incomplete, we would collect enough from the State of New York to help our financial status a great deal. I approached President Ruopp with my idea of revamping the requirements for completion. He supported my thinking, so I worked with the faculty to develop new requirements. President Ruopp didn't think I'd be able to reach my goal of $50,000, which was a great deal of money at the time, but I never gave up. At the end of the first year with the new requirements, we almost doubled my expectations. Dick was more than pleased and showed his gratitude that year with a nice unexpected bonus.

I was enjoying my position at Bank Street and I could feel the results of my leadership. It felt good. I was able to create new approaches to our curriculum. One of my fondest memories was the time I designed and offered a multicultural workshop for the summer program. The workshop was so much fun. New York is filled with so much diversity. We were able to travel throughout the city to learn about the history of this great city and the involvement of the different ethnic and cultural groups. Students came from all over the country and represented a diverse group, and we capitalized on the background and experience of our students. We formed a close working relationship among the students. We took buses and subways, and walked to the different sections of the city. We listened to lectures on the street from people who knew the neighborhoods. We enjoyed the food in the restaurants in Harlem and the Lower East Side. We even went to Brooklyn. Bank Street was coming alive and so was I.

There were no more stomachaches. I looked forward to entering the building each day. The faculty had warmed up. They became more positive as they worked with me.

One day, as I was about to take the elevator to my office, a lady walked up to me and asked if she could talk to me for a minute. I moved to the side of the elevator so we could talk. Through the gossip mill she had learned that my secretary, an energetic young woman named Marla, was also serving as housekeeper for me in the evenings. She assumed this was a strain on both Marla and me. She worked in one of the cafeterias for the New York Public Schools. She told me her granddaughter was a student in the Bank Street School for Children. She picked up her granddaughter, Janine, every day after school. Because her day finished an hour or so before Janine was ready to be picked up, some days she had to wait more than an hour to take her granddaughter home.

She offered to work for me every day during her waiting period cleaning my apartment. Both Marla, my secretary, and I were so pleased! Ms. Jimmie James started working for me immediately. The fact that my Bank Street apartment was one short block away from the school made it convenient for both of us. Marla was relieved and satisfied with working as my secretary. Ms. James, Jimmie as my friends and family called her, worked for and with me for over eleven years. As I changed positions and moved around New York City, she was someone I could always depend on. She cleaned, did the laundry, and cooked the most delicious fried chicken, biscuits, and apple pie. She prepared the food when I entertained and as she served she became one of the party.

I must say, Jimmie James spoiled me. I think my family members, especially the young ones, thought of her as my other mother. One weekend when one of my nephews, Brandon, who is now an attorney, and one of my nieces, who is now a mother, were visiting me, they heard me say "shit" when I spilled something. Later that day they went to Ms. James and quietly told her that Aunt Gwen had said a bad word. She told them she would take care of it. We still laugh about that to this day.

Janine, Jimmie's granddaughter, was only a few months old when Jimmie discovered that her mother had put her in a county home because she couldn't take care of her. Janine's mother had problems she could not overcome. When Jimmie discovered where her granddaughter was, she immediately adopted her. She managed to put her through private schools like Bank Street and Dalton. I went to Janine's graduation from Cornell University. Janine recently resigned her position as one of the editors of the Thursday style section of the *New York Times* and is working in Italy. Jimmie sacrificed twenty-one years to make sure Janine had the best. What a remarkable woman she is. If I had not taken the position at Bank

Street, I would have missed my introduction to one of the most important individuals I have ever known. She is still living in Manhattan, and we often talk and laugh about our days together.

After three years at Bank Street I was feeling quite attached. There were times when I thought about staying in my position until President Ruopp retired. I was enjoying New York. I loved the theater, the concerts in the parks, the restaurants, the fabulous stores, and I liked my change of lifestyle. Yes, it was inconvenient at times not to be able to shop at giant grocery stores, but I soon got used to what was offered. I missed having a car at my disposal, but I learned very quickly how to flag a cab, use the subway, and order a car for something special. I even adjusted to the prices for just about everything. I was becoming a real New Yorker.

My personal life was beginning to take shape up. I was meeting new people connected to the college and others at both professional and private affairs. I loved to entertain, and with Ms. James's assistance I gave lovely cocktail parties. I was still in touch with Elmer, who called me at least twice a day. During that time I was also in touch with my friend Reg in California. We continued to be cross-country friends. I was reminded of what my friend Margot said before she died, about how I would need ten men in my life. She was right. It was possible to have several men in one's life if the relationships were bonded in friendship and not sex.

However, Elmer was becoming more than a close friend. He didn't live in New York, so that helped me manage my friends. He came to visit at least once a month. I had met his family and it looked like we might have a future together. Elmer had never traveled out of the country, and said he would like to take a trip to Europe. That was all I had to hear. I loved travel and had been to Europe several times. My friend Jacque Owens in the State Department was now in Togo, Africa. I always managed to visit Jacque when she was assigned to a different country, but I hadn't yet visited her in Togo. Before Elmer knew it, I had planned a trip for us to Paris, Rome, and, yes, to Africa to visit Jacque. At my suggestion we agreed to split the expenses of this trip. I felt this would make it easier for both of us.

He joined me in New York a few days before we were scheduled to leave. He arrived with a headache, which should have been a signal for me, but I ignored it. He was ill until we were finally in the air. We had a great flight.

I was so thrilled to have a male companion on a trip with me. Since my divorce I had either traveled alone or with female friends. That was fine, but this was especially nice. I managed to select very nice hotels, and our first hotel in Paris was no exception. Dinner was excellent, and we both slept well after a long flight. The next morning, however, I noticed my friend's mood had changed. He became quite irritable. His company was anything but enjoyable. I didn't enjoy Paris with him and hoped the trip to Togo would be better. Italy would be our last stop after Togo. In the end, he could not adjust to foreign travel and all that it entails. He cut his trip short and returned to the United States without me. I canceled Rome to stay in Togo for the remainder of the trip. It took almost two years before we could communicate with one another again.

After I'd been at the college for three years, I received a phone call from a search firm. The caller, Anne Hyde, told me that I'd been recommended for a position in New York by the Women's Division of the American College of Education in Washington, DC. When I asked a question about the name of the organization, I was told that she couldn't tell me until I agreed to be interviewed. She did tell me that it was a large national women's organization that was located in New York. The position was for the national executive secretary of this organization. She broadly hinted at the salary and it sounded like it was more than my current salary. I told Ms. Hyde I would think about whether or not it was something I was interested in. As I thought about our conversation and perhaps a new challenge, I was pleased that if I was fortunate enough to be appointed to this position I would be able to stay in New York. After a sleepless night weighing the pros and cons, I called Ms. Hyde the next morning and agreed to the interview. Her response was most pleasant and she immediately arranged for us to meet in the dining room at the Hyatt Hotel in the city. I could hardly keep my mind on my job for the next two days. I went to the hairdresser, had my nails done, and carefully chose the correct suit to wear. The time for the interview finally arrived. Off I went in a cab on my way to the Hyatt, with my nerve in one hand and the excitement of what my future might encompass in the other.

I was a little shaky as I stepped onto the escalator at the Hyatt, trying to look cool and executive in case Ms. Hyde saw me slowly moving up to the second floor. As I walked through the gigantic lobby to the dining room I was feeling calmer. And then I had a thought: I didn't contact this person for a job, she contacted *me*. With that in mind, I walked up the few steps and into the dining room. A very impressive woman stood up at one of the tables and walked toward me, smiling, and extended her hand.

I could tell immediately that Anne Hyde and I would get along fine. After I ordered a glass of iced tea and we went through the niceties that two people go through in situations like this, Ms. Hyde said, "I'm sure you would like to know the name of the organization I represent." She paused, and I said something that sounded like yes I would. When she told me it was the Young Women's Christian Association (YWCA), I couldn't believe my ears.

When I was a teenager, the YWCA in Ann Arbor wouldn't even let me through the doors. I had to join the Girl Reserves, which later became the Y-Teens, through the Dunbar Community Center. I took a deep breath and tried not to look too surprised. During the interview I learned more about the organization's adoption of its "One Imperative": the elimination of racism. I shared some of my past history and experience with the YWCA. I also acknowledged that I was very interested in the position. I told her that if an organization could come full circle with regard to its racial practices, I would like an opportunity to work with and share in its new commitment.

Ms. Hyde paid me several compliments and told me she would submit my name to the board for their consideration. We agreed that if the board was interested in going further, which meant meeting with the search committee, I would agree to another interview. We shook hands, and she promised to get back to me as soon as possible. As we left the hotel together, hailing cabs to go our separate ways, I kept thinking, here is an organization that would not let me into its building when I was a teenager and now it is willing to consider me, a black woman, to serve as the head of the oldest women's organization in the world. I could hardly contain myself.

It didn't take long for me to hear from Ms. Hyde. Yes, the search committee was interested in talking to me as soon as possible. I asked her to send me as much background material about the YWCA as possible. The date they had set was less than two weeks away. I knew I had to do a lot of reading and research about the national YWCA.

The next day I received a large package of materials about the organization from its headquarters located in New York. I dug into the pile immediately and spent most evenings reading and making a list of questions I needed answers to. I had learned from my somewhat hasty acceptance of the Bank Street offer to be more thorough in what my responsibilities and their expectations would be. I was particularly interested in their fiscal status.

I said nothing to my colleagues at Bank Street except to Eddy Bayardelle. He and I had become friends and I needed someone to confide in who was close at hand. I had also shared this news with two or three friends outside of New York, all of whom thought this was a wonderful opportunity. The more I learned about the YWCA, the more excited I became. I hadn't realized the extent to which this organization reached around the world. The international component was exciting, especially because of my interest in the multicultural dimensions in and of learning.

The date for the interview had finally arrived. It was early March, when the weather was usually pleasant, early spring kinds of days. To my horror, I woke up to an unusually cold and snowy day. In New York this meant difficulty getting car service. Taxis were nearly impossible to find. I had planned to take the day off, have my hair done, and spend a little more time on my appearance. I made sure that my choice of outfit had not been left to the last moment. I gave everything my best attention. I felt that because I would be interviewed by all women, my appearance would be something the committee would comment on. I even made sure my briefcase was one of my best and matched my outfit. I don't know why my appearance was so important but it has always claimed my attention. Someone once told me that how one presents oneself is an indication of how one feels about oneself. I made sure the questions I wanted to ask were organized and reflected my thorough job of preparing for the interview.

Attending to all of my preparations did not take my mind off the weather. It began to snow harder than I had ever seen it snow in New York, especially in March. I knew I wouldn't be able to get a cab. Taking the bus to Midtown would not ensure a prompt arrival and by now I knew I would have to wear boots. And oh, my hair! I called several car services, especially those I used frequently, but nothing was available. I should have reserved a car the night before but I didn't know it was going to snow. This taught me a lesson. When an appointment is important, take no chances. Order a car even if it's three blocks away.

What to do? I thought of Eddy. He usually drove to work from Brooklyn.

My appointment was at 1:00 p.m. Even if the roads were not good, he should be in by noon. Fortunately, Eddy made it just in time to get me to Midtown, dry, but a little uptight. Thank God for Eddy. I was five minutes early.

What an experience. A wonderful experience! Two women greeted me when I entered the hotel lobby. I'm sure they'd been told what I looked like. They were very gracious as they led me to the elevator and to the interview room, where eight or nine other women waited. They all stood and introduced themselves to me individually. They offered me a seat and a cup of tea. Then the show began.

The woman in charge asked me to tell them about myself, which I always enjoy doing. This allows me to ward off questions that may seem awkward. The questions they asked were a pleasure to answer. When they had finished their questions, they asked if I had any. I answered yes, and reached down next to my chair for my briefcase. I opened the case and pulled out a small stack of papers. Several women exchanged glances. I was pretty sure they had not expected this.

I was very thorough in covering the waterfront, so to speak. It was obvious I had spent a lot of time reading the material and even more time formulating questions I needed answers to. I didn't want to accept a position and be surprised at issues I hadn't thought about. My experience with Bank Street taught me this, especially as it related to finance. This part of the interview took about three hours.

I was then introduced to a different group of women who had gathered in another room in the hotel. We had more tea and lots of introductions. This was more informal than the earlier part of the interview. I was finally allowed a few minutes to catch my breath and freshen up before dinner at a nearby hotel. There were only three other women besides myself. I hadn't expected a dinner, and assumed I must be passing the test. I knew this was the final part of the interview, to determine how and what I would order to drink and how I would handle dinner situations. I had no problem with any of this.

Later I was told they wanted to witness my drinking habits. They were pleased when I accepted to share a bottle of wine. My grandmother had long ago taught me how to use proper silverware and the many other little things important in formal situations. At last, the long afternoon was over. The farewells were most gracious. I managed to hail a cab in spite of the unexpected snow. The taxi drove me home to the Upper West Side. Although exhausted, I felt I would be offered the position.

I didn't have long to wait for my expectation to be confirmed. Anne Hyde called late the next day to tell me the search committee had taken a vote of the executive committee by phone earlier that day. Ms. Hyde had been given permission to offer me the position. I was so excited I didn't know what to do first. Call my very close friends and family members, or tell Dick Ruopp I was going to resign? I chose the latter. Dick was not pleased, but he agreed to all the particulars, including my last day at the school. I needed time to find another apartment because the one I was living in belonged to Bank Street and was part of my compensation.

I've always been quick to organize. In a couple of weeks I had located an apartment in Riverdale, in the Bronx, that was perfect. I had everything I needed and wanted, and the price tag fit my purse. I'd become accustomed to a doorman but felt I could adjust to not having one. It's strange how sometimes we get used to and expect things we never had. I didn't give much thought to the distance I would have to travel every day without a car. Even though I could catch a train or a bus, or take a private car, the distance would become a major problem and source of discomfort in the early days of my new position.

Before I had to deal with the transportation problem, however, I had to deal with another major issue, salary. I was told that the salary spread would range between $65,000 and $75,000. My salary at Bank Street, with apartment and benefits, was $65,000. I assumed that I would receive the $75,000. I have since learned never to take a position on my assumptions about anything, especially salary. Unfortunately, after Ms. Hyde had discussed my salary with the president of the organization, I was offered $65,000. The president's reasoning was that if I came in at the top there would be no room for advancement.

After hearing this, I realized I should not have assumed a higher amount. It also told me something about the leadership. There was no flexibility in the organization's decision-making process at that time. If I continued down this path, I would have my work cut out for me. I had also bought an apartment based on my expectations of a salary increase. My budget would have to assume severe cuts. I was not a happy camper. However, my pride was great, and I had already submitted my resignation. I couldn't change my mind.

So, with my nerve in one hand and a $65,000 position in the other, I moved forward in my career. In September 1984, I became the national executive director of the YWCA USA.

NINE

Leading a National Organization

I was almost overwhelmed at the magnitude and importance of my new responsibility. The more I learned about the YWCA, the more impressed I became with the history of this great organization and the impact it has had on the lives of so many women. Almost every black woman I knew had some contact with the YWCA, and the involvement had been significant and encouraging. In many instances, this organization took up the slack for women who were not able to participate in mainstream organizations. Also, there were many issues facing women that emerged during the late seventies and most of the eighties that the YWCA faced on behalf of women.

In reviewing an issue of the *National Board YWCA News*, I was reminded that this 125-year-old organization represented some two and a half million women and girls, with 450 community and student YWCAs operating in more than 5,000 locations in forty-nine states. Jane Pinkerton, director of communications and public relations, described my responsibilities in this newsletter: I would head a staff of 135 at the New York City headquarters. I would also be in charge of YWCA facilities and staff in Phoenix, Arizona, and in Washington, DC.

In 1983, the new $6 million National Leadership Development Center would open in Phoenix to serve as a major training center for YWCAs in this country as well as those throughout the world. I knew all of this before I was appointed, but somehow now that I had the position I could hardly sleep at

The Manhattan Chapter of Link Inc. honored me with an award in 1989. Mary Rockefeller, a trustee of the YWCA, attended the affair and presented me with a bouquet of roses at the luncheon. She was joined by Joyce Dinkins and Elizabeth Moore, who was also a trustee.

On behalf of the YWCA, I visited South Africa with Ann Stallard, YWCA president, and Mary Brown, director of the Boston YWCA. It was our pleasure to meet with President Nelson Mandela in his office.

As executive director of the YWCA, I was invited to a reception at the White House. I was greeted by President and Mrs. Clinton. Jo Uehera, director of the Washington office of the YWCA, accompanied me.

night thinking of all the possibilities for expanding programs that existed and creating even more to serve the needs of women.

The fact that the organization had adopted "the elimination of racism" as an imperative was extremely important to me. As I prepared for my new responsibility, I couldn't forget that there had been a time when I was not allowed to participate in the YWCA in Ann Arbor because of my race. The YWCAs that did accommodate the needs of black women were located mostly in the southern states. I now had the position of leading this organization on the national level. Later, as I traveled throughout the world, I discovered that there were separate YWCAs in some countries for whites and blacks. This was most obvious in South Africa, where I witnessed this situation early in my tenure as executive director.

During my final months while I was still at Bank Street College, the American Association of Colleges for Teacher Education (AACTE) invited me to attend a conference in Bangkok, Thailand. I was ending my term as a board member of AACTE. Although my new position at the YWCA did not focus specifically on education, the Association had YWCAs throughout the world. I decided to accept the invitation for two reasons. First, I thought it would be a wonderful opportunity to meet and learn from educators throughout the world. And second, it would give me an opportunity to visit the YWCA in Thailand.

As I prepared for this trip I realized how near I would be to Hong Kong, China, and Japan. I worked with the staff in New York who helped me obtain letters of introduction to the YWCAs in these countries. The New York YWCA staff and volunteers were excited that I would have this opportunity before I actually came on board. The more I learned about the YWCA's history and outreach around the world, the more excited I became.

My earlier travels, especially to Europe and Africa, taught me how to travel in foreign countries. I learned not just what and how to pack, but how to respect the differences in the cultures and lifestyles of other countries. Because of my work with the AACTE, I knew most of the individuals in the group I would travel with. Interestingly, my first research article had been published in the association's monthly journal and had helped me gain tenure at the University of Michigan. The conference for educators was a wonderful experience and a fine introduction to this part of the world.

After I said good-bye to my conference colleagues in Bangkok, I left for my appointment to visit the YWCA in that city. My reception could not have been more cordial. I was able to spend two days learning about their programs and the girls and women they serve.

A similar arrangement had been made for me to visit the YWCA in Hong Kong. This was a very different experience because I had asked to stay in the YWCA residence there. I wanted to get a sense of how a young girl or woman would feel living for a few days and sometimes longer at a YWCA residence. In Hong Kong the volunteers were very wealthy women. This was most apparent at the luncheon held in my honor. The hand-delivered invitation was in red and gold velvet. I wasn't sure I had the correct outfit to wear for what appeared to be a special affair. It was. The luncheon was held at an exquisite hotel. Everything was done in silver, including the chopsticks. I relaxed and enjoyed the charm and warmth of these volunteers.

Before I left Hong Kong, I made plans to spend time in China. I had been there before my position with the YWCA. Now I wanted to learn how the YWCA had fared during the Cultural Revolution and how it was functioning currently. With the help of the World YWCA, I found a young woman who was trying to reorganize the association after the ten years of upheaval. What was especially interesting was that although they had no actual building, volunteers were trying to design programs to serve the girls and women who needed so much. They met in a large room in a very old building. It was exciting to see what these women were doing with very few resources.

Because there was no residence, I stayed at a Sheraton Hotel. I could hardly wait to return to the United States and share my enthusiasm for this association, for there was so much we could help them do. I was also excited because the Chinese board of the YWCA invited the American board to visit China. I was very happy to be able to increase the knowledge and interest in what the YWCA was doing around the world to meet the needs of the populations we were prepared to serve.

In Japan, the residence at the YWCA was quite different. Although very sparse, it provided me with a clean and caring environment. YWCA USA is a major supporter of the well-respected World YWCA, which supports many associations around the globe. That respect certainly was extended to me in these two associations and when I visited the YWCA in Japan. At each association I had the opportunity to talk to staff and participants as well as volunteers. The president of the board of directors invited me to have tea with her and several other board members at her home. This was truly an honor.

As my trip was coming to an end, I planned a stop in Hawaii. I was eager to see how the YWCA of Hawaii in Kauai compared to those I had just visited. I stayed in one of the residences and, as I had expected, was greeted most cordially. My accommodations were very adequate and pleasant. The programs offered in all four of these associations were similar and were geared to the needs of the girls and women in these communities. Those needs varied, depending on the environment and on cultural necessities. I returned home even more excited about my new position after having visited the YWCAs in Thailand, Hong Kong, Japan, China, and Hawaii. How would I use these experiences?

Soon after my return to New York and before I started my new position, my uncle Mallory raised his thoughtful and generous hand again. This time it was a reception in my honor for being appointed executive director of the Young Women's Christian Association. The reception was held in New York at the Faculty Club of Columbia University. Uncle Mallory invited some of the Bank Street College staff and several executive staff members of the YWCA. Many friends were also included. We had live music and wonderful food and drinks. I felt very special and enjoyed it all.

While I was impressed with the lovely hospitality afforded me during my visits to the associations in other parts of the world, the welcome I received from the YWCAs in the United States was almost unbelievable. The outreach to me from the volunteers and staff of the national board was exceptional. There is something truly unusual about the women who serve as volunteers for the YWCA. Most of them are thoughtful and exceptionally gracious. From almost the first day of my appointment, I received an outpouring of phone calls, letters, notes, and invitations from members of the national board. The national staff was not far behind. They too were extremely hospitable and became involved in making sure I was comfortable in my new work environment.

One of the invitations I received early after assuming my duties was to a luncheon given in my honor by Mary French Rockefeller, who had been a member of the national board for many years. She was a most gracious and generous person. She and her husband lived in a multifloor apartment on Fifth Avenue in New York. Mary, as she insisted we all call her, had invited me to her home for tea prior to the luncheon invitation. I was greatly impressed with the beautiful furniture and original artwork that adorned their home.

The day of the luncheon in my honor is one I shall never forget. I must confess my knees were a bit shaky, but I managed to meet and greet the guests as cordially as I could. Mary had invited several longtime YWCA volunteers, some very senior, and a few newcomers to the luncheon. She also invited a few of the more senior staff, which made an interesting gathering of fourteen.

The first course was a clear soup. As I finished my soup, I carefully placed my soup spoon on the side of the bowl and casually watched how others finished their serving. To my surprise, Mary and several of the older and very gracious women picked up their bowls and finished the soup by drinking what they could not consume with a spoon. I had never seen this before, but realized I was entering a new and somewhat different world than I had ever known. I sat quietly waiting for the server to remove my plate and bowl. I did notice that the staff members and one or two of the younger women did as I did.

I shared this incident with several friends. I told this story once when I was having a bowl of soup at a hotel in Mexico. One of the women decided if drinking soup from a bowl was good enough for Mary Rockefeller it was good enough for her. I was most surprised when she picked up her bowl and finished her soup. A few people around us looked as if they couldn't believe their eyes. I now sometimes finish my soup in this manner, but only in my own home.

Not all of the entertaining at the gathering of YWCA women was at this level. I often find myself smiling when I recall my first meeting with the national board. The meeting was held outside New York City at a retreat center. I was told it would be an informal meeting so the board members who were not on the interviewing committee could meet me. I wasn't quite sure what informal meant, but I remember selecting an off-white pants suit for the occasion. In the early eighties, wearing slacks was not as common as it is today. I thought a pantsuit would be between casual and formal dress.

Again, an occasion I shall never forget. As we enjoyed the refreshments of fruit punch, tasty sandwiches, and sweets, I noticed small groups of two or three would gather off to the side. Something was going on that I didn't understand A while later I was listening to one on the members playing the piano when two women approached me with a somewhat crumpled brown paper bag. They quietly offered me a "little something" to spike my punch. I almost dropped my cup as I quietly refused. I couldn't believe such sophisticated women were sneaking around with liquor in a paper bag. I didn't want to appear shocked, but I was. I thought about this for some time. Before the next board meeting I asked two or three of the officers if they would object if we had a social hour after the meeting. We would serve wine during the social hour. Smiles came across their faces as if a burden had been lifted from them. I later understood that previous administrators had not approved of serving alcohol at YWCA functions and so those who wanted something stronger than fruit punch found a way of spiking their drinks. After that incident we almost always served wine at YWCA functions.

The red carpet continued to be rolled out whenever I was invited to visit a local YWCA or speak at a YWCA function. I was remembered on holidays and on my birthday. On one of my birthdays, the vice president responsible for the associations gave me a radio for my shower with a note attached that read, "Perhaps if you listen to the radio while taking a shower you will not think of things for me to do." Several staff members and I had a long laugh about this. I did come up with a lot of ideas while showering.

Seven months into my first year, the association was scheduled to have its triennial convention in San Jose, California. Most of the planning for this national gathering had been completed. All I had to do was prepare to be introduced to the delegates in attendance. Most of the almost four hundred associations were expected to participate.

This meeting was extremely significant because it was the only opportunity the national board had to emphasize the importance of the YWCA vision, imperative, and mission. Commitment to the mission was crucial for volunteers and staff if individual associations were to be successful and therefore financially stable. Forty percent of the budget of the National Association came from dues each association was required to pay. The amount each association paid was determined by the number of members in the association.

The convention surprised me. The organizers obviously needed some help in planning a meeting of this type. I wondered what the regional meetings were like. I made a promise to myself that the next meeting would be very different. What a wonderful opportunity to help women in the YWCA understand how important the organization was to the needs of women in the United States and around the world.

As the convention came to a close, we were told there were not enough funds to send more than one representative to the upcoming World Meeting for Women to be held in Nairobi, Kenya. The convention decided that the executive director should be our delegate to this meeting. My mind started to click. I knew that the world meeting of the YWCA would soon be held in the United States at our Leadership Development Center in Phoenix. In my closing remarks to the attendees, I said I felt very strongly that the newly elected president of the national board, Glendora Putnam, should also attend. I promised to find the additional funds needed for the two of us to attend. The response was supportive. I felt I had made a substantial impression on the audience and felt my commitment wouldn't harm my working relationship with the newly elected president.

Deep in my thoughts was how everything that had occurred during the first year of my tenure was giving me ammunition for how I could help broaden the intent of the YWCA vision. There would be many opportunities to introduce more women in the YWCA to the world. The organization's World Council had been active and was very supportive financially of the World YWCA. However, the council's activities were limited to those who could afford the membership and were invited to join.

Early in my second year as executive director, I was invited to attend the yearly meeting of the National Association of YWCA Executives (NAYE). This meeting was held at the Ritz Carlton hotel in Atlanta. Because the group had chosen this hotel for the meeting, I considered it another opportunity to interject a sense of the world into their leadership. When I gave the closing speech, I presented them with a challenge. I shared how meaningful my experiences had been during my visits to the YWCAs in the Far East. I suggested they hold their next meeting in Europe. I could hear the audience gasp. A few applauded. When the cost of such a trip was brought to the attention of the group, I responded by referring to what the current meeting was costing. I did not mention the lavish Ritz Carlton but they knew exactly what I meant.

I encouraged them to think about such a trip by elaborating on a tentative agenda. I suggested they visit the YWCA in London. Then go to Paris by train. Although there was not an association in Paris, we could meet with a group of women I knew who would tell us how the needs of women were met in France. I continued by suggesting we end the trip in Switzerland and learn more about the World YWCA. By the time the meeting was adjourned I think some of the women were ready to pack their suitcases. The next year the meeting was held in Europe and the itinerary was the one I had offered when I made the suggestion. Elizabeth Boyd, then national director of field services (Elizabeth Boyd retired and died in 2011), worked with a planning committee of executive directors during the following year. Approximately fifty of us made this historic journey on behalf of the YWCA of the United States. While the trip was extremely successful, it did not meet with the unanimous approval of the national board. However, with a bit of politicking around the edges, most of the opposition disappeared once the participants returned and shared their excitement over what they had learned and experienced. I now had help in my endeavors to increase the leadership's awareness of the YWCA's work around the world, as well as the members' awareness.

There was more work to be done over and above my desire to involve the membership in the activities of the world. Just before my appointment, the national board had sold the national headquarters building, located on Lexington Avenue next to the New York YWCA. Today the selling price of $600,000 for this piece of prime property in the middle of the city would be considered a steal by the buyers. The board in turn purchased two floors of space in the lower part of Manhattan next to New York University.

When I toured the new space, I knew immediately this had been a poor decision. There was simply too much space. The cost of building out the space had far exceeded the estimate. There had been little supervision and some staff members had made their own decisions about what they desired in their office space—a door here or there, and other things. While the income from the endowment was tapped to help pay for the overruns, this meant less for the ordinary expenses I was responsible for. At my very first meeting with the staff, I told them not to get too comfortable with the space they were calling their own because there would be some changes made and soon.

One of the first actions I took was to identify one of the city's outstanding space engineers. He agreed with my thinking that half the space would be enough to run our national office. We did a cost analysis before I even discussed what I wanted to do with the executive committee of the board. The committee was in a state of trying to adjust to the cost of the overruns on the build-out. It appeared that no one had been in charge. They didn't want to hear what I was asking permission to do. They didn't want to spend another two million dollars to undo what had been done.

The architect and I presented the numbers on the savings that would occur if we sold one of the floors, converted the work space that was more open, and used the space that was not occupied. The planners had saved a large amount of space for the main computer, but by this time computers no longer required a thousand square feet. A computer could sit on a desk. Some members didn't want to lose the space even though they now realized it wasn't needed for a main computer. They wanted the space for board meetings. We presented the savings if the board met in a hotel. The discussion took a while, but eventually I convinced the leaders on the board. Accepting my suggestions meant saving close to $700,000 a year. It also meant I wouldn't have to raise that amount of money. When it comes to fund-raising, the executive is the main person responsible for revenue.

In the process of awarding the construction contract, I reminded the board that we had to make sure we were supporting our mission. This meant we would include a provision in the contract to make sure that 50 percent of the workers involved in the remodeling represented people of color. The president, Glendora Putnam, was 100 percent in support of this provision. Some said we would never achieve this.

Not only did we achieve the provision of 50 percent, but the head supervisor was a person of color. The project started and ended on time. We achieved our projected savings and actually spent less that we had estimated to reduce the space. The work went well, but several staff members were definitely not satisfied. I could feel the hostility.

During this period we had a lot on our plate. Because of the space savings, we needed to redo the budget. The reduction of space affected almost every line in the budget. The budget was the main item on the agenda for the coming month. I will never forget that meeting. We were still meeting in the computer room because the work had not started there yet. We sat at round tables grouped according to departments. The directors had presented their budgets to me, and with my approval they were ready for presentation.

Once the presentation was made with overheads and hard copies, I asked for questions before the board gave its approval. A hand went up. "When do we go over the budget and make our suggestions?" Another board member spoke up, "If we don't get started we'll be here until midnight." It was at this point in the budget review process that I realized what happened in previous processes. This began my learning of what it meant to work with volunteers. I had never witnessed this kind of behavior from volunteers.

I immediately told them what I thought my responsibility as the executive director was. I also stated what I expected each of the directors to present to me for my approval. I made sure that if we had staff responsible for budgets who could not handle the task, that person would not have the responsibility. I pointed out my own responsibility for the budget, and acknowledged that if I, as executive director, could not manage this important task I should not be in charge.

The room grew very quiet. Several volunteers whispered to each other. "I am asking you to approve what we have presented," I said. "If you do this and change the review process, you'll have time to see a play, go to a fine restaurant, shop, or do whatever you do on Saturday night in New York." The motion was made and accepted. The meeting was adjourned. This was only one of the processes we changed. Some of the changes were minor, and some were very significant.

The next item on my list of things to work on was how to pull these 450 community and student associations together. It didn't take me long to decide after reading my mail and visiting associations. I traveled to many YWCAs across the country. There was no way of telling when you were approaching an association. The logos on the front of the buildings were all different. The logos on the stationery were different. Some of the YWCAs had a logo for each season. I thought about this for a few weeks and worked with Jane Pinkerton, our director of communications. Jane knew almost everyone in the business. She suggested that we talk with Sam Jones in California to see if he could help us design a plan for consolidating the approximately eight hundred logos into one. What a great suggestion that was. We made the trip to California. The meeting with Sam and his colleagues almost set me on fire. Their suggestions and ideas were excellent.

I had hoped we could adopt a new logo at the next triennium conference in Chicago in 1987. By the time Jane and I returned to New York, we had the outline of a plan. We knew that whatever we did had to involve as many members as possible. We had regional meetings so involvement would be extensive. With Jane as the top staff member in charge, we began immediately. We traveled back and forth to California. The consultants traveled to regional meetings. It was an exciting project. The day I saw the boards containing all the samples of the different logos that were used, I not only laughed, I cried with joy knowing that one day soon we would adopt a new logo that every association would use. The consultants did the research with help from staff members around the country. I had learned it was necessary to include the staff and volunteers in the research. And we needed approval from all the delegates at the Chicago convention.

So there I was with the space project fully progressing, overseeing the logo project, balancing fund-raising, budgeting projects, hiring and firing staff, and oh so much more. I was pleased that I was able to balance it all. I arrived early at the office and worked until dark. I was excited and very happy. And then the criticisms began to mount. I hoped that at the convention we would complete the space project, finalize and accept the logo, and accomplish more of what we needed to do. I thought about what was happening and decided that after the convention, I would resign.

Fortunately there were staff and board members extremely supportive of my leadership. I quietly spoke to several of them at the next board meeting, held at the Leadership Center in Arizona. What did I do that for? Lo and behold: during one of the breaks they kidnapped me and took me to one of the meeting rooms at the center, complete with champagne and snacks. They wanted to talk to me about my plans for retiring. They made a list of the changes and accomplishments I had made during my first three years. I told them I didn't understand the negative reactions or the criticism I'd received.

Through the crying and shouting—and I did most of the crying—the answer became apparent. The list of responsibilities the board had given me and those I had identified myself were not intended only for me, Gwen Baker, to do by myself with the staff. The volunteers were used to taking charge of whatever was being done, and now, the new executive director had eliminated their involvement. This group convinced me to stay in this position, but to work on changing my approach to what needed to be done.

After drying my eyes and taking a sip or two of champagne, I agreed to stay, but only if they would help me. In all of my other leadership positions, I alone was expected to do what had to be done with paid staff. I needed help identifying when and where volunteers could be useful. I left that meeting with the women who wanted me to stay and who were more than willing to help me.

At the Chicago convention, one of the first items on the agenda was the logo. We planned to present more than one, so three were presented. Sam Jones did a fabulous job reviewing and reporting the outcome of the research. As he presented the first two logos, he shared the reasons why they didn't completely reflect the mission. By the time he unveiled the third logo and told the audience why and how that logo was created and chosen, my stomach was having its own tornado.

I usually sat on the stage next to the president in our meetings. For this meeting we sat in the front row. While everyone knew this new logo idea was mine, it was important for me to let the president preside over the remainder of the presentation. When Sam finished his presentation, he asked President Putnam to join him for questions. Anyone who knows the YWCA knows that it can take forever to get a decision out of a group of YWCA women. I was ready for a knock-down, drag-out reaction. As Glendora approached the stage, I was almost afraid the tornado in my stomach could be heard to the last row. The president asked for questions. There were none. Then she asked for a motion to accept the new logo. I would say the response was unanimous, though I did hear one or two objections from the crowd. My stomach quieted down, I relaxed, and the tears slowly rolled down my face. I could not believe what had just happened. I knew then that I was not going to leave. However, during the remainder of my tenure with the YWCA there were several times when things became so pressing I was ready to run out the door.

With the convention behind us, we turned our attention to other issues. Living in New York City is an experience of its own. The television, newspapers, radio, and magazines almost set the agenda. One day I received a phone call from my friend Patricia Campbell, who told me that a friend of hers wanted to nominate me for a position on the New York City Board of Education. I couldn't understand why. She told me her friend's name was Dr. Terry Baker. We were not related. He had observed my career and felt I would be an asset to this seven-member board.

The mayor, David Dinkins, had appointed a thirty-five-person search committee to recommend three people for his consideration. Dr. Baker wanted to know if I was interested. I never thought I would or could live long enough to serve on this seven-member board, overseeing some thirty individual school districts. Of course I was interested. I sent Dr. Baker my résumé by messenger. In less than a week I was notified that I would be interviewed by the search committee. I was so excited I could hardly keep my mind on my YWCA duties. I checked with the president to make sure if I was selected she and the board would approve. She gave me her support and felt that the visibility would be good for the YWCA. I wouldn't need to spend more than a few hours a week as a member of the board. I felt I could make up any time I took away from my YWCA work by working late and on weekends. I was already doing this.

The day finally came when my interview was scheduled. So many great things were happening to me that I was learning to calm the tornadoes inside when I was excited. At my interview I was introduced to the group, and the chairwoman, one of the state senators, questioned me. Before I answered, I said, "All of you around this table know me but I don't know any of you. Madam Chair, could we take a few minutes so the members of this committee could introduce themselves to me?" She agreed. I noticed a few smiles. I did this to have some time to settle in. I also wanted to know who I would be talking to.

I recalled the time I was being interviewed for a school principalship in Ann Arbor. I was taken into a room with twenty-five fourth-graders, no chairs, and I was the only adult visible. I immediately sat on the floor (I could do that then), and asked the children to join me. This tickled them. They smiled and sat around me. I asked them their names, and the interview was fun. So was this interview.

When I left the interview with the Board of Education committee, I felt I had left a group of friends. I knew that if I was appointed to this wonderful position I would need friends. It occurred to me that the one thing that might keep me from going further was my relatively short residence in New York. Obviously that didn't matter because a week or so later, I was called and given an appointment with the mayor.

David Dinkins is a delightful man and very comfortable to be with. I soon learned from the newspapers that I was one of the finalists. I have no idea how I kept my mind on my work at the YWCA.

One day following all of this, I was attending a conference in Denver. When I opened the door to my hotel room during an afternoon break, the phone rang. I had no idea who would be calling me in the afternoon other than perhaps the office. (This was the time before cell phones.) I answered the phone. It was Mayor Dinkins offering me the position. The afternoon session of that conference continued without me.

There was one major requirement the mayor put forth. I had been living in Riverdale in the Bronx after I moved from the Bank Street apartment. The mayor had a requirement that his two appointments live in Manhattan. This requirement did not bother me because a move to Manhattan would make it easier to get to work. I soon found a suitable living space on the East Side. This made it possible for me to walk to work, which was great for my weight and my budget.

Once again, so much was happening at a fast pace. Uncle Mallory came for the swearing in and held the Bible that my grandmother, his mother, had given to me. I invited several close friends and some senior staff members at the YWCA to attend the swearing in ceremony. What a lovely occasion and celebration.

If I thought my plate was full before this, now it was overflowing. I had another office to manage, and another staff to hire, an assistant and a secretary. I had almost forgotten that board members were allowed a car and driver until I was introduced to my driver, Leroy Pierson.

My five years as a member of the New York Board of Education was an experience all of its own. The following chapter will cover this experience in more depth. However, there were several incidents that occurred during my tenure with the two organizations, the YWCA and the Board of Education, that impacted each other.

I had hardly gotten my feet wet trying to get used to serving in two positions. I was getting up earlier and going to bed later. I was always working, in both offices, at home and in the car. Mr. Pierson, my driver, found a large board I could use as a desk in the back of the car. I even kept the basics I needed to freshen up for an appearance or a change of clothes. My phone rang constantly. I couldn't believe the mail. Requests for my appearance at various occasions and for speeches seemed unending.

One morning I received a phone call from a reporter at the *New York Times*. I don't remember if it was a man or a woman, but it makes no difference. The reporter asked me what I thought about the school board distributing condoms to students. I couldn't believe what I heard. I hadn't know about this. I covered up my ignorance by saying I had just joined the board and was not aware of this issue, and that I opposed it.

This was the late eighties, and it was a difficult issue to deal with. I was a feminist. I had raised three children and had not changed my thinking about young people having sex. I'm sure that my early pregnancy had a great deal to do with my response to the reporter. I had no idea this conversation was about to change my thinking on the issue; it almost changed my life. I was still naive about how to respond to reporters concerning student issues.

Some of my comments were almost militant when it came to the distribution of condoms to black students. I realized that my response was inappropriate for a member serving on any board of education, especially in New York. The position I took on this issue was also not appropriate for the executive director of the largest organization in the nation serving the needs of women and girls.

I was angry that this was happening in the school district, but also that no one had told me about this issue. I think I was also angry because I felt embarrassed; I should have known about this and didn't. I found out I didn't know what embarrassment was until the following morning.

I had hardly gotten out of bed before my phone rang. One of my staff members asked me if I had seen that morning's *Times*. "No," I said, "what's in it?" She told me to look on the front page of the city section. It was early and I hadn't yet picked up my copy of the paper, which was usually just outside my door. I quickly hung up the phone, rushed to get the paper, and turned to the section Lorraine had referenced. My mouth fell open. I flopped down in the nearest chair. There, on the front page of the *New York Times*, was not only the homeliest photo of me anyone had ever taken, but almost a word-for-word quote of the telephone interview regarding the distribution of condoms in the schools.

I sounded as though I had all the answers as to why the schools should not do this and made a clumsy excuse for why, as a school board member, I was not aware of this. I was not ashamed of my position but did not approve of how I presented my view. I swallowed hard and finished dressing. But I was totally unprepared for what awaited me in the outside world.

Mr. Pierson was waiting for me at the front of my apartment building. After he opened the door for me and was sure I was settled comfortably in the backseat, he too asked if I had seen the morning *Times*. We chatted about the publicity. He mentioned that this was only the beginning as far as publicity was concerned, now that I was a member of the Board of Education.

I remember the day a copy of a letter I wrote to the editor of the *Times* appeared in the paper. One would have thought I'd written a book on the best-seller list of the paper. I was so proud. My name was in the *Times*! Not just my name, but my letter with my thoughts in it had appeared in this great newspaper. A few years later, my photo, a summary of a telephone interview, and my name were there for all to see. I silently wished all of this could have been over some other issue. But how was I to know that in my future I would have mornings when I perused the *New York Times*, the *Daily News*, and other local newspapers, hoping there would be nothing in any of the papers about me. The publicity would have been welcome if it all could have been positive, but so many times it was not.

That morning almost every person I met as I climbed out of my car, rode the elevator, and sat down at my desk made some kind of reference to the article. The phone calls began. By noon, I wanted to bury my head under a pillow. All of the reactions were in opposition to my opinion. Other reporters wanted me to explain my thinking. I soon began to realize the world had changed since I had been a mother of three children. I could never have survived, or so I thought, if I had learned that my son and even worse my daughters had condoms in their book bags or in their pockets. Possession was an indication they were using or about to use a condom. I gave no thought to the fact that using a condom was an intelligent way to protect two individuals from what could be something much worse. A pregnancy, a disease, what else?

I think the most important reactions came from the president of the national board of the YWCA, Glendora Putnam, and from members of various feminist organizations like the National Organization for Women (NOW). President Putnam was a lawyer; she approached me as though I were a client. She was very direct when she told me that I no longer spoke for Gwendolyn Calvert Baker, that when I opened my mouth I was speaking for the YWCA and for the Board of Education. Her remarks were very similar to those of David Dinkins. Mayor Dinkins said to me, "When you open your mouth people listen, so say something significant." I realized saying something significant did not mean sharing what I thought was important. What had I gotten myself into? How would I maintain the respect of my friends, especially the women I interacted with throughout the organizations that worked for the rights of women? I had always been on top of my thinking of what was right for children, women, and people of color. I gave this situation a lot of thought and finally came up with an idea.

My idea was to do a brief research project. The project would be to interview students, parents, and teachers about their thoughts on whether the school system should distribute condoms to students. If yes, for what reason and under what conditions. I limited my visits and interviews to three high schools in Manhattan, Brooklyn, and Queens. I think I should say I did an informal survey rather than a research project, because what I did what very informal.

However informal the survey, I did not discover anyone, student, teacher or parent, who agreed with me. The parents and teachers were clear about not wanting to encourage students to have sex, but they also felt the distribution was teaching protection against unwanted outcomes. Once I concluded my survey, I summarized my findings. I did not call a press conference but reported the results of my summary at a meeting of the board, and further understood what I had not taken the time to examine before. I reported that I agreed with the students, teachers, and parents.

The papers reported on my survey results and said a good word or two about how I managed to gather enough information to make a change in my opinion in favor of the distribution of condoms in the school system. In some small way, I think I gained respect from the community for the manner in which I handled the situation. With this issue behind me, I was able to turn my attention to my other responsibilities.

One of the most important issues for the YWCA was raising enough funds to support our plans for pre- and post-breast-cancer activity. As I write this portion of my memoir, the October Cancer Month has just concluded. This is the time when everything, at least it seems like everything, is decorated with the famous pink ribbon. Even the Beverly Hills Doggie Day Care is covered with pink ribbons in honor of the breast cancer raffle it is sponsoring.

Over the years, this ribbon has been used to call attention to other situations or issues. The one I see most often is Support Our Troops. Not many individuals outside the YWCA are aware of how the pink ribbon came to represent fund-raising for breast cancer. Whenever I recall its origins I am reminded of how important and how significant a sincere thank-you can be.

I had a friend named Donna Blackwell who was on the board of the Avon Foundation. She suggested we have dinner together to talk about some of the YWCA programs that Avon might be able to help us with. I was excited about the upcoming dinner engagement and immediately began to sort out our needs. Our number one need and priority was raising enough funds to develop a video for the breast cancer pool program. Our dinner meeting was most pleasant and we appeared to be on the road to a successful fund-raiser.

Not too long after my meeting with Donna, the YWCA received a check for twenty thousand dollars for the video. While I was very pleased with the contribution, the cost of the video was twice that amount. I thought I had made it clear during our dinner discussion that we needed forty thousand dollars. What to do?

I discussed our dilemma with the director of development, and suggested we make an appointment with the president of the foundation for the purpose of "thanking the foundation for the twenty thousand dollar contribution." In addition to expressing our appreciation to the president, I would be able to let him know in a subtle way that we still needed an additional amount. I was eager for the meeting. As I thought about Avon, I remembered another time in my life when Avon helped me fulfill a need. Here we were again.

So with my nerve in one hand and my Avon history in the other, the director of development and I hailed a cab and went to the Avon headquarters on Fifty-Seventh Street in Manhattan. The building seemed enormous. The foundation headquarters was most impressive.

After we were escorted by several staff members to the office of the president, I was beginning to settle my nerves. There is something about making a request for a financial contribution that always puts me on edge. After the introductions, we began our discussion of why we were there. For some reason, I very tactfully mentioned how important Avon had been to me in the early days of my life. I had not planned to do this, but the discussion seemed to make it appropriate. I shared with the president the fact that I had been an Avon representative when my children were small and I was attending the University of Michigan. I even mentioned that I gave Avon parties when this was not something that Avon was doing at the time. But my potential clients were student wives who had babysitting problems as well as a shortage of cash to spend on Avon products. The party idea allowed the women to bring their babies, win prizes, and book parties of their own. I was helping these young mothers and they were helping me. For a couple of years I too could use the products I could not have afforded otherwise, and in spite of my overhead, my Avon income helped me clothe my children and myself. I remembered the beautiful beige winter coat I bought myself with my Avon money. And how I occasionally bought my husband a pair of socks. We all laughed and turned our attention to why we were there. My story seemed to break the ice.

During the conversation I never really revealed how much more money we needed for the video because the discussion took another turn. The president asked questions about the work of the YWCA. He wanted to know about other plans we had for helping women in all phases of breast cancer. After a lengthy meeting, he turned to me and asked if I would return to Avon headquarters for a luncheon with some of the staff. He wanted them to hear about the work of the YWCA, especially in the area of breast cancer.

A few days later I received an invitation to a luncheon at Avon for the purpose of sharing with the invited staff the work of the YWCA. When I arrived at the headquarters for the luncheon, I was greeted with such accord I felt very special. I also felt this luncheon would be very special. The private dining room was welcoming. The table was set for twelve, complete with linens and a lovely floral centerpiece. I made a short presentation and encouraged questions from those present.

Near the end of the luncheon, the president spoke about Avon's outreach to nonprofit organizations. He specifically talked about the cancer research project Avon had contributed to in Great Britain. He then stated that Avon had created a small piece of jewelry that was sold through the Avon catalogue and whose proceeds went to cancer research in Great Britain. The sale of this piece of jewelry had netted approximately three million dollars. I almost fell off my seat. Here I was worried about twenty thousand dollars and the president was thinking in millions. It didn't take long for me to understand where he was going with this information about jewelry and cancer research.

He ended the meeting by stating that he had invited the present staff to hear about the work and plans the YWCA had for its Cancer Outreach Program because he wanted them to design and create a small piece of jewelry to be included in the Avon catalogue to assist the YWCA with its work with breast cancer. The entire audience, including me, applauded. I was so excited.

After we shook hands and said our good-byes, the president invited me to take a walk through the retail shop located in the headquarters. Once there, he instructed the staff member in charge of this shop to assist me in selecting any item I might like to have as a gift from Avon. All I wanted to do was fly back to the office and share the good news. But I did take advantage of selecting a few Avon products in the retail shop. After hearing the mention of millions of dollars that went to the cancer research project, I stopped thinking about the twenty thousand I had hoped for when I went to say thank-you for their original gift.

Soon after the luncheon experience with Avon, the national board of the YWCA held a board meeting at its Leadership Center in Phoenix. In the middle of a business session, one of my staff members handed me a note that said I had a call from the Avon Foundation and they were holding the call from New York. I handed the note to the president, who was presiding. She read it quickly, smiled, and nodded agreement for me to leave the meeting and take the call.

The person calling had been assigned to work with the YWCA to prepare a video about its work. When the video was finished they would send us three hundred thousand dollars. They needed more from us. After returning to the meeting and sharing the news, we prepared what Avon had asked for. We learned it would be used to help design the piece of jewelry Avon was creating for the catalogue.

Our plans for supporting the needs of women who had or might have breast cancer soon increased. We wanted to make sure that all of our approximately four hundred YWCAs throughout the country would have an organized support center for breast cancer. The staff and I visited many breast cancer centers throughout the country. We were definitely on the right track. Our plans were structured to provide what women needed.

What followed soon after is almost magical. We were not told what the piece of jewelry would be, nor were we consulted. We simply were not at that end of the project. We would be happy with whatever design was created to support our need. The day the Avon catalogue came with the pink ribbon pin, we could hardly believe our eyes. The YWCA had been the catalyst for the development of the pink ribbon design. One can hardly move through a day without seeing this symbol in a window, on an envelope, a car, or wherever. This design exploded and is not restricted to the color pink. However, the pink ribbon is very popular throughout the month of October, which is Breast Cancer Month.

As a result of this project, the YWCA received more than three million dollars from Avon. The sale of the pink pin and other items bearing the symbol was so profitable, we are told, that Avon included other nonprofits in its distribution of the income from the sales.

Several years after I had resigned from the YWCA and was serving as president and CEO of the United Nations Development Fund for Women (UNIFEM), I had my yearly mammogram. I usually selected a different clinic or center for the experience. I had become involved in what was available for breast cancer diagnosis and treatment during the YWCA/Avon project. This particular year I selected a center that was located on the Lower West Side of Manhattan. As usual, I had my mammogram and was waiting in a small dressing room for my results. When the curtain was pulled open I had expected the staff member to tell me all was well and I could get dressed.

This time the result was different. I had to have a second mammogram. The second time was different. I had cancer in my left breast. I was in a state of shock. I could hardly get dressed. I made it back to my office and called my internist. I told him my situation. The clinic where I'd had my mammogram that morning had already made an appointment for surgery for me later that month.

My doctor insisted he send me to a breast cancer specialist within walking distance from my office, at New York University Hospital. Although it was late in the day my doctor was able to get me an appointment with a specialist. Within the hour the surgeon examined me and called another specialist in to see me. They validated the results of the mammograms.

I was alone. I was frightened and confused. What did all of this mean? For years I had worked to make sure women who could not afford mammograms could go to a nearby YWCA and have their needs met. I had insurance. I could afford my yearly mammograms. Why did I have to end up with cancer? I had just started my new position with UNICEF. After shedding many tears, I meet with the surgeon in his office. He spent a great deal of time with me that evening. He helped me understand my cancer and planned a surgery schedule for me. At the time I was traveling out of the country several times a month, and schedules other than mine had to be considered.

A week or two later I went to the hospital for a series of tests. One of the nurses was wearing a pink ribbon pin. It was like a bolt of lightning striking me. I started to cry. I was crying so hard the nurse had to help me to a chair. I think I was crying for several reasons, but most of all for remembering that the magic of a thank-you was real.

I have attempted to do some research on the YWCA/Avon project but my attempts were done some twenty-five years later. I did make a trip to Avon headquarters several years ago and spoke with the director of the unit that now assists other nonprofits in their outreach. The ribbon sales had netted an unusual amount of income. All the people I had interacted with had retired or moved to other corporations.

As I looked around the Avon headquarters on Fifty-Seventh Street in New York twenty-five years later, nothing around me seemed as huge. And nothing around me seemed the same, except the excitement I could still feel when I worked with the YWCA and Avon helping women manage their breast cancer needs.

TEN

An Opportune Platform for
Multicultural Education

When my appointment to the New York City Board of Education was announced, my world changed. I'd never dreamed of having such an opportunity in my entire career. And in the short time I had lived in New York, I learned that people who attained high appointments in government had been involved in neighborhood and community governance for years. Some, along with me, even wondered why and how an outsider could be selected for such a position; by "outsider" I meant a person who hadn't lived in New York for more years than I had.

New York had the largest school district in the world. Not just the nation, the world. In the early 1990s, the student body consisted of over one million students in the five boroughs that make up the city. Each borough was different. Manhattan, the largest, was the home of hundreds of national corporations. Beyond the center of Manhattan, ethnic groups made up smaller subcities. In 1986, Queens was perhaps the most diverse borough, while Brooklyn served students who spoke over seventy languages. Staten Island and the Bronx claimed many varied ethnic groups as their own, each with distinguishing characteristics. The teachers' union served more than enough individuals to incorporate two separate cities, each with over fifty thousand residents.

When I was appointed to the New York City Board of Education, I was sworn in as a board member by Manhattan borough president David Dinkins. My uncle, Mallory Thomas, held the Bible my grandmother gave me on my eleventh birthday.

Each borough elected its own president. The presidents of the boroughs at that time had the authority to appoint one individual to the city Board of Education. The mayor was allowed to appoint two members to the board. Most members were political appointments, but mine was somewhat different. David Dinkins had a nominating committee to interview candidates who were nominated by groups or individuals.

During the 1980s the school system consisted of thirty-five districts. The total budget was in excess of several billion dollars, several times larger than most individual school systems. In the late eighties, Ed Koch was the mayor of the city, and had served in that position for several years. One of his two appointments at that time was Robert Wagner, a former mayor's son.

Each appointee to the seven-member board had some history and experience in the governance structure of their borough. I had none. There were times when this was a great inconvenience, but in other situations it was a blessing. I lacked historical knowledge. I also came to the position without any political debts.

The new board would need a president. The jockeying for this position began even before our first meeting. Most people assumed that Mayor Koch wanted Robert Wagner as president. David Dickens wanted me to be president. I was caught between a rock and a hard place. I was well aware that I did not have the necessary experience or knowledge about the city to take on such a responsibility.

By the time Mayor Koch finished making deals with other borough presidents, he had all the votes he needed to have Wagner elected president by the other board members. I did not feel bad at all about the election. I knew I needed more experience. I decided I would work hard and learn all I could. Perhaps one day I might be elected.

There was so much to do. I was very lucky to find two excellent staff members to help. Almost as soon as realized I needed an efficient secretary who was familiar with New York, I came across a distant friend of mine from Michigan. Lorraine West was looking for a job as a secretary. Lorraine had lived in New York for several years and had previously worked for the school board. She was a perfect fit.

Next, I needed someone who could serve as my assistant, someone who knew the city and was also familiar with schools and education. I had met Eddy Bayardelle when I was vice president of the Graduate School at Bank Street College. I worked with Eddy and promoted him to assistant vice president at Bank Street. When I approached Eddy about working with me at the Board of Education he accepted immediately. Once I had these two important positions filled I could turn my attention to other concerns as the new Manhattan appointee to the board.

One of the fringe benefits of being a member of the New York City Board of Education was having a car and driver at my disposal. Having an assistant, a secretary, and office space in the Board of Education headquarters were perks I was grateful for, but a car and driver? These were a great help as well as a privilege. Moving around Manhattan was a challenge to my time and energy. I often needed to go from one side of the city to the other. I also had to respond to school district invitations in the other four boroughs. I had to plan my daily and weekly schedules carefully.

The driver assigned to me was truly a blessing. Leroy Pierson drove for me until he retired. He was a very responsible driver and a gentleman in every way. As I write this, I am still in touch with Mr. Pierson and his wife Dolores, who retired to North Carolina. The driver who followed, James Ray, was also a most responsible and respectful person. Just this month I had a letter from his son, James Ray Jr., telling me of his father's passing.

The cars for the board members were generally in better shape than the offices. I can honestly say that the school system up to that time did not spend money on even inexpensive office furniture. What was there was pitiful. The YWCA was in a much better position in this regard. When I became president of the board, I moved to a larger office. I requested that the drapes be removed and discarded, for they were about to fall off the windows. Washing or dry-cleaning them would have resulted in shreds. I did ask to have the blinds and windows washed. Once the walls were painted I called the art department and requested several student paintings for my office. I personally purchased two or three large plants to fill up space where furniture was needed. The space eventually shaped up nicely.

There was one last thing I did not need but wanted. There were times when I needed to freshen up. The only possible space was the latrine. In a hundred years there had only been one woman president before me. There was no thought for accommodating the needs of a woman who might occupy that office. When I asked to have the latrine removed, it caused an uproar. Very few people even knew it existed. Once it was removed, I at least had a mirror to comb my hair and a lavatory where I could wash my hands.

Becoming president not only required more office space, but also more assistance. I was able to appoint another fine assistant, Lori Acala, who added her personality and skills to Eddy and Lorraine's, providing me with excellent support.

It took a great deal of effort to get used to the brash way things were done on the Board of Education. Fixing up our offices was minor to what needed to be done to the board meeting room. When I was escorted to the boardroom early in my tenure, I couldn't believe my eyes. This was the meeting room for the board that governed the largest school district in the world? We had a large oblong table that barely provided space for the seven members. The table was in disarray, as were the huge uncomfortable chairs around it. Even more appalling was the lack of space for citizens to attend meetings. It sent the message that we didn't want the public here when we conducted board business. Our much-needed assistants often couldn't find a seat in the room near the member they were serving. When I became president, changing the board meeting space was one of my priorities.

I was not prepared for the kind of publicity board members received.

There seemed to be a regular schedule for reporters to attack the fact that each board member had a car and driver. Not only did reporters focus on stories about the cars, they also sought opportunities to take embarrassing photos. I was very careful and never had the driver take me to a personal appointment. I became somewhat paranoid over the frequency of coverage as well as the aggressive approach.

Some reporters had an uncanny ability to make something out of nothing. The headlines of one page of a popular New York newspaper said that I had spent ten thousand dollars to refurbish my office. I was furious. But how could I refute this accusation? The individuals who read such falsehoods were not privileged to know the truth.

Checking the newspapers early in the morning became a daily ritual. I had to be prepared for reporters waiting for me in the lobby of my apartment building or on the steps of the Board of Education. One little slip in a response to a reporter about something that appeared in the papers on a given day could make or break not just my day, but several that followed. I made mistakes, but I learned quickly how to respond to a reporter's question in my favor.

At the time I accepted the appointment to the Board of Education, I didn't realize how much time I would spend fulfilling the needs of two full-time positions. The YWCA National Executive was certainly more than a forty-hour-a-week position. I thought the Board of Education position would be part-time, but it wasn't long before it too became more than a full-time responsibility. Part of this was because I was a new face in New York and on the Board of Education.

The black community was very proud of my appointment. Almost every week an organization honored me with an affair that, although pleasant, added to my busy schedule. There were also numerous requests for the presence of board members. When I became president my attendance at functions was even more important. Dressing for these affairs, especially the semiformal evening events, meant I often had to change clothes at the end of a long workday. I learned to take one black skirt and turn it into several different evening gowns with the help of two or three tops. A pair of black evening pumps and a string of pearls went a long way.

The work of the board was very time-consuming. I spent hours reading the material that accompanied the board agenda. Soon I began my days

I am sworn in as New York City Board of Education president by Mayor David Dinkins. Glendora M. Putnam, national president of the YWCA of the United States, holds the Bible my grandmother gave me in 1942.

earlier and ended later. Even with support staff at the YWCA, the Board of Education, and in my home, I was still short of time and energy. Jimmie James, my housekeeper from Bank Street College days, was still with me. I couldn't have managed as well as I did without Jimmie and the other dedicated staff members who did more than expected.

The first four years of serving on the board were filled with challenges. Almost every item on the board agenda's called for political warfare. I soon discovered that the purpose of board meetings was to report decisions that had already been made behind closed doors or on telephone calls. These decisions were also subject to change at any moment.

While David Dinkins was not the first African American to serve as the president of the borough of Manhattan, he had appointed an African American woman to work with him on the business of the board. The climate I had to work in doing board business was not pleasant. There were times when I wasn't sure why board members refused to support me. In some cases they wouldn't even listen to my opinions or suggestions.

The climate became worse when David Dinkins was elected mayor and I became president of the board. Now the city had two "firsts." David was the first African American mayor of New York City; I was the first African American woman elected president of the Board of Education, and the second woman to serve as president in a hundred years. While it was difficult for me to work in such a hostile environment, I can't imagine how burdensome it must have been for Mayor Dinkins.

Although the atmosphere was at times difficult, I like to think I was able to add a "touch of class" to our meeting environments, besides bringing some warmth and spirit to the meetings. I had the location of the meetings moved to a much larger room with enough space for those in attendance to sit comfortably during the meetings. The arrangement of the members and their assistants was given some care so the business could be conducted in an environment that reflected concern and good stewardship.

Despite the difficulties, serving on the board included many positive experiences. I enjoyed the accolades that came with the appointment. Newspaper articles and television appearances were usually pleasant. When my picture was on the front page of the *New York Times* I was more than excited. However, when I recall some of the situations I had to work through to even suggest a change, the cost was at times almost more than I thought I could endure.

One of the most embarrassing situations had to do with the budget. Most nonprofits usually have difficulty with their financial status. The school board, or should I say, the city of New York, was no exception. During David Dinkins's administration, finding ways to reduce the budgets of various departments within the city was almost a daily consideration. The school board was no exception. I didn't worry too much about being asked to take a budget cut because of my close relationship with the mayor. By close I do not mean personal; rather, we had developed in a short time a close professional relationship. If asked, I was sure I would be able to negotiate a lesser amount. I knew he probably felt he could not exclude asking the school board to take a cut. If he did, some would think it was because I was African American.

Surprisingly, the board was asked to take a sizable cut. After working very hard to find areas where the budget could be reduced, the board asked me to go to the mayor and request that he reduce our proposed budget reduction by 15 percent. In coming up with this solution to our problem, some of the board members used the very reasons they felt the mayor would agree to our request—because of our relationship. Politics was raising its ugly head. They did not make any comment about the fact that we were both from the same ethnic group: they were not dumb. They knew better than to voice anything even close to that except to infer we had a collegial relationship. Most of the members were on the board because of their relationship with their borough presidents. My stomach only did a short churn. I was able to tell it to calm down because I knew that while I might not be able to convince him to allow us a 15 percent cut, I was almost sure he would agree to my suggestion of proposing a smaller one. I had not mentioned this to the board; I wanted it to be a surprise.

I rarely had a problem getting an appointment with the mayor, so I was granted an appointment almost immediately to discuss the proposed budget. This added to my confidence in his positive response to my proposal for a budget cut of a smaller amount. When I entered his office, he was, as usual, most gracious. He acknowledged the presence of Bill Lynch, his assistant, and the three of us sat in a semicircle, discussing the state of affairs of both the city and the school board. I made a few brief remarks about the obvious lack of support and cooperation I was receiving from the board. I also thought that if I could take the mayor's agreement to a smaller cut to the board, this would lessen the board members' hostility toward me.

I presented the board's reasons for our inability to find ways to cut the budget by 15 percent. I gave the mayor a written report that justified our reasons for not finding places to cut. After listening to me, he glanced quickly through the folder I had given him, stood up, walked behind his chair, and placed his hands of the back of the chair. He took a deep breath and looked at me. I almost smiled and extended my hand to thank him when I heard him say no. I can't remember exactly what I said, but I knew better than to appeal. A David Dinkins no, especially with his right-hand man Bill Lynch present, meant just that.

I was not only embarrassed, I was angry. All the reasons I was so sure he would reduce his request meant nothing. In fact, the African American aspect may have worked against me. I was embarrassed because I had taken too much for granted. I had expected the mayor to respond to me for the reasons I identified because they were the same reasons I would have used if I had been in his shoes. Or so I thought. But I was not in his position. I was angry because I had to report to board members who would feel I did not have the support of the mayor, the very person who thought I should be president but did not or was not able to support me. I felt I had been betrayed.

After the budget crisis, my working relationship with the board appeared to get worse. In fact, one time I asked the board to meet in executive session in my office and four of them refused. Of the seven board members, five represented each borough and two were appointed by the mayor. Westina Mathews and I had been appointed by him, so whenever I needed support on a motion, I could always count on Westina and the Manhattan borough representative. I had to work to gain control of a fourth vote.

One member came on during a term to replace a member who had resigned. I knew after our first meeting he was going to be trouble. One of the issues we were dealing with was a professional staff member who acted most unprofessionally when working with individual board members. This situation was causing a lot of trouble. I was aware that the new board member had a very good relationship with the person causing trouble. I finally decided this individual should be fired. I polled the board and believed I had a fourth vote. I learned that the new board member would not be present at the meeting I planned to obtain support for the dismissal. When I asked for support to dismiss this individual, I received unanimous approval. I was so relieved I could have jumped for joy.

I left my office and prepared to fly to a meeting in Chicago the next morning. When I reached Chicago and was registering at the hotel, I received a phone call at the check-in counter from my assistant, Eddy Bayardelle. Eddie always called me "Boss." He said, "Boss, you'd better take the next flight back to New York." When I asked him what the problem was he said, "The problem board member returned to New York and learned of the dismissal. He called a meeting to overturn that decision." I didn't think he could do this, but I felt I needed to be there. I returned to New York.

At the board meeting in New York I was stunned. This problem board member had convinced the four board members to work against me. The reason was obvious. The "two firsts" represented much of what he was against. I looked each of the four in the eye and asked how they could have changed their vote overnight. They all had one reason or another.

Working in this hostile environment was difficult. I realized I was spending more time on board business than on YWCA business. One evening, shortly after the staff dismissal issue took place, I went home after an unusually long day. When I walked into my apartment I almost lost my balance. I was exhausted. I was frustrated. I had to make a change, but I wasn't sure what to do.

I had four more years to go as president of the board. I simply had to get the business of the YWCA in better shape. I could no longer afford the kind of time I was giving the board. Salary didn't matter—my income from the board was merely twenty dollars a month. But I realized from the city's response to my attempts to reduce the budget cuts, and the board's response to the member dismissal, that I had little or no support from the city or the board. I closed my eyes and took a deep breath. I no longer wondered what to do. I knew what to do.

I submitted my letter of resignation to Mayor Dinkins. He gave me a lovely reception at Gracie Mansion. When I greeted the guests and later looked over the crowd from the podium, I knew that the support I had lost was felt within, but I had gained much more than I realized.

ELEVEN

More Challenges:
Inside the United Nations

Resigning from my position as president of the New York City Board of Education was not as simple as I've made it sound. The press conference Mayor Dinkins held so I could announce my resignation and my replacement was a disaster. In a city as large as New York, it doesn't take long for news to spread. Mayor Dinkins was quick to arrange a press conference in City Hall and quicker to select my successor. I'm not sure if he was displeased with my performance or not. He praised me whenever he introduced me at public events. I assume that in his position he always had a list he could turn to. And there is no shortage of qualified African Americans in the city of New York.

I had attended many press conferences in the same room, so appearing once again was almost a pleasure. The room was crowded with cameras, reporters, Board of Education staff members, and those who were there just for the sake of it. This news item was especially interesting because David Dinkins was the first African American mayor and I was the first African American female president of the Board of Education.

Rumors abounded about why I was resigning, and few people were aware of who the mayor would appoint in my stead. I was very comfortable as I approached the front of the room near the podium. The mayor introduced

When I resigned my position on the Board of Education, Mayor David Dinkins gave me a lovely reception at Gracie Mansion, the mayor's official residence. During the reception he presented me with a beautiful inscribed crystal bowl.

me. As I took the five or six steps to the podium, I wanted all of this behind me. I made my statement, which included some niceties about the mayor. I gave a simple statement about why I was resigning, then I took the same five or six steps back to my place on stage. As the mayor announced Carl McCall as my replacement, I happened to glance at my feet. That look gave a very aggressive reporter with his camera an opportunity to capture me with my head down. I didn't realize at the time that one of the rumors was that I had been fired by the mayor. Of course that was not true, but when the photograph of me looking down appeared on the front page of the *New York Times* the next morning, it gave visual credence to the rumor.

The transition of returning to my full-time position with the YWCA was most unpleasant. I had an idea where some of the negative rumors were rooted, but once a rumor is out, good or bad, there isn't much to do except hold your head up and move with the flow of things. For several weeks I was not happy.

The deeper I plunged back into my work and the responsibilities of my position at the YWCA, the more I thought about my departure. I didn't give this a great deal of reflection because I was very involved not only in the work of the YWCA, but also in the revision of my textbook, at my publisher's request. *Planning and Organizing for Multicultural Instruction* had seen me through my move to Washington, DC, and my divorce. To revise the book would take time and energy. I soon forgot all I'd been involved in at the Board of Education and focused on revising the textbook. Things at the YWCA were moving in the right direction.

Early in my settling-back-in period, as I refer to my return to my full-time position, I received a phone call from a firm looking for someone to fill a position as a director on a local bank board. I casually asked them what kind of person they were looking for. I made notes during the conversation and thought about whom I could recommend. Nearing the end of the conversation, the gentleman who called said that the average income for a board member was about fifty thousand dollars a year for two days of meetings a month. Without hesitation I told the headhunter I was interested in the position. He said he had hoped that I would be interested. We made an appointment to meet over lunch the next day. I felt somewhat the same as I had when I became interested in the position with the Board of Education.

In a few days I had committed myself to an interview with the president of the bank and with the current members of its board. Before the interviews I did a quick study of Brooklyn Savings and Loan. I familiarized myself with the background of the board members. I also learned that the current board needed to expand by one member. They had made it clear to the firm working with them that because the current board members were all men, they wanted a woman for diversity.

They had interviewed five women. Four of these women were white and the fifth was African American. The existing members were all white, as was the president. After doing a little more homework I discovered the women candidates were all under fifty. This made me the oldest. I decided not to let the age issue get in the way of my interest in the position.

Before I interviewed for the position I talked with Glendora Putnam; I wanted to make sure I had her support and that she would understand the need for me to be away from my position at the YWCA a couple of days a month. Glendora was very interested in the possibility of my serving on the board of this bank. I remember during our discussion she said to me, "Don't think they are interested in you just because of your position with the YWCA. Remember what you have gained by serving on the board of the largest school district in the world." We both agreed that I should go through the interview process and hoped the results would be beneficial.

Prior to being presented to the board of Brooklyn Savings and Loan, I met with the president of the board, Gerald Keegan, an impressive young man in his mid-forties. Mr. Keegan had moved up from a position of teller to the presidency of this bank. We had a most amiable conversation. For some reason I am never nervous when I have an interview. I guess part of this is because I always do my homework. I know names, goals, and of course the history of whatever organization interviews me. At the end of our conversation I told Mr. Keegan that I hoped the decision to fill the board position would not be made on any consideration of my sex or ethnicity. With that we proceeded to the boardroom.

I knew I had dressed properly for the occasion. I am a conservative dresser so I usually fit into any type of business or professional situation. The introductions were courteous and pleasant. I would say the average age of the board members was mid-sixties. Most had backgrounds in financial banking or real estate. I felt good about the questions and noticed that the two attorneys serving the board were silent and taking everything in, especially my responses. After I asked my questions they thanked me and told me I would hear from the president in the near future.

The next day I received a call from Mr. Keegan. He offered me the position. I was ecstatic. Once again I was moving into another exciting arena. I thanked the president and said I would respond as soon as I conferred with my attorney. Meeting with my attorney was very important. This bank had been in a bit of financial interplay with the federal government. My attorney assured me that I would not be financially responsible in any way. Once again with my nerve in one hand and the desire to become involved in a new and different world, I graciously accepted the offer to become the first woman on the board of the Brooklyn Savings and Loan Association who just happened to be African American.

Before my interview I had purchased several books about stocks, bonds, and the basics of banking that I needed to know. This was a completely new experience for me, and I had a lot of hard work to do, for I was moving into a new and different world. It doesn't take much to learn the basics of the banking industry, but it takes a long time to grasp the business of the industry. I had received several nice fringe benefits when I was on the Board of Education, and several of these continued. I went through an orientation with the bank lawyers and Mr. Keegan. I would be picked up by car before each board and committee meeting. and would be expected to meet with the board for lunch and dinner meetings at the bank's expense. This was truly a pleasure. Cafeterias were not on the list for bank board members.

I worked hard to be a contributing board meeting and spent hours in the evening preparing for meetings. I was extremely busy but enjoyed every minute of my new experience. I found time to read the *Wall Street Journal* in addition to the *New York Times* and couldn't get to the stock reports fast enough. Some of what I learned about the stock market and investing has made my retirement more comfortable. There are times when I wish I had been more aggressive, but a short visit to memories of losses makes me feel more satisfied.

Balancing both working the YWCA and serving on the bank board was not easy, but I was doing it. I felt the YWCA was about where I had hoped it would be before I resigned. The budget was on target. Development was not where I wanted it to be, but it was supporting the national office along with the memberships from our associations. The member associations paid a percentage of the fees they received from memberships, and this constituted a significant portion of our total budget. It was greatly dependent on the income from our portfolio. At that time there were few nonprofits that received income from investments. The YWCA had been in such solid financial condition when I took over the leadership that I knew even if I didn't raise revenues, I couldn't put them out of business. When I resigned I was pleased with the results of my administration.

My next challenge didn't come from a phone call but from a letter. The letter was from a search firm representing the United Nations Children's Fund: UNICEF.

When the letter came to my attention, I gave it a quick once-over. It asked me to recommend someone for the position of president and chief executive officer of UNICEF. All I knew about this organization was its trick-or-treat collections on Halloween, though my children had been trick-or-treating long before UNICEF became involved. Therefore I knew very little about the organization. As I began a quick run-through in my mind of individuals who might be interested, I thought I would call the person who signed the letter and get a bit more information about the position, including the salary and location of their national office.

When I spoke with the person heading up this particular search, I discovered the office was in New York. When he told me the salary was in the neighborhood of two hundred thousand dollars, I stopped thinking about whom to refer and immediately suggested that we set up an appointment. I indicated that I was interested. I didn't waste any time clearing my calendar so we could meet soon. This opportunity came exactly during the time I was thinking about my next position. I was very excited and started scanning anything I could find about UNICEF. I didn't want to wait for the materials the search firm was sending. As per usual, I wanted basic information so I could ask intelligent questions. The more I learned, the more excited I became. I could hardly wait for the appointment, which came soon after the telephone conversation.

The gentleman I was to meet was staying at the InterContinental Hotel in New York City. I had been in most of the large and impressive hotels in the city but had not been in this one before. It is a lovely building. When I entered the lobby I could feel that I was embarking on a new and different journey. My body felt somewhat queasy. I wasn't nervous, I think I was just excited. The gentleman, and he was indeed a gentleman, greeted me graciously. I wasn't sure whether he knew I was African American or not. But I realized if he was conducting this search he had probably done his homework and knew a great deal about me. As soon as we shook hands and were seated comfortably, the interview began. It wasn't a series of questions but an interesting conversation. It did not take long for him to tell me he wanted me to meet the board's search committee as soon as possible. My schedule was tight because I was leaving for a meeting in Ohio the next day. He said he would need to check with the chair of the committee to find a convenient time.

When I left the interview and stepped into the elevator I felt as though I was walking on clouds. I was so excited. I liked all I had learned about the responsibilities of this position. If all went well, I would not have to leave

New York because the national headquarters was within walking distance of my apartment and near the United Nations. The position required a great deal of international travel, which I really enjoyed.

Later that day I received a call from the gentleman who interviewed me. The day the committee wanted to meet with me was one of the days I had planned to be in Ohio on YWCA business. The only way I could meet the interview schedule would be to fly to New York and return to Ohio on the same day. I knew that would probably be out of the question because of the cost. My mind never considered anything without seeing a price next to it. I had worked for nonprofits for so long I didn't realize that some were more privileged than others.

The response to my need to travel to New York and return to Ohio in one day was met with approval and a very gracious expression of thanks for my going out of the way to accommodate the search committee's schedule. I was beginning to feel very positive about this position. If they were willing to pay this kind of money to transport me to the interview, the results of the interview with the search firm must have been quite positive. I quickly organized myself and my work, and left Ohio early the next morning for the interview.

I arrived in New York City just in time to stop by my apartment, freshen up, and change clothes. I wanted to make a good impression. I was somewhat nervous but as usual I had plenty of nerve in one hand and enough excitement in the other over the possibility of having a new assignment that I was ready to go.

The chair of the board was Hugh Downs, the former television personality. The chair of the search committee met me at the door of the meeting room. The committee had chosen a somewhat obscure meeting place, but I could understand that. They certainly didn't want to hold the interview at the organization's headquarters. Once I was introduced to the group members, I felt quite comfortable. I had once again reviewed the material that was sent to me, as well as information I had retrieved. None of the questions were difficult or unfamiliar. My previous positions had prepared me for almost everything the members of the committee asked. It was a pleasant couple of hours.

Interestingly enough, there was one question that I still remember. This question came from one of the members of the committee who later became one of the least supportive board members. She asked me what I would do if I felt I could no longer contribute to the position I had accepted. This was a question I had no problem answering because I had been thinking thoughts along this line regarding my position with the YWCA. I had provided YWCA leadership for approximately nine years. When I accepted their position I told the board I would stay as long as I felt I had made significant progress in adding my brick to the organization's foundation. And I was currently feeling it was time for me to move on.

My answer to this question in the UNICEF interview was the same. We concluded our round of questions. I was excused. The following day the staff member of the search firm called. He had a question. The committee wanted to know if all the information reported about me when I was appointed to the Board of Education was correct. I knew immediately what he was trying to find out. Because I received my bachelor's degree later than most, I appeared to be ten years older than most. If that was true then I was somewhere in my early sixties. From the remaining information I appeared to be in my early fifties. At the time I looked like the latter. I knew what they were trying to discover but he knew and so did I that if he even mentioned age, I would never have to work again. Questioning my age was legally not appropriate.

Shortly after we hung up I received another call in which I was offered the position. I could now resign from the YWCA and start my new position as president and chief executive officer of the National UNICEF.

This all took place in late spring of 1993. My official starting date was in September. However, as soon as the appointment was announced, calls for earlier appointments and appearances began to trickle in.

I had no regrets about resigning from the YWCA. As I mentioned earlier, it was time for me to move on. The nine years spent with the association had allowed me to give my best to help strengthen and move the association forward. Providing leadership in a changing world was becoming more than just a challenge. Trying to justify the female-only requirements of the YWCA was demanding legal justifications. Questions about sexual relationships between and among women were beginning to surface. Even though the imperative of the association was to "eliminate racism," at times trying to implement that was just as difficult internally as it was externally. So when I accepted two dozen yellow roses in a glass vase from the board as their thanks for my nine years of dedication and work, I said thank-you. I had no regrets.

There is no way I could think of UNICEF without recalling how important Audrey Hepburn has been to this organization. Audrey died a few years before my appointment, and almost everyone who congratulated me on my position mentioned how dedicated she had been to UNICEF's mission. I conjured up pictures of her holding a child, along with scenes from her movies. At that time I never dreamed I would learn more about her through her son and her most recent companion. I did have the privilege of visiting her gravesite in Sweden and visiting her lovely home. A bottle of wine made from her vineyard still adorns a table in my sitting room. What an introduction to my new responsibility.

Like any new position, there were lots of people, places, and routines I needed to become familiar with as soon as possible. The national office was close enough to my apartment that I could walk to work. And the office was a few blocks from the United Nations Plaza and UNICEF's world headquarters. The national office was spacious. There were over one hundred staff members. There was also a much smaller office in Washington, DC. One of my first trips outside New York was to meet with the staff in Washington. The federal government contributed over one million dollars to the total World UNICEF budget. It was our responsibility to lobby, a word I do not like to use. Instead I will say we had to continue to work with Congress to ensure the passage of legislation necessary to support this contribution. Once I met the staff in DC I knew our support system was in good hands. During my tenure with UNICEF we were able to move the staff into more suitable offices in a more impressive building.

Almost immediately I made an appointment with the general secretary of UNICEF, Mr. James Grant. I was told he would meet with me for two or three minutes. My staff was shocked that my first meeting with Mr. Grant lasted over an hour. Mr. Grant's wife had been an active member of the national board of the YWCA, and he was impressed that I had served over nine years as their national executive. We talked about issues, laughed about challenges, and enjoyed the time together. This was a crucial meeting for me. It helped set the tone for working with World UNICEF. I had no refusals for future appointments with him. Unfortunately, Mr. Grant had cancer and died midway during my appointment. This was a great disappointment. His replacement never supported my efforts. I will not say much about her administration, but I credit her with contributing to my resignation.

Becoming acquainted with the United Nations was important and also exciting. I was informed during my interview that I would be expected to speak before various committees within the UN when necessary. I looked forward to opportunities to speak to groups and was eager to become involved. The UNICEF building seems overwhelming but quite attractive. The flags of the member countries on the building's exterior signal a welcome that is all-encompassing. The interior tells many stories of the UN's work. It is all very impressive. One cannot overlook the beautiful gowns and robes of the visiting members as well as of the staff. I considered it an honor to become part of the United Nations through my involvement with UNICEF. (Throughout this and the following chapter I use USC and UNICEF interchangeably. USC is the United States Committee subdivision of World UNICEF.)

Like most jobs, there are certain items that need the attention of the person in charge. I met individually with each board member. It didn't take individual meetings with the board members to realize I had some work to do. This board was anything but diverse. Diversity did become an issue, and required some delicate work. I was able to add some diversity by identifying individuals whose credentials could not be questioned.

Hugh Downs was as gracious as he appeared on television when he was part of 20/20. I soon learned that he expected to conduct the board meetings along the same lines as scheduling a television show. I was able to learn how to script his participation, including the opening greetings. He read everything and seldom spoke extemporaneously. I had to keep him and the board on time. He checked with me constantly to make sure everything was going as scheduled. I rather enjoyed this. We got off to a great start. Unfortunately as time passed we did not work as harmoniously as I had hoped. I will discuss the reasons for this later in the chapter.

The major responsibility of the individual countries that compose World UNICEF is to raise funds to support its work. Having recently been involved with the New York Board of Education, whose budget at in the early nineties was approximately nine billion dollars, I was shocked to discover that UNICEF had a yearly budget of only around one billion. I could not believe the work this organization does for the children of the world depended on such a small budget. The Board of Education's budget served the needs of about one million children.

My responsibility became even clearer when I discovered there were approximately forty countries supporting the work of UNICEF. It also made me realize how important it was for me to get to know the people providing leadership for the organizations in these countries. This was an interesting part of my responsibilities. Some countries didn't need to raise funds because their governments paid their total contribution to UNICEF. The size of the country determined how and how much they could contribute. The United States had the largest financial responsibility. The majority of the countries that had to raise funds did it through the sale of greeting cards.

The sale of greeting cards demanded my immediate attention. I had worked through the screen of diversity all of my life and in all of my positions. It never occurred to me how important multiculturalism was in selling greeting cards. Most countries sold large numbers of cards. However, it was somewhat easier for other countries to sell cards because their countries, at that time, were homogeneous. That meant the cards they sold were intended for one population. Germany could sell many cards designed for Germans. We had to have a multitude of different types of cards because of our diverse populations. In fact, in New York City alone we had to have cards that fit many cultures. Brooklyn, for example, had a population that spoke over seventy languages. The cards we needed to sell in Manhattan had to be different for the different sections of the city. A card that was appropriate for Midtown held little appeal for Harlem. Card design and selection was the work of several staff members. The greeting card staff of the national office worked very closely with that of the world office.

Having worked in large organizations before, I knew I needed to spend time with the board early on. Meeting the board members was just a beginning. However, as I noted earlier, I immediately recognized the need to identify individuals who could add diversity to the board. I was not interested in diversity for diversity's sake, but in individuals who could provide the expertise needed.

For example, UNICEF included work with Africans who had various diseases that caused river blindness. I had recently met an African American ophthalmologist who was interested in the work of the organization. It was not easy working with the board nominating committee to have them accept Dr. Samuel Guillory, who to my knowledge was not only the first ophthalmologist, but also the first male African American board member. I had lived in New York for twenty years and had met some very special people. I was successful in having Mayor David Dinkins join the board along, with Toni Fay and several representatives of other ethnic groups.

I soon realized there was serious work to be done with the United States Committee for UNICEF. It was not just about the greeting cards or the lack of diversity within the board. There was so much dissension within the organization including board members, staff, and even in some volunteer groups. While it may have looked as though I brought a bag of problems into this arena, I served more as a catalyst for preexisting problems.

I was the first woman to serve in my position, although not the first African American. I discovered there had been a great deal of racial discontent during the administration of a former executive director who was African American. The very nature of UNICEF requires a multicultural perspective. The more I worked with the board, and particularly the staff, the more discontent became obvious. Many groups and individuals throughout the organization strongly resisted change. Before my first year was out I decided I needed professional assistance.

At the YWCA I had discovered a wonderful young woman named Alceste Pappas who ventured out on her own after working for years with one of the largest consulting firms in the country, KPMG Peat Marwick. I had engaged her services as an alliance with Peat Marwick to help reorganize the YWCA. Although it had needed new thinking and reorganizing, the YWCA was nothing like what I felt was needed for the USC. I contacted Ms. Pappas to help us redesign UNICEF. We referred to the process as Project Redesign in the YWCA; it became Project Redesign in the USC.

By December 1994, the USC had gone through an extensive study that left no stone unturned. Although much needed, it was not an easy undertaking. It would take another book to fully disclose the process and results.

The project was designed to take sixty months, and would lead to a totally new and different USC. It required intense work with the board and staff members. During the next two years I received wonderful support from some board members and staff. Eddy Bayardelle, the CEO, and Helen Corrado, my secretary, were two of my senior staff who witnessed situations too tense for me to shed tears over. Yet in spite of all that was occurring, I enjoyed implementing the organization's mission.

The US Committee for UNICEF works for the survival, protection, and development of all children worldwide. It does this through education, advocacy, and fund-raising. The nature of the organization requires a great deal of international involvement.

Approximately 50 percent of my time required traveling abroad, which delighted me because I always enjoyed traveling. I still give my mother credit for contributing to my fondness for exploring other cultures. The incident with the coffee visits me often when I pack for a trip. She had told me one of the benefits of travel was exploring the tastes, sounds, and lifestyles of others, so why take your own coffee?

My first traveling assignment was to visit the projects we funded or were interested in supporting in South Africa and Mozambique. I was eager to go. I had visited South Africa when I was working with the YWCA. However, the focus of this visit was entirely different. I invited two of my assistants to accompany me. None of the staff in the seventy-five USC chapters had ever traveled to one of our sites. The director of the Boston chapter expressed his desire to join us, so the four of us left for South Africa.

Our first stop was Johannesburg. I experienced a city different from the one I had visited a few years before. The transformation that had taken place after the release of Nelson Mandela from prison was amazing. It looked like many of the downtown areas in today's cities in the United States. On my first visit there had been a lovely two-level shopping area either near or attached to a first-class hotel. The area now lacked upkeep, but the hotel seemed in good condition. On my earlier trip, we had stayed at a hotel just outside of Johannesburg—we did not trust our welcome at the five-star hotels. Five-star hotels in this part of South Africa were few but not expensive. However, I was interested in what had happened to the racial restrictions since Mandela had been released and the apartheid ended.

Once again with my nerve in one hand and my title in the other, I made reservations to stay at a lovely five-star hotel. From my experience, the lobby of a hotel usually represents the style and decor of the sleeping rooms. When I arrived, there was not one indication that I was a black woman. I was received almost more graciously than hotels in the United States. Comfortable with my reception, I picked up the phone in my room and ordered a massage. Almost anyone who knows me will not find this a strange request. It was a wonderful experience. I found it somewhat difficult to understand how such change could take place after so many years of hatred and exclusion. But there was definitely a change. As a girl who grew up in a small Midwestern town, I was witness to a major change in the world.

I looked forward to visiting Soweto again. The changes that occurred after apartheid were felt rather than witnessed. People appeared more relaxed as we moved through the streets. Some of this may have been because our vehicle had UNICEF on the sides and almost everyone the world over, except in our country, is aware of what those six letters imply. We attended a large celebration in the stadium. I always thought the University of Michigan football games were colorful and exciting, but this group of excited Africans was unbelievably colorful and loud.

We visited schools and spoke with children when possible. The neighborhoods were mixed by skin color and types of housing. The coloreds who were light-skinned lived in one section. The darker-skinned individuals lived together in still another area, but adjacent to those of Asian descent. More modern, newer homes were mixed in areas with living quarters more like shacks.

We were invited into several of the older, smaller homes, which were generally one large room with a cooking area in a corner. Clothes were hanging inside, but all appeared to be well organized. On our way out of Soweto we saw Nelson Mandela's home. I had seen it on my first visit, and enjoyed seeing it again. At that time there was gossip about the Mandelas not getting along. Although it was a short visit, we were able to observe and record what we needed.

We arrived in Mozambique by plane, a four-engine craft. We landed just outside the capital city of Maputo, were met by some of the UNICEF staff, and were taken to our hotel. We drove up in front of a large white attractive building that was our hotel. We could not have asked for any place to stay that would have been more wonderful. It was located on a small body of water, which added to its charm. Part of our shock with the hotel was the fact we were expecting to visit a country that was very poor. After the first day of our arrival we saw the real city. The UNICEF representative, Mr. Shob Jhie, and his team briefed us and we visited a children's health center as well as other projects sponsored by the United States and the Netherlands.

Mozambique was occupied by the Portuguese for several centuries.

After considerable attempts to gain freedom, the country finally won its independence in 1975. However, there had been a great deal of internal unrest since then. We were told that when the Portuguese finally gave up the occupation, they were so evil they poured cement in the pipes of a large hotel under construction so the building could never be used and provide much-needed income from tourism.

One day the three of us visited the northern part of this interesting country. We went by plane because of poor roads. None of our delegation was really comfortable with this arrangement, but we clung to the floor of the plane and dared one another to look out the window when we could. We needed to land to visit a province outside of Maputo. The pilot had to swoop down close to where we wanted to land in order to clear it of children and animals. When he finally felt no one would be in danger, he landed. What a welcome we received. Not many people visited this area, especially in the manner in which we did.

This was an exciting visit. We joined some of the children while they were working in the fields tending the crop. We visited the *maternidade*, a maternity clinic, following the birth of one of the first babies to be born in a facility and not in the field. The staff was eager to show us how they weighed the progress of the babies, which clearly was not the kind of scale we were used to. It was more like how meat is weighed. We stayed overnight. Our hotel for the evening was a very old building. My room had a small bed with clean bedding but little else, only a bent tin cup on the sink. I thought of my friends who assumed I traveled first-class for UNICEF; this would counteract that kind of thinking. I had an extra glass of the local wine so I could fall asleep quickly. The day had been an exhausting one. My work was not about luxury, it was about helping. And we did.

Before we prepared to leave Mozambique, those in charge of our visit made sure we met as many of the leaders in the country as possible. We met the governor of the province we visited, the minister of education and health, and Lady Graça Machel, head of international affairs in Parliament who later became Mrs. Nelson Mandela. I was also introduced to the head of state, President Joaquim Alberto Chissanó. What a thrilling first international experience with the USC. I learned so much on first trip, and gained experience that gave me an immense enthusiasm for my work with UNICEF.

One of the many interesting aspects of working with UNICEF was meeting celebrities associated with it. Through their involvement we gained visibility that greatly helped our fund-raising. One of the first individuals I had the pleasure of meeting was Harry Belafonte. Harry and his wife had a long and involved relationship with UNICEF. Shortly after our meeting, Harry invited me lunch. I was honored and excited. He is a most amazing person. He suggested we meet for lunch at the Water Club, one of my favorite restaurants, right on the water in Manhattan.

I arrived at the club before he did. While waiting, the maître d' approached me and said, "Mr. Belafonte called to say he will be a few minutes late." Once he arrived with all of his flair, everyone knew him. Until then, I was just another customer. After that day, whenever I arrived or called to make a reservation, the staff knew who I was.

Harry and I had traveled to London together to discuss possible events and plans with World UNICEF. Because of the relationship I was developing with Harry, I felt comfortable asking him to make a trip to Africa for us. He didn't hesitate. His only request was that his wife travel with him. (Ordinarily as the CEO, I would have made this trip. However, I was just recovering from breast cancer surgery and could not travel.) Of course that was no problem. His wife had long been involved in the work of the organization. The results of that trip to Africa netted us TV interviews, newspaper articles, and more. Our financial gain was great. We at UNICEF needed both visibility and funds.

Implementing the mission of UNICEF came about as the result of visiting some of the countries on our proposed list of core countries. These countries had already received UNICEF funding or were being considered for support. One of the countries selected for support in 1995 was the small country of Haiti, which needed much. We felt in some small way we might help improve its educational system. Whenever possible, we invite a celebrity to accompany us when we visit the country. On our trip to Haiti, Julia Roberts joined us.

Eddy Bayardelle, Nancy Sharp, and I accompanied Julia Roberts and her agent, Nancy Seltzer, on a five-day visit to Haiti. Ms. Roberts attracted an enormous amount of press coverage and exposure, which helped us advocate on behalf of the children in Haiti and also raise funds. While there our delegation enjoyed two audiences with President Aristide. During the first meeting with him, I announced the board's decision to provide three years of funding for UNICEF-assisted education projects in Haiti. I think the media was more interested in the pillowcase Julia had made, slept on, and presented to him. I did receive a grateful appreciation response from their governing body later the next day.

Traveling with a celebrity has its ups and downs. I found it difficult to strike up any real sense of conversation with Julia on the plane or in Haiti. Part of my responsibility, when traveling with a celebrity, is to include myself in as many photos with the celebrity and children as possible. It was most difficult for me to do this with Julia. I told my staff it was almost as though she didn't want to have any photos taken with me. On the evening prior to meeting with the president, I arranged a meeting with my staff, Julia, and her agent. There were several protocol issues to discuss. Ms. Roberts said she didn't need this meeting. I had to insist that she attend. I remember saying something to the effect that even President Clinton needs a briefing before he sets foot in another country. I discussed the fact that those involved in the meeting were not to wear shorts in spite of the very warm weather. We were lucky. Ms. Roberts did have one dress in her suitcase. She did not appear to be a happy camper.

Thanks to her visibility and popular appeal as one of the most well-known actresses in the world, word of UNICEF's work in Haiti spread through every major wire service, most of the top circulation newspapers, and many of the most widely viewed television programs. In all, the trip generated 145 television segments nationwide, including her television appearances on the *Oprah Winfrey Show* and on CBS's *This Morning*. In addition, there was a good deal of coverage in major magazines, including the premiere issue of the new political magazine *George*, which was published by John F. Kennedy Jr., and the *Ladies Home Journal*. The fund-raising from this effort included a $25,000 corporate contribution from Warner Brothers.

Julia's interest in UNICEF was precipitated by a long visit she had aboard an airplane with Audrey Hepburn shortly before her death, during which Audrey spoke passionately about her work with us. Inspired by this conversation, Julia contacted us.

For my trip to Vietnam, singer Judy Collins, a recently appointed USC representative, and her companion, Louis Nelson, led the delegation. Dr.

Westina Matthews, a vice president of Merrill Lynch, Robert Brennan of UNICEF, and Denver Collins, a photographer and Judy Collins's brother, joined us. This was an extraordinary opportunity for us to see the country, observe the kind of work UNICEF was doing there, and become familiar with the projects USC supports. Visiting the schools and going into the homes of the women we were helping, even seeing the pigs and smelling the chickens, helped us better understand the importance and necessity of what we were accomplishing,

Judy Collins is a very gracious person who is deeply committed to the work of UNICEF. Louis Nelson, a distinguished designer, helped us open new channels of fund-raising. We appreciated the support that came from Merrill Lynch.

Following the visit to Vietnam, I left the group in Ho Chi Minh City to meet Nancy Sharp in Beijing. We had planned to meet at the luggage area in the airport there, and we actually found each other at the exact time and place we had agreed to. When we saw each other we laughed and gave each other a big hug. It was always a pleasure working with Nancy. She had worked almost a year with the office of Gertrude Mongella, secretary-general for the Tenth Conference on Women, to ensure USC involvement.

I had attended the Conference for Women ten years earlier in Nairobi, Kenya, and was gratified to see so many women leaders on the world scene. They included the president of Iceland, the only female vice president on the continent of Africa—who was from Uganda, one of our Core Countries—the prime minister of Pakistan, and a host of others.

This official nongovernmental organization (NGO) conference was thirty miles from Beijing. Nancy and I spent a day at the general conference, which gave us a flavor for some of the issues being discussed. The NGO conference had set aside one day to focus on female children. This was the first time the World Conference on Women included a special emphasis on the plight of the female child. I was invited to make a presentation and delivered a speech entitled "The Way Forward: Commitments for Action."

I had the distinction of representing all the national committees for UNICEF. I remember this experience as a "grand" one. I met so many new and interesting people involved in the same work we were, focusing on children and women. We also ran into some American colleagues at a restaurant one evening. I was excited to see Jo Urehara and Alpha Alexander, who had both worked with me at the YWCA. The trip to China also gave us an opportunity to spend some US dollars. I bought a lovely beige embroidered cashmere stole that I enjoyed wearing for years.

At this time in my career with UNICEF, I was trying to develop a relationship with the China Business Council. During my stay in Beijing I met a member of the Ministry of Foreign Trade. I wanted to see the work that Johnson & Johnson was doing in Shanghai. Under the guidance of a member of the UNICEF Beijing office, we traveled to Shanghai, where Johnson & Johnson and the Shanghai Welfare Institute were our hosts. We visited the Baby-Friendly Hospital initiated by Johnson & Johnson at the International Peace Hospital. I took great pride in the work sponsored by one of our board members and his company. We also visited schools and clinics in Shanghai, and observed many projects funded by UNICEF.

A footnote to Shanghai: When I had visited Shanghai with the YWCA, I stayed at a Sheraton Hotel. It was modest but nice. I wanted to visit it while there this time but couldn't find it. I asked one of the staff of the extremely large Sheraton where we were staying, and was told that the hotel I was looking for was the front entrance and lobby of the hotel I was staying in. It was almost unbelievable how in a few short years the city had transformed itself. It looked like New York City.

My first trip to China had been in 1982. This trip, in 1995, was my fourth trip there. In thirteen years the major cities I visited became comparable to any of our large cities in the United States. In 1982, crowds of young people would gather around when you spoke English to purchase something. In 1995, almost everyone we met in Beijing and Shanghai spoke fluent English.

As I recall, my first trip was with a small group from New York. I was divorced and had decided to take a trip by myself to see if I could do it. My second trip was with a group of educators from the American Association of Teacher Education (AATE). The third trip was with the YWCA and was led by my dear friend Audrey Lam, who died of cancer in 2010. The fourth and possibly not the last trip to China was with UNICEF. I say possibly not the last because I had never thought I'd travel to China once, let alone four times. I am writing this shortly after my eightieth birthday. Who knows what is in my future.

In 1995, Eddy Bayardelle and I had attended one of the joint meetings of the UNICEF National Committees held in Tokyo. By this time I knew the names and countries of some of our colleagues. I was feeling rooted in the international aspects of my work. I remember having a brief conversation with Graça Machel, whom I had met the previous year in Mozambique. (This was before she married Nelson Mandela.) I also met the representative from Myanmar, formerly known as Burma. He invited me to visit his country.

The UNICEF staff found family living quarters for us in Myanmar. We didn't have time to take full advantage of staying with families because of our schedule, but it was a nice change and added value to the experience. We visited health centers, schools, and water projects. We also met with members of the NGO community. I was impressed with the partnerships that UNICEF had established, given the challenging political and human rights circumstances in this country.

When we learned about actress Jane Curtin's interest in UNICEF, we invited her to join us on a visit to El Salvador. We arrived at our hotel just prior to an affair that was taking place in the hotel. As I watched a parade of elegantly dressed couples enter the hotel, I couldn't believe we were in a country that needed our help. I soon learned that El Salvador was no different from a number of countries. The wealthy are there and so are the poor.

The following morning we started on our journey. We traveled in a Jeep. I was glad I had my jeans and comfortable athletic shoes. I will never forget the ride. We bounced up and down and all around. I held on to my seat and gasped with the rest of the passengers. We rode deep into the countryside to see the schools; many had been recently erected with the help of UNICEF. We interacted with the teachers and the children. Jane Curtin was her usual charming self. The children loved her. The USC attorney had also joined us. He was amazed at what he saw. This was his first trip sponsored by UNICEF. I often remind people when we talk about travel experiences that when you travel with UNICEF you see the real world. What we are allowed to witness is totally unlike a trip most people take. There is much behind the scenes. During that excursion I remember taking time out and to have our lunch under a group of trees.

All I could think about while in El Salvador was how we could help. Once again I was grateful to a celebrity for giving us the support we needed. The media coverage always helps our visibility and our fund-raising.

The next time I went to Africa, it was to assess the need for UNICEF's assistance with river blindness. Because of board member Dr. Guillory's expertise in this area, we invited him to join us. We had already assisted programs in Ghana and had been asked to consider the educational needs in Cameroon, so we added a stop there. Once in Africa, it made sense to cover as much territory as possible. The results of this excursion would help us solidify our funding for the coming year.

In addition to Dr. Guillory, Dean Richard English from the School of Social Work at Howard University joined us at his institution's expense. He wanted to make student exchange contacts while there. Fortunately, there were two teenage women who wanted to join our group, and whose parents were willing to cover their expenses. I felt this was a great opportunity to give these young women the experience for their own development and to help us organize a youth group for USC. Kyle Godfrey-Fraebel was the first to volunteer. She was the daughter of Neale Godfrey, a board member and friend. Kyle had traveled throughout the world with her mother and brother so I knew I wouldn't need to hold her hand. Ashley Smith also volunteered to come. She too was the daughter of a board member.

Our first stop was very meaningful. The tribe of Africans afflicted with river blindness was aware of our visit, and greeted us warmly. They knew there was a doctor traveling with our group and eagerly gathered around him. It was amazing to see Dr. Guillory examine several men and women. I was unaware that he had medicine with him, and after a few minutes he was treating people. We were there long enough to assess what was needed, and reluctantly moved on to our next stop.

Wherever we stopped, we were met by UNICEF staff. Our visits were well planned. We traveled to and from sites that were either receiving or needed assistance. Thanks to UNICEF director Danielle Fignole Benjamin, in Cameroon we were able to visit several sites. Danielle was Haitian and had lived in the United States. She had personality plus.

The visit that impressed me most was a women's banking group. The women were lent a small sum of money ($50) to set up a for-profit business. They kept a notebook of their transactions, and most were able to repay the loan so others could participate. Some of the women sold fish on the road side. Others baked bread. It was wonderful to hear their reports and to hear them sing a familiar hymn after they prayed and ended their weekly meeting.

We visited other equally encouraging sites. I spoke to a large group of children. They understood English and responded warmly to me. I always wore a UNICEF shirt to identify myself. We also distributed small gifts whenever we could. We had such a pleasant time it was difficult to leave. However, we were looking forward to visiting Ghana.

Our reception in Ghana was wonderful. The UNICEF staff received amazing support from the Ghanaians to prepare for our visit. We met many officials in Accra. The president's wife had a school for upper-class Ghanaian children. She spent an entire day giving us a tour of her facility and the schools that needed support. I learned much from this visit.

At one point I saw truckloads of lumber being shipped to Europe. Of course this was profitable for the Ghanaians for the moment, but there were no plans to replace the forest for the future. I had the feeling that the leaders in some of the formerly occupied countries wanted to emulate the style of living they had observed from their oppressors. They wanted big fancy cars and houses, but in some cases it seemed they had not given much thought to the future of their countries.

I have a dear friend, Jacque Owens Briggs, who lived in Accra. Jacque was with the State Department and stationed in Ghana. During my stay there I was her houseguest along with Dr. English, whom she also knew.

I was also able to visit the Quashis, the family I met during my first trip to Ghana in the early seventies. Our friendship has lasted over the years. The memories of these friendships remind me of how fortunate I am to have met such wonderful people throughout the world.

We left Ghana for South Africa. We were told it might be possible to meet Nelson Mandela. I had met Nelson Mandela and visited him in his office when I was in South Africa for the YWCA in 1993. I thought it would be wonderful for Kyle and Ashley if they could meet him and give him a gift. We worked this out with the UNICEF staff and it happened. I'm sure Kyle and Ashley will never forget that experience.

My assignment to Uganda was a separate trip from the one just described. As I listen to the news during the writing of this chapter I am reminded of how empty I felt after the trip to Kampala, the capital of Uganda. The current situation appears to be more disastrous than it was in the nineties. My visit was about ten years after the terrible reign of Idi Amin. The country was in great need. Not only was Uganda trying to recoup some of the losses as a result of the internal strife, but AIDS was rampant throughout the country.

I visited homes, or rather huts that were called homes. I spent a great deal of time in the schools. I wanted to cry when I saw the outdated and inappropriate textbooks the teachers and children used. The schools I visited had prepared a program for us. Each song, poem, or skit by the children was about the AIDS epidemic and how it had affected their lives. The children had lost parents and older siblings.

After the program, the teachers asked if they could speak with me. This happened on two occasions. As we sat under the trees I tried desperately to answer their questions. Every teacher wanted to know what they could do in this terrible situation. I was told that many of the families were led by the oldest child, some as young as seven or eight. Many girls were still stunned by the sexual abuse of the soldiers during the war. I searched for the right responses. There was nothing I could suggest. As I looked at their faces I could see some relief from just talking to someone who would listen. I seldom come away as distraught as I did on my trip to Kampala and the surrounding villages. The need was so great. All I could do was pool what we could contribute from the USC with other countries who were interested and pray it would help.

Ethiopia was the last of the core countries approved for funding during 1995–98. I was very interested in visiting this country. I had helped my first assistant, a very capable young woman, receive a promotion as a UNICEF staff member in Ethiopia, and she helped organize our experience there. When I remember Ethiopia I think of children, women, and water. Not that I don't think of these things during my other visits, but Ethiopia was different. The capital as I recall was not as modern as South Africa.

For some reason I felt a close kinship with the people I met. Perhaps it was the large Hilton hotel that reminded me of the United States. I remember the lovely shops in the hotel lobby, mostly jewelry. Ethiopian 18-carat gold was exquisite.

Early in our visit we were introduced to a woman who had built and developed a large orphanage in the city. She told us that the got its start one day when someone left a child on her doorstep. She accepted care for this child and soon after found the need to care for more children. She left her husband and began step by step and brick by brick to develop a most impressive facility. She had sleeping rooms, a dining room, a kitchen, and showers. She also added everything to make this orphanage completely independent from the city. She grew her own vegetables and built a huge laundry, sewing room, classrooms, and more. I was so impressed. We earmarked our support for this orphanage.

One woman sought me out and wanted me to visit a center she and others had organized to eliminate female circumcision. I listened to their stories and the plans they were working on to carry out their goal. They invited me to watch a video they had developed to show interested individuals how the process is done. I knew what circumcision was but had no idea until I saw this video how inhumane and horrible the process is. I could not watch the entire video and nearly fainted as I left the room while an old lady in the video took a razor-type knife to a two- or -three-year-old female child. Of course we focused our efforts on eliminating that terrible process in Ethiopia wherever we found it. Unfortunately it was quite prevalent.

I was also introduced to a hospital organized by a white married couple, both doctors, to help women going through a terrible result from unsupervised pregnancy. The baby, when born dead, goes through the woman's body leaving a hole from her vagina and through her rectum. The process is called a fistula.

The hospital needed a water system. When they heard UNICEF was in the area, close enough for me to visit, I was approached to take a tour. The husband had died but the wife remained, assisted by young dedicated doctors. These doctors received little pay for their work but chose to be there to assist. When the doctor walked me through the small facility, there were approximately twenty young women and beds. The entire facility, including the bedding, was immaculate. As we walked past the beds, the young women called this doctor's name and extended their hands as if worshiping her. After I learned why they were there I could better understand their reaction.

The doctor was scheduled to interview a young woman for admission to the hospital. She suggested I join her for the interview. The young woman had become pregnant at the age of fourteen. She lived in the upper part of the country, in the wilderness where there were no doctors. Small groups or tribes gather together and form small camp-type communities far from larger communities. When a baby is born this way the infant is allowed to go right through the woman's body, leaving a hole where her vagina and rectum were. The women cannot hold their elimination and are shunned because of the smell and waste. If they are lucky enough to have someone wrap them in a blanket and put them in the back of a bus, they can be dropped off at the hospital.

This young woman we were about to see had arrived with her body tied across a horse. As I listened to the doctor talk to her about her care and stay in the hospital, she picked up a pencil and a blank sheet of paper. She took the pencil and made a hole in the center of the sheet of paper. The doctor said to her, "This is what has happened to your body. We are going to put it together for you." As she said this she took her fingers and gently closed the hole in the paper. Then she leaned over and picked up a beautiful piece of cloth and she continued with "We will make you a new dress." The young woman's face lit up. We all smiled as we left the office.

I joined the doctor for tea in her lovely home, adorned inside and out with beautiful plants and flowers. I had no idea where I was at that moment in time. The experience had taken me far away to a place where there were people who cared enough to help others who were in great need. Of course the hospital received the funding of $15,000 for a new water system.

The following day we were taken, once again by a four-engine plane, to the tip of the country. We wanted to see the child-care center, partially supported by UNICEF, and the ways of the Ethiopians living in that part of the country. The child-care center was quite sparse, consisting mainly of a few bottles of baby supplement on sparsely filled shelves, a table and a few chairs. The focus of the center's two rooms was the scales used to weigh the babies. The staff was as sparse as the facility—no doctors, two or three minimally trained nurse assistants. As in South Africa, babies were weighed in the same manner as grain or chunks of meat. The mothers waited patiently in a long line for their turn at the weigh-in station. I couldn't help compare this situation to my visits to our pediatrician when our three children were babies.

After visiting the child-care center, we went to a lake developed by the men and women in the community. What a marvel! Water was almost like gold in this part of the country. In this community there was one major water source other than the lake. This "waterhole" was located in the center of the main part of the town. The women and girls were responsible for carrying the water from this source to wherever they lived. For some, carrying large containers of water on their heads meant a trip every day from this water source to their homes. The containers were as large as a clothes basket we use for carrying laundry. Perhaps the shape was more oval than round. I tried to lift one of these empty vessels and could not get it up to my waist. How these women, young and old, could carry water in this manner for miles was almost unbelievable. If necessary, the young girls were taken from schools to help transport the water supply. The men and young boys mainly took care of tending the crops the villages depended on.

In 1996 I was invited through the U.S. Department of International Education to travel to Minsk, the capital of Belarus. I was asked to speak at the Ninth International Congress for School Effectiveness and Improvement. My address was entitled "The Impact of Societal Change on Curriculum Development." JoAnn, my oldest daughter, traveled with me. Because of the uncertainty resulting from the recent portioning of the Soviet Union, JoAnn suggested that we travel with a picnic basket. I am so glad we did because if it had not been for the crackers, peanut butter, sardines, and wine, I'm not sure we would have made it. I did lose a few pounds. The restaurants were few; the meals in the hotel were not good. Even the coffee was not to my liking. It was just colored water, as was the juice. Once we found a restaurant that served spaghetti and salad, we thought we were in heaven. We ate there several times in spite of the cost: one hundred U.S. dollars is a lot for spaghetti and salad, especially in 1996. In addition to being hungry most of the time, we were very cold. Actually I cannot remember being that cold at any other time in my life. When it snowed it was like a heavy rain. We had to walk backward to go forward. I seldom eat spaghetti, but today whenever I eat linguine with a spaghetti sauce I remember how much I enjoyed the spaghetti in Belarus.

While there I had a free day and asked to see a school. Because it was a Saturday we visited a children's hospital that treated children who had been victims of the Chernobyl disaster. It was not a pleasant sight to see these children who had cancer as a result of having lived in the province where this disaster had occurred. We were told that it had not only affected the children but had disrupted families, and many women were left caring for these sick children. I asked what UNICEF could do to help. The director of the unit told me they needed vitamins. She said, "Most of the patients are too sick to die."

When I returned I learned that World UNICEF had not approved sending vitamins to any country. However when I told them that Johnson & Johnson had responded to our request for vitamins, World UNICEF gave us permission to send the three hundred cases of the needed vitamins to Belarus. What a wonderful feeling it is when a cry for help is heard. This time the cry from the children of Chernobyl was heard by UNICEF and Johnson & Johnson.

Our international trips took a great deal of time but were essential to our work. Monitoring projects and attending professional meetings were part of my responsibilities. I am not complaining at all. I enjoyed every part of it. And the international experiences not only helped me in my work, they helped me grow as an individual. In addition to these experiences, there was a great deal to do on the home front.

When many people think of UNICEF in the United States, they also think of Trick or Treat for UNICEF. I had expanded this event from one day, Halloween, to the entire month of October. This month was a lot of fun, especially when we had a brief morning appearance on NBC with several children from schools in Washington, DC, all dressed in costumes. In 1995, actress Meg Ryan was the chair for that month. Her appearance with children from schools in New York and at the United Nations for a luncheon program was most successful. National UNICEF Month received wonderful visibility in the media, including coverage in *People*, *Time*, and *Parent Magazine*, as well as a front-page story in the *Wall Street Journal*.

I was having such a wonderful time with the events we had planned for the Fiftieth Anniversary of UNC that I didn't have time to deal with the negative things that were happening. One of the major events was the launch of Olympic Aid-Atlanta, a partnership between the U.S. Committee and the Atlanta Committee for the Olympic Games (ACOG) to help eighteen million children caught in civil conflicts in fourteen target countries.

The Olympic Aid Team for Children, a core group of top athletes representing a variety of sports, was launched to help raise visibility and funds for the program. The team included Johann Olav Koss, speed-skating gold medalist and UNICEF representative for sports, Michael Jordan, Edwin Moses, Bonnie Blair, Hakeem Olajuwon, and Summer Sanders. Eddy Bayardelle, my COO, worked very hard at making all of this come together. I give thanks to Andrew Young for his help in putting the necessary glue on this project.

As I write about this project I am reminded of something that happened

My first trip for UNICEF in 1993 to Mozambique. Staff members and I visited a school with a farm. During this trip I visited with several of the young students.

during our work on Olympic Aid. Andy Young's wife had died before this occurred. As I mentioned earlier, Andy was a strong supporter of USC. My staff, especially Nancy, decided to play cupid. Nancy and some of the other staff members thought I might make a good companion for Andy. To this day I am not sure how they arranged for me to have lunch with him in Atlanta. They thought this might be the beginning of more than just a USC friendship. Well, we had lunch together in a lovely restaurant in Atlanta, complete with a tour of the sites for various sports activities. I'm not sure if he had any idea why my staff insisted on this meeting. We had a very pleasant time, and we even went to the headquarters of the *Atlanta Constitution* for an interview and to meet some important individuals. It wasn't long after our lunch together that I learned of his plans to marry one of his wife's friends. We continued to stay in touch when we were in DC, but plans for what my staff had hoped for were shattered. And maybe some of mine too. Andrew Young is a very fine person.

In February 1996 we held a fiftieth-anniversary salute to UNICEF at the Warner Theatre in Washington, DC. President and Mrs. Clinton served as honorary chairs of the event. The program was a show entitled Children First. I was thrilled because it featured Sir Peter Ustinov, Phylicia Rashad, and Rory of the Learning Channel, with a special video and musical tribute to the Muppets and their creator, Jim Henson (who died six years earlier). The video was introduced by his daughter Jane. I had the privilege of meeting Jane and Mrs. Henson prior to the show. They presented me with one of Jim's books. A real treasure. To add to my excitement, we learned that Mrs. Clinton would attend the event and stand with me and the other participants at the end of the show, prior to the gala that followed. When I heard this, I was concerned about what to wear. The staff told me to wear something with color that would stand out in a group. I went shopping and purchased a bright red St. John slack suit.

Before the show began, I was to wait in a room and, when appropriate, Mrs. Clinton would come to meet me. She was most pleasant. That was the first of several times I had the pleasure of being in her company. When she greeted me she commented on the beautiful suit I was wearing. Guess what? That suit is still in my closet sixteen years later.

Another one of our major events that year was the 1996 Child Survival Awards held in Atlanta. President and Mrs. Carter attended. We had photos taken with them and with UNICEF goodwill ambassadors Liv Ullmann

Upon my retirement from UNICEF in 1996, I had the honor of appointing Maya Angelou to the position of UNICEF ambassador for the United States and honorary chair of the 1996 Trick or Treat Monthly Campaign.

and Johann Olav Koss. Ullmann and Koss received the 1996 Child Survival Awards. It was a special night and I was pleased that my good friend Dr. Adrianne Austin also attended. I had met Adrienne when I was working during the Carter administration in Washington, DC. She was a member of our Proposal Review Committee and soon became a close friend.

Somehow, Project Redesign was moving along well. The organization-wide strategic planning process was to be launched in April with plans for completion by the year 2000. Alceste Pappas and her group had done a wonderful job moving through the steps of the process. We would now be referring to our project as New Directions.

In addition, the results of my most recent African trip were bearing fruit. One was the founding of the youth group organized with the help of Kyle Godfrey-Fraebel and Ashley Smith. The day the group was recognized, Maya Angelou was in New York for USC. They were able to meet her and have a photo taken with the newly appointed ambassador for the United States Committee for UNICEF. Having the pleasure of naming Maya Angelou an ambassador was one the most important and exciting acts during my tenure. It also was the last official act before my retirement that same month of December 1996. Maya Angelou was the chair for the annual Trick or Treat for UNICEF during the month of October, for which she wrote a poem entitled "Daughters and Sons."

DAUGHTERS AND SONS

If my luck is bad
And his aim is straight
I will leave my life
On the killing field
You can see me die
On the nightly news
As you settle down
To your evening meal.

But you'll turn your back
As you often do
Yet I am your sons
And your daughters too.

In the city streets
Where the neon lights
Turn my skin from black
To electric blue
My hope soaks red
On the gray pavement
And my dreams die hard
For my life is through.

But you'll turn your back
As you often do
Yet I am your sons
And your daughters too.

In the little towns
Of this mighty land
Where you close your eyes
To my crying need
I strike out wild
And my brother falls
Turn on your news
You can watch us bleed.

In morgues I'm known
By a numbered tag
In clinics and jails
And junkyards too
You deny my kin
Though I bear your name
For I am a part
Of mankind too.

But you'll turn your back
As you often do
Yet I am your sons
And your daughters too.

Turn your face to me
Please
Let your eyes seek my eyes
Lay your hand upon my arm
Touch me. I am real as flesh
And solid as bone.

I am no metaphor
I am no symbol
I am not a nightmare
To vanish with the dawn
I am lasting as hunger
And certain as midnight.

I claim that no council nor committee
Can contain me
Nor fashion me to its whim.
You, come here, hunch with me in a dingy doorway,
Face with me the twisted mouth threat
Of one more desperate
And better armed than I.

Join me again at today's dime store counter
Where the word to me
Is still no.
Let us go, your shoulder
Against my shoulder,
To the new picket line
Where my color is still a signal
For brutes to spew their bile
Like spit in my eye.

You, only you, who have made me
Who share tender taunting history with me
My fathers and mothers
Only you can save me
Only you can order the tides.
That rush my heart, to cease
Stop expanding my veins
Into red riverlets.

Come, you my relative
Walk the forest floor with me
Where rampaging animals lurk,
Lusting for my future
Only if your side is by my side
Only if your side is by my side
Will I survive.

But you'll probably turn your back
As you often do
Yet I am your sons
And your daughters too.

The evening at the United Nations when I bestowed the title of ambassador on Maya Angelou was the first time I felt the sting of my arthritis. I had to ask for someone to assist me as I walked up the two or three stairs. The sting is still there, but now it is more of a bite than a sting.

During these many interesting events, I had to somehow deal with the nastiness of what some of the staff members were causing. Added to this was my displeasure with how UNICEF was responding to my plea, and those of a few others, on staff assignments in other countries. As early as 1995, I was aware of the concern the African professionals expressed about their lack of involvement in the organization. I had expressed my support to the director of UNICEF, but my concern was not received well. In fact, my position on how assignments were being made was shared with some of the USC board members. I will not go into the details, but during a meeting with the president of our board (who was not supportive of my position), I heard myself saying, "I realize the USC is not the NAACP, but I cannot allow this board to control my thoughts and my behavior. You will have my resignation before the end of the day." I resigned my position in writing on September 6, 1996.

This was a special year, not only for USC but also for me. I celebrated my sixty-fifth birthday on December 31, 1996.

From the day I submitted my resignation until the end of 1996 seemed like an eternity. There were so many tasks I needed to complete. My thanks to Helen Corrado and Maurin DeSoto for their assistance. They did the impossible by working after hours and on weekends. I had boxes of saved materials to sort and ship. I did not have space in my apartment. My daughter JoAnn, who lives in a large house in Michigan, allowed me to store my materials in her basement. I was so grateful.

I did not think about another job. Had things been different and more

In El Salvador we visited an elementary school and distributed gifts from UNICEF.

This is my attempt to lift one of the pots that the women in Ethiopia put on their heads to carry water. I could not raise this pot to my waist. Women often carry these pots from a watering hole several miles from their villages.

Visiting Baby Friendly Hospital in Shanghai. The children's ages range from a few months old to three years.

The First Lady of Ghana was eager for us to visit the private nursery school she had organized and raised the funding for.

pleasant, I would have continued in that position for who knows how long. At one point I thought about going to the *New York Times* and sharing my concerns. But I did not want to do anything to disrupt the good the organization is doing in developing nations.

I must say there were a number of staff members who were very supportive and wrote letters to the board on my behalf. Generally these were individuals who had been with USC for many years and had seen some negative behaviors resurfacing. I am still in touch with several who were friends or who became friends, including some of the board members. Of course Eddy Bayardelle was a friend before he joined me at USC and continues to be a close friend today.

I will never be able to thank Neale Godfrey and Dr. Samuel Guillory for their support. Nancy Sharp Zuckerman was the very first staff member I met. Nancy and her family are close friends. My personal lawyer was the husband of Chris Carty, the attorney who worked closely with me when I was at the YWCA. It helped having individuals who knew me well to guide me through some of the decisions I made regarding my separation from the United States Committee for UNICEF.

TWELVE

A New Chapter in My Life

It was not easy starting a day with no place to go. It seemed as though I had worked all my life. As a matter of fact, I had some kind of employment in seventy of my eighty years. I truly missed getting dressed for a day doing something for others or for myself. As I gazed out the windows of my Street apartment in Manhattan, I felt guilty about not joining the crowds gathered at the bus stop across the street from where I lived. After the guilt trip I felt jealous that all of those men and women had someplace to go. I joined the New York Health Club a block or two from my apartment. I even engaged the help of a trainer to organize what I needed. The times I went to the club it was almost empty because most people were working. However, I had learned to enjoy my own company, so working out and sitting in the sauna did take some of the emptiness out of my schedule.

Shortly after the beginning of the new chapter of my life, I again received a phone call that made a lasting impression on me. The call was from the Office of the President at the University of Michigan. Before I could even think of what the call might be about, the voice on the other end was telling me that I was to be awarded an honorary degree in law from the University of Michigan, which would take place at the 1996 graduation ceremony in December. I thought it was someone playing a joke on me about my recent retirement.

One of the reasons I thought someone was playing a joke on me was because in June 1991, I had received the prestigious University Alumnae Council Award. This award was presented to me at a lovely luncheon held in the Michigan League. Approximately 150 people, all of whom were friends, relatives, or colleagues, were in attendance. Vice President Henry Johnson presided over the affair. It wasn't until I received a letter in the mail a few days later that I realized it was not a joke. It was really true! And so much came with this honor. There would be dinner at one of the prestigious guesthouses on campus with President and Mrs. Lee Bollinger, former president and Mrs. Robbin Fleming, and former interim president and Mrs. Homer Neale.

I had worked for President Fleming as his assistant for affirmative action. What a pleasure that the Flemings would make the trip from Florida for the event. I was pleased to come across a recipe recently from Sally Fleming for a delicious desert I had in their home when her husband Robin was president. Unfortunately, I recently learned they are both deceased.

I was also overjoyed to hear that Homer and his wife Jeanne would fly in from Switzerland to attend the event. I later learned that Homer and Jeanne had supported the nomination for my honorary degree. This was very special for me because my former husband James and I had been friends of Jeanne's parents before they were married. I had watched Homer's climb to the top of the academic ladder with much pride.

In addition to these prestigious individuals, a longtime friend and administrator of the University of Michigan, Percy Bates, and his wife Jan would arrive with one of my closest friends from New York, Kay Clanton. Kay and I had met shortly after I joined the faculty at Bank Street College in the early eighties. What a lovely evening.

I invited all my family members and close friends. The event was even more special to me when I learned that another Ann Arborite, Ken Burns, would give the address. Since then I have watched with great pride the wonderful historical contributions he has made through his work in film. This special honor gave meaning to my retirement. It also highlighted my achievements for me. I am told that to this day I am the first and only African American woman who was born in Ann Arbor, attended Ann Arbor public schools, and received three degrees from the University of Michigan as well as an honorary degree in law.

During the latter part of my career at UNICEF, I began to have serious pains in my lower right leg. I remember the day I awarded the National UNICEF ambassadorship to Maya Angelou in the dining room of the United Nations, I had difficulty stepping up to the podium without help. After moving from one doctor to another, I finally had an MRI. The results of this test dictated surgery. I had severe spinal stenosis.

I turned to my good friend Dr. Samuel Guillory for help. Samuel had helped me when I had a lumpectomy. Now I was depending on his help as a friend and physician. After doing research to find the best surgeon for this problem, we were able to get on the schedule of Dr. Andrew Casden, one of the two best surgeons in the country for spinal stenosis.

It took some time to recuperate from the surgery, but with the help of good friends like Dr. Guillory, Eddy Bayardelle, Nancy Sharp, former staff members, Liz Dopman, and my sister in-law Catherine Baker, as well as others, I recovered well. The experience with the staff at Beth Israel in Manhattan, on the other hand, left much to be desired. Unfortunately, many hospitals in metropolitan cities depend on newly arrived immigrants to fill service positions. Many come from countries where they have lacked access to good health care. I am aware of this because of my work and travel with UNICEF. So it was not shocking to me to experience the negative reactions from some of these individuals who openly refused to assist me. I finally had to hire twenty-four-hour private nursing care because the black staff did not want to help black patients. I took the time to write to the administrator of Beth Israel and the director of nursing to suggest some multicultural training for the incoming staff.

Dr. Casden and his staff did a fine job on my spine. He followed my case for several years after this surgery, from 1998 through 2005.

This operation convinced me to put my tennis rackets on the top shelf in my hall closet and think seriously about golf. I had the time, and my friend Elmer Beard was a wonderful golfer. He became my personal instructor. My friend Evelyn Moore had tried several times in the past to convince me to take golf seriously. I finally did when I realized I wouldn't be able to move around the tennis court as I had before surgery. The only difficulty playing golf in Manhattan is that it just can't happen. Simply to find and play on a practice area takes most of a day to get there and back on a bus. Whenever Evelyn and I could, we took our clubs with us on a plane. A phone call that came one day without notice did lead us to more opportunities to play golf than the two of us realized at the time.

When I served as a member of the Brooklyn Savings and Loan Association, I became friends with one of the lawyers for the bank, Robert Curry. I had helped his son to be appointed to the student slot on the UNICEF board of directors. Occasionally Bob and I had breakfast together and talked about our work. One day he called me and said he wanted to talk to me about a position on another board. I was interested until he told me it was a nonprofit. All my previous work had been with nonprofits, and they take a lot of effort. I was tired.

Bob insisted on meeting with me to discuss the Howard Gilman Foundation. I told him I would only meet with him in Central Park for coffee. I walked to and through the park every morning and I didn't want to interrupt my routine. When we met in the park, I was in my navy-blue running suit and he was in a suit and tie. We got a couple of strange looks. When Bob told me about the foundation and described Howard Gilman, who was deceased, I became interested. During our short meeting he mentioned White Oaks Plantation several times and tickled my curiosity. This fifteen-acre facility on the border of Florida and Georgia had an office in Manhattan, and appeared to be well funded. The real truth came later. I agreed to submit my résumé and as we hugged each other I said, "We shall see."

I soon received a phone call from the office of the foundation. The caller wanted to schedule an appointment so I could meet CEO Bernard Bergreen and CAO (chief administrative officer) Natalie Moody. We arranged a date. A car would pick me up and deliver me to the CEO'S Fifth Avenue apartment. That meeting would be followed by a site visit to the White Oak Plantation. I was invited to bring along three members of my family or friends. This visit would take place very soon, after which I would tour the New York office. There would be no cost to me or my guests. I invited my friend Evelyn Moore, her sister Roberta, and her husband, Ivan Moore.

The weekend at White Oak was a remarkable experience. We were met at the Jacksonville, Florida, airport by a most gracious driver from the plantation. The site was about ten miles from the airport. The driver's greeting alone indicated we were in for an unusual experience. Once there, we were taken to one of the eighteen lovely houses on the acreage. We were told President and Mrs. Clinton had stayed in the same house when they visited White Oak. The visitors to the plantation were board members and friends of Mr. Gilman. There was also a very nice nine-hole golf course on the acreage. The Clintons and Vice President and Mrs. Gore played golf at White Oak.

We were given a quick introduction to this beautiful facility and whisked away to have dinner with a group in the lodge. The group included a board member and the two staff members I had met in New York, Mr. Bergreen and Mrs. Moody. White Oak Lodge was Mr. Gilman's former residence. It had the appearance of a museum. After a delicious dinner and excellent wine, we returned to our quarters, exhausted from the entire experience but looking forward to the next day.

The next morning a chef and his assistant greeted us and prepared breakfast in our kitchen. Then we toured the plantation, met the staff, and saw most of the animals on the grounds. Mr. Gilman had taken an interest in animals that were becoming extinct. He met John Lukas on one of his trips to Africa. They had similar interests in wanting to preserve certain species. Gilman and Lukas decided to establish a wildlife preserve to conduct medical research and provide a home to extend the lifelines of certain animals that were becoming extinct. We only had the weekend, but there was much more to see and to learn about the foundation and White Oak.

We had another fabulous dinner in Roseland, our residence, and the following morning were again served breakfast by the chef and his assistant. There was time for horseback riding, a tour of the golf course, time at the pool, and finally massages in the massage room. After watching a movie and having a cocktail, we weren't ready for our departure the next morning.

The question of whether I would join the board of directors was no longer a question. After examining the possibilities to help the foundation achieve its goals, my answer was definitely yes. The investment in the animal preserve was only one aspect of the foundation's work that I found interesting. I also supported their focus of providing support for the arts. What an amazing opportunity.

I experienced much more with the Gilman Foundation and White Oak than I could include in this chapter. I met many wonderful people through the foundation. The chair of the board, actress Isabella Rossellini, was Ingrid

Bergman's daughter. Just getting to know Isabella was worth the experience. The board was made up of many fine individuals, including Donald Bruce, a longtime friend of Mr. Gilman, and Justin Feldman, an outstanding New York attorney who was married to one of my favorite authors, Linda Fairstein. Linda and I were also members of the International Women's Foundation. Once I became familiar with the generosity and care Mr. Gilman imparted to the staff, I better understand the staff's devotion to the Gilman Foundation and all the foundation embraced.

My invitation to join the board of directors came about as a mandate from the State of New York to broaden the membership of the foundation. Several members of the staff and the state suggested the board needed more diversity. There were no members representing the nonprofit sector, and I certainly added that experience to the group. There was no mention of adding ethnic diversity to the board, but with one glance around the table at my first board meeting, it was obviously needed.

It didn't take me long to assume my responsibilities as a board member. I was almost overwhelmed at the outpouring of gratuities. Board members had the privilege of using one of the New York offices for personal and professional needs. I was encouraged to use the facilities in New York and at White Oak for meetings of organizations I was attached to. For example, as a member of the advisory committee of the One Hundred Black Women, I was allowed to invite two dozen women to meet and reside in the guest lodge at White Oak for an entire weekend at no cost, including meals and all the amenities available in any five-star hotel. This occurred on several occasions.

The Gilman Foundation was supported by several paper mills in the Northeast and in south Georgia. When I joined the board, the paper industry was undergoing severe changes that threatened the foundation's income. The board meeting agendas became overloaded with how to continue the mission and still maintain the generous activities at White Oak. At one time there were four hundred staff members providing services needed in the New York office and at White Oak.

I learned about the financial history of the paper industry in the United States and Canada, but more importantly, about the need for the board to make some serious decisions. We thought long and hard about the nine-hole golf course that was used for clients. How could we best use the beautiful houses located on fifteen acres? With the decline in income, did the board need to rethink the office space in New York? At what level would we be forced to consider reductions in grants? And what did this mean for staff? We had to think about the number of staff needed in a declining situation as well as the current level of salaries and benefits. There were other extremely important decisions that needed to be made about the financial holdings of the foundation.

At the beginning of my tenure with this board, things were very pleasant, but the more drastic decisions we needed to make, the more difficult participation became. Serving as chair of the audit committee made my responsibility even more important. When the list of decisions to be made finally reached the level of salary reductions, I had problems when the options presented did not take into account salary levels. Individuals in the lower salary levels were asked to take a much larger decrease than those in the higher income brackets.

After much thought, I decided I could not approve the plan for such salary decreases. As much as I respected the foundation's mission and what it had achieved, rather than approve this option, I felt I should resign from the board. Soon after my resignation, other members of the board resigned over similar situations.

Many of the staff at White Oak had become friends. I always looked forward to making a trip to the plantation. I enjoyed the golf facilities, and the golf staff was very helpful. I took my daughter for a photo opportunity during a courtesy weekend at White Oak.

My retirement agenda was becoming quite full. I felt physically stronger and found more time to work on a few other projects. I had continued working on my book. I had decided to address my friend Margot Ellis's suggestion before she died, that perhaps I would need ten men instead of a second husband. I thought about this for a long time, especially after my experience with the various men I had some kind of relationship with. I didn't make a list of ten, but I was coming close. To follow up my thinking, I decided to write a book about the possibility of women needing ten men. I explored this idea with several women and decided to try my hand at developing a book entitled *It Takes Ten: Some Women May Need More Than One Man*.

I organized my thoughts and developed a table of contents for the manuscript. I wanted to include a section on the results of interviewing individuals. Why not? I had the time to do this. I listed the questions I wanted to ask men and women alike about their dating and sexual experiences. Then I made a list of people to contact. It took a great deal of time writing letters, asking permission, and making appointments for lunch, dinner, or a visit for the interviews. The entire experience turned out to be a great deal of fun. I was well into writing the early chapters of the book when a telephone call offered me another challenging experience.

My good friend and colleague James Banks, who was president of the American Education Research Association (AERA), called me with an offer I could not refuse. He and the board asked if I would consider a position they had recently created. I had previously been defeated for the position of president of this association. This position was to assist with the social justice concerns of the association. I wouldn't need to move to Washington, DC. I could work as many hours as my schedule allowed. And to top it off, I could set my salary. What a deal. I was dedicated to the mission of the association, I liked the thought of traveling to Washington once or twice a month, and felt I could do the assignment justice by working half-time on it. I immediately accepted the offer. I became excited about this possibility. Several issues had disturbed me during the time I had been involved with AERA, and this was a wonderful opportunity to help the board members resolve some of the issues on their agenda and on my list.

My first board meeting was held at an annual meeting in Canada. I enjoyed it very much. I made new contacts with younger members of the association and renewed friendships with members who'd been my colleagues when I was involved as a board member in several special interest groups (SIGs). It had been several years since I'd been active in professional educational organizations. My work with the YWCA, the New York Board of Education, Brooklyn Savings and Loan, and UNICEF did not leave me the time I needed to do more with AERA than pay my dues.

I was traveling to board meetings several times a year in different cities throughout the country. Annual meetings held in major cities provided an opportunity to do more than work. One aspect I enjoyed was that I was not the boss. It had been a long time since I had reported to anyone other than a board. Working with the CEO was convenient, for he generally agreed with the manner and substance of what I felt needed to be done. AERA was no different from most professional organizations. It had only been a decade or two since the need for integrating diversity throughout these organizations had been acknowledged. AERA had done a good job of integrating the membership in more ways than establishing the Black Interest Group and the Women's Interest Group. I had been and still was a financial member in these groups, so working with them to accomplish even more diversity throughout the association was a pleasure.

However, I found it somewhat difficult to change the way the board and the CEO felt about certain things that needed attention. For example, the association headquarters was housed in an old multistory house. All of the staff was young and able enough to climb from one floor to another. I felt strongly that consideration be given to make the headquarters more accessible for the physically challenged. I was not able to convince the administration to give this need serious consideration. This was not acceptable to me and the lack of positive movement on these issues gave me much concern. I had friends who had never thought they'd be physically challenged, yet became so almost overnight.

My previous work with the federal government at the National Institute of Education was successful through the grant-making process. I felt this was something I could help AERA achieve, for the association had a positive record in receiving funding for various programs from the government. I saw a need for funds that would assist women and minorities in their research projects. With the help of one or two staff members at AERA, we put together a proposal to achieve this purpose. I made some necessary contacts to get the funding process moving.

Obtaining funding from the government is not easy. We were asking for approximately ten million dollars. Sometime later, at one of our field meetings, I learned through the grapevine that the project I helped initiate had been funded. This wonderful news would be announced at one of the general meetings of this field meeting. When the announcement was made, however, my involvement was not acknowledged. The leadership for this project had been appointed when the announcement was made. I don't have a lot of ego, but this did not sit well with me.

During the two years I worked with AERA, I made several significant changes. But I was beginning to feel that my work as a volunteer was more rewarding than my work with AERA.

Before I decided to resign my position with AERA, I had thoughts about writing a memoir. My introduction to this manuscript describes the experience I had when I was a young girl. That experience provided the purpose for writing my life's history. It also provided the distinct purpose and direction for my life. Even in retirement, I am always interested in trying to instill the philosophy of multiculturalism whenever and wherever I can.

So in the early years of my retirement I added yet another project to my list of things to do. There were times when I wondered how I had found time to work a full-time job. At the turn of the century I found myself completing work on *It Takes Ten: Some Women Need More Than One Man*. I had developed an outline and had a draft of the initial chapter of *A Hot Fudge Sundae in a White Paper Cup*. I felt that if I'd been able to rewrite my textbook *Organizing and Planning for Multicultural Instruction* during the days when I was leading the YWCA, I could certainly work on my memoir in my spare time. My spare time, however, was beginning to slip away.

During my time with the YWCA in the 1980s I had been elected to serve as one of the eight public sector members of the board. What an experience. Let me explain why I was even considered for a position on this prestigious board. When I was heading up YWCA, I was fortunate enough to appoint a young woman named Alpha Alexander as director of our health and physical education program. Alpha was a recent PhD who was eager to develop the YWCA's interest and involvement in sports.

With my support, Alpha submitted an application to the U.S. Olympic Committee on behalf of the YWCA for membership. We were pleased when the YWCA was admitted. As one of the nonprofit members, we were eligible for a position on the board of directors as a representative of the public sector. Alpha became a member of the board. A remarkable young woman, she soon was known by almost everyone in the U.S. Olympics community. One of her supporters and a former board member was Andrew Young.

When Alpha's term expired in 1996, she and Andy nominated me for a position on the board, essentially replacing her as one of the public sector members. I was delighted and found myself in the midst of a completely new and different environment. Of course I enjoyed sports as a spectator, but I had never thought about the administration of this giant in the arena of sports.

I soon became almost as involved as Alpha had been. I did my homework and read as much as I could about the history of the Olympics. I was eager to attend board meetings and took advantage of many opportunities to learn about the organization. At the time I took my seat on the board, there were only seven public sector board members. Before our reorganization, an additional position was added.

I had the privilege of serving on several committees. My first appointment was on the audit committee. This important committee was chaired by Roland Betts, an unusual individual with many skills. Roland was the chairman of Chelsea Piers Management in New York City. It was a pleasure to work with him. Shortly after my appointment to the audit committee, I was asked to serve as a member of the international committee under the leadership of Dwight Bell and Dale Neuberger.

I was becoming quite involved and enjoyed the work. After my first four years, I was invited to serve a second four-year term. During this quadrennial I served as a member of the CEO search committee. This was an honor and a privilege. Through the process I met some very talented individuals.

I attended the opening ceremony of the 1996 Olympics in Atlanta and was so thrilled I could hardly sit still. I remember that evening very clearly. Eddy Bayardelle and Nancy Sharp Zuckerman accompanied me. We were able to walk from our hotel to the stadium. It was a warm but pleasant evening. This was so special I bought a bag of French fries and a huge cold beer, something I almost never allowed myself do, except when I was in other countries and sometimes drank beer instead of water. For whatever reasons, I allowed myself to enjoy the special treats.

UNICEF had been involved with the organizing committee through the support of Andrew Young, the cochair of the Atlanta Games. The committee established the fund-raising booth to raise money for children whose lives had been affected by war. We met with several athletes and media representatives to achieve the publicity we needed. At that time I never thought I might attend another Olympics.

I was still on the board when it came time for the games to take place in Australia. Some board members volunteered to work at the games, and some of their expenses were covered. Some public sector board members even rented their own apartments. I knew I could only stay two weeks. I was able to make my own arrangements for air flights and lodging. I didn't have to convince Alpha Alexander to travel to Sydney with me. She was already there in her head. By the time we got our plans together, trying to locate lodging became difficult. Fortunately for us, I was a member of a private women's club in New York City. I soon learned that there was a sister club in Sydney. I contacted the club in Australia and was able to reserve a room for two for the two weeks we would be there. The club in Sydney was a block away from the office of the U.S. committee and across the street from the main entrance to the underground train to the sites of the games.

The staff at the club was very gracious. Whenever I travel, I unfortunately always wonder how I will be received. The club in New York was 99 percent white. I did not have trouble gaining membership after extensive interviews primarily because I was the executive secretary of the YWCA. Women like Mary Rockefeller, a YWCA board member, were my sponsors. They had encouraged me to join the club because so many YWCA contributors were members, and membership would help me get to know these important women.

At the club in Sydney, the staff practically rolled out the red carpet for us. During this time, I had become a board member of the Gilman Foundation. Once I let the staff know this, I learned that Natalie Moody, the CAO of the foundation, had a friend in Sydney. Natalie immediately put in a call to her friend, Ann Summers, and Ann offered us her apartment in Sydney for the latter part of our stay. Ann was leaving town for a month and insisted that we accept her offer. Ann is an outstanding supporter of women's rights and a fascinating author. How fortunate Alpha and I were to meet Ann and stay in her lovely apartment. The view of the city at night from her sitting room window was one I shall never forget.

We arrived a few days before the games began, which gave us time to do some sightseeing in that beautiful city. The tour of the opera house was so exciting. We attended art shows, ate delicious foods in wonderful restaurants, and drank the wine. By the time we made it to the games, we were worn out. Unfortunately I had waited too late to make reservations for tickets to the opening ceremony, and was disappointed that we could not obtain tickets. However, we viewed the ceremony on a very large screen in the U.S. Olympic Office along with a room full of people who were in the same plight.

Soon after the games in Sydney, the U.S. committee was faced with a charge to take a look at itself. Some things were occurring that caused concern from several quarters, including the federal government. (The U.S. Olympic Committee exists because of federal legislation.) A task force was appointed to take an in-depth look at the organization. Over time there were changes and practices that needed to be examined. I was asked if I would serve on this ten-person task force.

After several months of working to reorganize the Olympic Committee, one of our last tasks was to appoint a nominating committee for members of the new board. I felt strongly that I needed to be included in making the selections to ensure diversity. I don't think there was another member of this task force as committed as I was to ensure someone on the nominating committee would make sure diversity was a consideration. This was not easy, but I nominated Dr. Samuel Guillory.

By the time the work of the task force was complete I found myself involved in more and different types of activities. This did not include the Olympic Committee, not because I didn't want to continue my work with them, but because the task force decided that to completely reorganize and leave former practices behind, no one who had previously served more than two years in a leadership role with the Olympic Committee could serve with the newly organized U.S. committee.

I learned a great deal about sports and met many fine individuals who had an impact on me. I've already mentioned how I appreciated working with Roland Betts. Roland is a friend of former president George W. Bush. Roland graciously included me on his list of invitees to the White House for a preview of the movie *Seabiscuit*. I invited my friend Dr. Guillory to accompany me.

We all mingled with President and Mrs. Bush. Other guests included Laura Hillenbrand, the author of the book on which the movie was based, director Steven Spielberg, and the young movie star Tobey McGuire, who played the leading role in the movie. The conversation was light and delightful. At lunch, I found myself standing in line behind President Bush selecting portions of the wonderful buffet dishes. After lunch we were invited into the presidential viewing room and were served bags of popcorn. It was like going to the movies, but a bit classier.

Donald Fehr, another individual I greatly admire, was a member of the Olympic board. In his role as CEO of the Major League Baseball Players Association, Don invited me to serve as an adviser for the Major League

Baseball Players Trust for children. I worked with his staff on several occasions to help identify directions the Players Trust might consider funding. Until I became involved with MLBPA I had no idea that players were interested in funding activities for children. This privilege didn't last long, but I met with staff, attended several trust meetings, and took great pride in completed projects. Meeting the players was a privilege.

Frank Marshall, chair of the reorganizing Olympics task force, was another board member I admired. He was also a film producer, and was at that time filming *The Bourne Identity* in Paris, France. Evelyn Moore and I planned to be in Paris during the shooting. With my tongue hanging out I asked if we could possibly visit the set. Frank graciously invited us to do just that. And he was kind enough to send a car for us. What fun this was.

Equally pleasurable was working with Gordon Gund, of Gund Investment Corporation. Gordon entertained the public sector members at a meeting in his suite at the stadium in Cincinnati. Former senator Bill Bradley always added levity to our meetings, and Dr. Henry Kissinger's intellect we could not have done without. Michael McManus, president and CEO of Misonix, and Donna Lopiano, executor director of the Women's Sports Foundation, added what was needed.

After I had retired in 1966, I wasn't sure what my future would hold. And yet I found myself pleasantly involved in areas where I had not tread before. Almost every organization I worked for included travel. And there were the trips I just wanted to take, like going to Spain and Morocco with Evelyn Moore. Evelyn had not retired when I had, so we planned our trips around her work schedule. There were times when we traveled professionally. One such trip was when People to People asked me to serve as the honorary U.S. cochair of the Citizen Ambassador Program. The purpose of this trip was to participate in the United States / South Africa Joint Conference on Early Childhood Education in 1997.

In 2000, People to People again invited me to serve as the leader of a delegation to Cuba. For the most part delegates really want to attend the conferences and explore the cultures of the countries involved. I met some lovely people through these trips. The well-known Italian chef Lidia Bastianich added spice to our Cuban trip. She was able find lobster and have it cooked on the beach when most of us had chicken. The young travel coordinator for the group, Pennell Skinner, was not only extremely efficient but a delightful individual. We have stayed in touch. We both currently live in Florida and have developed a lovely friendship.

Early in 2001, having ended early my second term with the Olympics, I became involved in yet another nonprofit organization. As much as I tried to avoid nonprofits, there was something about them that attracted me.

As a member of the USTA Olympic Committee I was expected to attend the board meetings. These meetings were held in various places, including Puerto Rico. I learned much about the operations of the USTA. It is an amazing organization, but it too needed to work on the diversity problem. I tried to nominate friends of mine to some of the committees but was only successful in having Dr. Guillory appointed to the technology committee. I felt the USTA needed someone who could help develop tennis programs for inner-city children, and they missed a golden opportunity by not appointing Evelyn Moore, who was then CEO of the National Black Children's Institute. I continued to serve as a volunteer for USTA until my appointment was over. My travel never stopped. And my professional luggage never retired.

Puerto Rico seems almost like home, especially during my early retirement days. I was there on several personal excursions. The organizations I participated in usually held one meeting every two or three years in San Juan or El Conquistador. One such group was the National Coalition of 100 Black Women. I was introduced to this coalition through a friend of long standing who was president of the national board and lived in New York. Betty Adams had worked as the CEO for the Jackie Robinson Foundation and knew almost everyone in New York—black, white, yellow, or red. It didn't take long for me to become a member of the coalition, and within a few years I was invited to join the national board. I continued to travel to membership and board meetings. The coalition has had a dedicated CEO in Shirley L. Poole. The founder, Jewell Jackson McCabe, was very active when I invited the coalition as guests of the Gilman Foundation to White Oak Plantation.

When I was on the New York City school board and Betty Adams was president of the national coalition, she allowed time on the monthly agenda for me to report on school board activity. This was very helpful to me. I needed to vent, and it was even more important when I became president. Sometimes the higher one climbs, the lonelier it is. I'll never forget the support I received from the coalition. (Note: My friend Betty Adams died after a long illness as I was completing work on this manuscript.)

THIRTEEN

My Retirement in Paradise

Who would have thought September 11, 2001, could have happened? Between that day and the early months of 2002, I'm not sure what I did or where I went. Everything was in a fog. I was no longer comfortable in Manhattan. It seemed as though, along with many others, I was just tiptoeing through the streets, doing what we had to do. It was a relief in the winter of 2001–2 when I received an invitation to speak in Sarasota, Florida, at an International Women's Celebration sponsored by UNIFEM (United Nations Development Fund for Women). I had a good reason for leaving the city. But I had no idea how this event would change the rest of my life.

I jumped at this opportunity not only because I needed a reason to leave New York for a while, but also because I needed a reason to use my brain power. I needed to think, and to create a presentation that focused on the work that has always meant so much to me. It was also an opportunity to visit Sarasota again. I had traveled to Sarasota several times for one reason or another when I was working, and had always enjoyed this beautiful and quiet little city.

I was excited about developing a speech that would differ somewhat from others I had given. I wasn't reporting on a recent visit to another country. My presentation would represent the intensity I felt when I experienced the plight and situation of women and children around the world. This had been the focus of my work for many years.

Two friends I had met while serving on the Board of Education in New York City, Dr. Carroll Buchanan and his wife Carol, were members of the Sarasota chapter of UNIFEM. In fact, Carol was the current president of the chapter. We had worked together when I was with UNICEF, and the two organizations had parallel goals: UNICEF focused on children and UNIFEM on women. The Buchanans invited me to be their houseguest during my stay in Sarasota, and I accepted their gracious invitation. On my earlier visits to Sarasota, I had always stayed in a hotel. In fact, I originally thought the city was in one key. This invitation allowed me to see a different section of the city.

The more I learned about Sarasota, the more I liked it. Each morning in New York I took my familiar walk from my East Side neighborhood through Central Park. I did the same in the neighborhood in Sarasota where my friends lived. I was impressed by the greenery, the smell of freshly cut grass, the chirping of birds, the colorful butterflies, and the beautiful flowers nestled among the bushes. The more I walked and experienced, the more I wondered if I could manage to live in a place like Sarasota.

The UNIFEM luncheon was held in a lovely restaurant, Michael's on East. There were approximately two hundred people in the audience, more women than men, but a warm and receptive crowd. I discovered that one of the sons of my friends Douglas and Catherine Williams of Ann Arbor lived in Sarasota. Kenneth Williams had also been my student at the University of Michigan. In fact I used to babysit him and his two brothers. I invited Kenny to be my guest and he was as proud of me as I was of him. All went well, a very nice affair.

I was in Sarasota for only three days, but I couldn't get the thought of living in Florida out of my mind. I even asked Carol for the name of a realtor. I enjoyed Sarasota, and it promised to give me more opportunities to play golf. As I've said, it's difficult to play golf in New York City, and almost impossible to find a practice range. I came up with more reasons why living in Florida was a good idea. I then explored the possibility of living in two places.

It didn't take long before my thoughts led to action. I contacted Peggy Hurston, the realtor Carol had suggested. Within a few weeks I was on a plane flying to Sarasota for a weekend. I kept my plans to myself, not discussing any of this with my children or my significant other, Elmer Beard, in Chicago. I was not entirely secretive; I did share my thoughts with Pete

Catenacci of Ameriprise, my financial adviser. His advice was to manage two living spaces for three years and then make a decision. I thought this was good advice. Of course Peter always gives me good financial advice, which is one reason I could even try this new adventure.

I arrived in Sarasota on a Saturday morning. A car from the Ritz Carlton picked me up. Almost as soon as I checked in, a representative arrived from the company Carol Buchanan had recommended. Before coming to Sarasota, I had discussed the type, size, and price range I was interested in. I wanted a condo or apartment near a golf course. The realtor had six places for me to see. The sixth was a villa I wasn't interested in. I had lived alone for several years and enjoy being near neighbors, so a single family home did not appeal to me.

By the end of the day we had looked at five units, none of which interested me. I'd hoped to find something near the Buchanans, but no luck. As we were on our way back to the hotel, the realtor suggested we look at the original villa I had said I didn't want to see. She told me that we had the time and it might be nice to see what a villa could offer. We made a turn off a major road and drove through a very lovely area. One of the important aspects of selecting a place to live is how calming the journey is on the way home at the end of a day.

Palmer Ranch Drive was very calming and beautiful. When we turned into Mira Lago and drove through the gate, I sat quietly, observing all I could. Pulling into the driveway I was thinking that perhaps I could live in a free-standing home. This villa was on a lake and across from a golf course, actually across from two golf courses. We entered the villa and I could not believe my eyes. It was as if I'd walked into my own living room. The former owner's taste was very similar to mine. I moved from room to room and fell in love with the place. None of the furniture had been removed by the owner's children. Even the closets were full.

By noon the following Monday, I had purchased this lovely villa for a bit more than I wanted to pay, but I bargained to save enough to buy a membership in the TPC Prestancia Golf Club across the road. Before I closed the deal I checked with a few friends and then told my family and significant other.

What surprised me was how much I liked the villa. Soon after making the purchase, I questioned whether I needed two places to maintain. Before the week was out, I decided to sell my New York apartment. A week later I sold it to my neighbor across the hall. I closed in July and planned to move in October. I waited until the fall because I had been asked to serve as a judge for the September 2002 Miss America Contest, and I wanted to stay close to the festivities in New York until then.

It didn't take me long after moving to Sarasota to understand why so many people refer to it as paradise. After living here for more than ten years, I am so happy I made the move. I enjoy the weather. The hot summers don't bother me. I enjoy the greenery, the intermittent showers, and the beaches. Living within five minutes of the golf club adds to my pleasure. I can walk to the spa and pool in less than five minutes.

I couldn't believe how much better I felt as I planned the move and the interior decorating. I found a reliable interior decorating company to assist me. It was so much fun choosing colors, new pieces of furniture I would need, and making all the decisions that contributed to my move. It was just what I needed after 9/11.

The Buchanans hosted a lovely reception in their home in my honor soon after my arrival. Many of the people I met that evening are now friends. Mary (Jackie) Davis and I immediately became friends, partly because of our interest in golf. We set aside Thursday mornings to play together. Even though I'm no longer able to golf, she keeps that time open in case a miracle decides to whiz through my spine.

The surgery I had on my back for spinal stenosis in New York had begun to lose its effectiveness. However, Jackie and I decided to keep our brains intact as well as our bodies, so we joined the Ringling Library Town Hall Lecture Series. This gave us an opportunity to meet and enjoy outstanding international speakers several times a year. The two of us continue to be interested in mutual activities. Jackie makes sure we renew our yearly subscriptions to the West Coast Black Theatre Troupe and Asolo Repertory Theatre.

I met another interesting person at the reception. Colonel Robert Fitzgerald was a fairly new resident in Sarasota. Bob and I became friends, and thanks to him I met other individuals who are currently in my larger circle of friends.

It was exciting to meet new people and discover we had mutual friends in New York, Washington, DC, and other places. One such discovery led to an introduction to Charlotte Scarborough. We were both educators and had several mutual interests. During one of our luncheons we came up with an idea that even eight years later still gives me pleasure. We thought it would be great fun and also give us an opportunity to meet others in the community. We shared the idea of hosting a pre-holiday luncheon to six other women. We became the Eight Bells. It took us a year of planning, which led to each angel hosting the eight of us in her home for a planning session, and each session involved delicious food and drink.

We planned our holiday luncheon and got to know each other better. Jackie Davis was the first person to accept our invitation to join the group. Judy Wilcox, Florence Jackson, Joyce Ladner, Jacqueline Jones, and Aileen Grifin also became Bells. Our luncheon was extremely successful. We held it in one of the loveliest restaurants in the city, Michael's on East. The decorations, delicious food, and live music all helped more than three hundred guests enjoy themselves.

I volunteered to make the centerpieces for each of the thirty tables. For a year I scoured the clearance racks in the best home household goods stores and came up with beautiful gifts. I decorated each one as a Christmas gift that not only adorned the table but became a gift to one of our guests. During one of the planning sessions Charlotte and I discovered our mutual interest in music. For several years we had annual subscriptions to the Sarasota Opera. I continue to attend and enjoy the performances.

I decided when I moved to Florida that I didn't want to repeat activities similar to those I was involved in earlier in my life. I quickly learned to say no to offers to join organizations. I did, however, stay attached to UNIFEM at a minimum level as a national adviser. This was the organization I helped reorganize when I worked with UNICEF in New York. A minimum level meant continuing my financial contributions and attending a yearly affair or so.

My involvement with the International Women's Forum also continued. This organization had given me a Strength of City Award when I served as president of the New York City Board of Education. It was presented to me at a prestigious luncheon at one of the finest New York hotels in 1989 by the New York Forum. Since my induction into this organization, I have attended several of their international meetings. My first was the meeting held in London. Members from around the world were in attendance, and the members from Great Britain organized an unforgettable meeting in London.

The meeting held in Israel was one I shall never forget. My friend Evelyn Moore traveled with me and we went on a trip afterward to Egypt. I was eager to make the visit to Egypt because one of my friends from Michigan worked there: Barbara Johnson was the superintendent of a private school in Cairo. The three of us had a wonderful visit. Barbara and I met during our freshman year at the University of Michigan. I remember attending her wedding in Detroit when she married Martinus Johnson from Liberia, who later became an ambassador. Since living in Sarasota, I attended the meeting held in Argentina. By this time my friend Evelyn had become a member of the Washington, DC, chapter of the Forum. We attended meetings together and made a short trip to Uruguay.

Learning about the world and traveling continue to play an important role in my life. My suitcase has always remained ready to hop a plane. I still think the earlier exposure to world travel through my mother laid a foundation for this.

Moving to Sarasota did not curtail my travel to Barbados, Morocco, or Nevis. These trips were somewhat different from those I did while working. I spent more time relaxing and exploring the cultural aspects of these countries than looking for ways to solve the problems we discovered.

My last trip was to Tuscany. I always enjoyed Italy but never spent time in that area. Several of us stayed in lovely villas surrounded by fields of grapevines and olive trees. In fact the villa I stayed in was built over a huge wine cellar. Tuscany was my last trip since moving to Sarasota in 2002, but not my last to be taken. As I write this final chapter, I am preparing to take a three-week cruise to celebrate my eightieth birthday. I plan to travel with my friend and neighbor, Suzanne Murphy Laronde. We look forward to exploring parts of India, Thailand, Malaysia, Singapore, Indonesia, and Bali.

While having no trouble adjusting to paradise, I have developed a rather new lifestyle. I enjoy swimming more than ever, and JoAnn, my oldest daughter, has been working with me to improve my strokes. I also decided not to let my hair control my life. I had my hair cut very short so it's easy for me to get my hair wet and run fast from a hot curling iron. Keeping my body in shape and staying on top of my weight is far more important than my hair. I also discovered that I don't like indoor exercise. I settled that by purchasing a three-wheeled bike. I didn't want to take the chance of falling. I may look like an old lady riding down the street on a three-wheeled bike, but I don't care. I enjoy it. Walking isn't so easy anymore, so I've had to leave the beach walks to my guests. But I will keep trying.

My children enjoy Florida and visit as often as possible. In fact my son Jim liked it so much he found a teaching position in a middle school in North Port, a small town about thirty miles from my home. I always enjoyed it when Claudia brought my granddaughter Amanda to visit. Her oldest son Marshall hasn't made it here yet. Perhaps when his two daughters, Makayla and Maya, get older, it will be easier for Marshall and his wife, Marcella, to make the trip. I visit Ann Arbor several times a year and this has allowed me to see family and friends. JoAnn comes whenever she can find the time.

As I was settling into my retirement lifestyle and enjoying paradise, life took its toll and reminded me that all does not stay the same. In 2007, my daughter Claudia discovered she had leukemia. When she called to tell me about her condition, I think I was more concerned than she was.

During the next twenty-four hours, my family and I began making the adjustments necessary to give her the support she needed. This was two nights before Thanksgiving. On Thanksgiving morning, my daughter JoAnn called to tell me to come immediately. Fortunately my son had just started his teaching position here in Florida and was staying in my home temporarily. The two of us somehow did the impossible and made the next plane that morning to Michigan. I was a nervous wreck. Jim and I were sitting in the airport when his phone rang. Before he handed me the phone, I knew what had happened.

My Claudia had died before I could reach out to hold her in my arms. With the support of family and friends, we put her to rest within four days. Jim had to return to his teaching position. JoAnn was remarkable. She handled most of the arrangements while I did what a mother needed to do. Our Lord did what he felt he needed to do. My family and I appreciated the thoughtfulness of over four hundred relatives and friends who came out in the ice and snow to show their love for Claudia.

Adjusting to Claudia's death was not easy. I didn't feel like doing much of anything except sitting and thinking. Depression was taking its toll. I finally decided to find someone to help me through this period. I never thought one of my children would die before me. I was fortunate to find a young woman psychologist with whom I felt comfortable. We worked together for over a year. I began to feel more comfortable with the thought of Claudia's death. At one point in our work together, this psychologist suggested I consider getting a dog. I did. My thanks go to my friend Jane Wright, who insisted on taking me out to look for a dog. It didn't take long for me to find a bichon poo, and we fell in love with one another.

Bami is my dog, my friend, and my companion. He is loved by the neighbors and several of their dog friends. I make sure he is not around seniors all the time, so he spends two days a week in the Beverly Hills Dog Spa. This gives me some time for myself and allows him to play with those of his own kind. In 2012 he had the honor of being named the Beverly Hills Super Dog of the Year. This award carried lots of gifts for Bami and me. I wanted to name him Obama, but didn't think it would be appropriate to name a dog after our president, so I came up with the name Bami in his honor.

Shortly before Claudia's death, my mother moved from Arizona back to Ann Arbor. She was living alone and depended a great deal on my daughter JoAnn, my brother, and his wife Doris. Visiting my mother was my primary reason for going to Michigan as often as I did. There were times when I combined a visit with her and my family with an event at the University of Michigan. I always took time to visit my old friends and my favorite uncle, Mallory Thomas.

Uncle Mallory was in his early nineties, however, and his health was declining. He meant so much to me over the years. At his funeral I told the gathering in the Second Baptist Church how much he had meant to me. He was my second father, and had been my Santa Claus almost all of my life. He was as proud of me as I was of him.

Shortly after the surgery on my back in 1998, I began to experience pain in my left thigh. After trying over fourteen years to find a physician who could recommend something that could relieve this pain, I did. Just before Mother's Day 2012, I had an appointment with a surgeon who was confident he could help me. Two days later, a tumor was removed from my right leg, and the pain I had endured for many years disappeared. How wonderful it was to have the relief.

I called my mother on Mother's Day to visit with her and let her know of the success with the surgery. During our conversation she told me she was having an uncomfortable day, with some light pain in her stomach. After suggesting some home remedies to help, I called Doris, my brother's wife, and asked her to take Mother some ginger ale. We both felt this would help. The following morning my brother Russell called to tell me that my mother was in the hospital in Ann Arbor. She was seriously ill. In spite of just having had surgery, I flew to Michigan almost immediately. My mother was not doing well. We knew that although she was six months away from her one hundredth birthday, she would probably not see that day.

My mother died the following week. I was very grateful that I'd been able to spend the entire week with her before she died. During the week I was with her, the surgeon who had removed the tumor from my leg called to tell me it was malignant. Since then I have been dealing with additional physical problems and grieving over the loss of my mother. However, my siblings and I have so much to be thankful for.

Mother did not make a hundred years, but we were blessed to have her for almost a century. I loved my mother very much, but did not realize how much until now.

The preceding chapters describe in some way where I've been and what I've experienced over more than eight decades. I'm still not ready to adjust to the changes aging requires. The physical changes can be depressing, especially when I put on a bathing suit! One that hasn't changed is my vanity. My daughter JoAnn reminds me that "black doesn't crack," and that always makes me smile.

It's not just the way aging makes one look, it seems as if there's always a new and different pain to deal with. My calendar and I know I'm not alone—it's filled with doctor's appointments. When I'm not having a massage, I'm trying out a new physical therapist. I imagine Karen Bennett, my masseuse, is probably a little tired of moving these old muscles around. She's been doing this for ten years, here in Sarasota. When my daughter JoAnn is here, she takes the time to give me a free massage.

My neighbor, Suzanne Murphy, has introduced me to a fantastic therapist. I don't really know what Mary Hart's technique is, but it certainly contributes to my well-being. Spinal stenosis and arthritis have given me more pain than I want to tolerate. Because I've become so involved in keeping my body in some kind of shape, I have Makeela Strait, my yoga instructor, meet me at the pool and tell me what I can do in the water to help relieve the pain. Recently, through a chiropractor who thought she could help me with some of my physical discomfort, I was introduced to Norman Jones, an outstanding therapist. I have added Norman to my schedule and he has helped me a great deal. And I wonder what I would do without Mark Abrams, who helps me plant my tomatoes and nurture my orchids.

Who would have thought I'd need help shopping for groceries and making my doctor's appointments? I met Peggy Dillon through one of my neighbors, and she not only helps me make my appointments, but makes sure my companion, Bami, makes it to the Beverly Hills Dog Spa. My housekeeper has become a dear friend. I met Phyllis the first month I moved to Sarasota. My house is her house. She comes every day to walk Bami so I can stay in bed an extra hour or so. All of these wonderful individuals add so much quality to my life. And they truly help me enjoy my retirement.

I have just returned from the trip I planned to celebrate my eightieth birthday. It took me almost a year to plan this experience. It was certainly well worth the time and effort. As I sat on the deck of the ship, I had time to think about my journey of eighty years. It was significant for me to take this opportunity to summarize my life's work. I have been and continue to be a spirited black woman in a white world. As I traveled through Mumbai to Bali, I was so often reminded of the relationship of skin color and poverty. The developing world is my world and it clearly looks like me. The lifestyle of so many individuals throughout the world needs so much. There were times when I almost felt ashamed as I lived a luxurious lifestyle on the ship. However, I reminded myself that I contributed what I could through my life's work.

I am grateful for all of the opportunities I have had to help make the world somewhat better than it was. My experience as a young girl with the hot fudge sundae in a white paper cup made me the person I am today.